70's Gla
and Pe

A WALSALL LAD HITS THE WRONG SIDE OF THE TRACKS

STEVE GRAINGER

YOUCAXTON PUBLICATIONS
OXFORD & SHREWSBURY

YouCaxton Publications
enquiries@youcaxton.co.uk

Foreword

'I have known Steve for several years mainly through his interest in football memorabilia and of course Man United. The late 1970's always reminds me of my Doc Martens days and travelling from Belfast to Manchester every weekend to train with Man United schoolboys - great times. Mainly through humour and sometimes heartache, Steve has certainly captured the mood of a teenage boy growing up in the turbulent 1970's. Anyone who was around in the 70's will immediately identify with Steve's book.

I just know the book is going to be a great hit and will sell like cup-final tickets'

NORMAN WHITESIDE
Manchester United & Northern Ireland Legend!

'Steve and I first met back in 2008 in very rowdy bar in Moscow. We were both in the Russian capital to see our beloved Manchester United win the Champions' League. We have kept in touch ever since.

Steve has been lucky enough to lead a very exciting and well-travelled life and whenever we meet up, Steve has always been wonderful company and has great stories to tell.

I'm not the least bit surprised Steve has decided to put his experiences down on paper and I am in no doubt that Steve's book will be a great success'

SHOBNA GULATI
Actor

Introduction

I wonder what my old English teacher, Mr. McLoughlin would say about all this? Probably something like, *'have you been copying again Grainger?'*

I decided to put 'pen to paper' or more like 'my fingers to the keyboard' after years of witnessing young kids living their teenage years in their bedrooms, when their only contact with their friends outside of school was via text messages in a virtual world. That said, I'm not looking to glorify my actions or encourage young kids to behave as I did when I was a teenager. I was a naughty little sod and at times a bit of a handful, but I was never truly wicked or vicious. I was just full of devilment and I loved to have the craic. With Irish blood on my mom's side and gypsy blood from my paternal grandma, I'm sure it was in my DNA to play the fool and get up to no good.

I would like to remind people that there's more to being a teenager than Play-Stations and mobile phones - and if your little cherub does turn out to be a little bleeder, hopefully they'll come out the other side better for it - like I did!

In a light-hearted way, I have done my best to share the growing pains of a young boy, turning into a young man. I've been as honest as I can when describing how I felt, riding the rollercoaster of life during my formative years. Besides telling of my wanderlust, I have also tried to capture what now seems to be the very laid-back and free-following spirit of the 1970's , to transport people back to a time when life didn't seem so serious and the world seemed a lot bigger place. As the book is mainly based around teenage boys, there's a fare bit of fruity and racy language between the pages, but I really couldn't sugar-coat that. Back then it was how us uneducated ruffians communicated with each other – don't you know.

I feel lucky and privileged to say I grew up in a time when teenagers were allowed a lot of freedom and all a teenager boy had to worry about was: when are we going to get a colour telly?, who your team would draw in the FA Cup? and would the game be on the box? who was No.1 in the charts? And your biggest problem was making sure you could listen to chart show on Radio 1 every Sunday evening or getting a Paper–Round, so you could buy the latest fashions, or, in my case, so I could go and watch United.

We didn't have faceless civil servants and bureaucrats (aka Big Brother) telling us what we should say and think. I was forced to stand on my own two feet at an early age and I was off exploring with my mates near and far, long before I became a teenager. But it seems today's teenagers won't go anywhere, unless they're dropped off and collected by their parents. These kids aren't just missing out on excitement and adventure, but also on character-building. I pity the kids today, whose lives are ruled by Social Media, I.D. passes and endless school exams. I dread to think how I would have coped with schooling in this day and age, where children are pigeon-holed and they all have to hit an expected level at the same time. We're not robots; we all blossom at different times. I'm certainly a great example. I like to think I was a bright kid, but I wasn't interested in school at all. Then at the age of twenty, a light went on in my head and I got an unquenchable thirst for knowledge that has lasted to this day.

The two things I would love to bring from the '70's into the 21st century are music and football. In the 1970's we were introduced to Soul – Heavy Metal and were the first to witness the outrageous and extremely entertaining Glam Rock scene, Disco, Punk and New Wave. Even the Teddy Boys made a come back. Now we have the X-Factor and a production line of wooden guitar players.

Whether you were at Old Trafford or Meadow Lane, White Hart Lane or Brisbane Road, in the 70's you were guaranteed a great atmosphere, even truly electrifying for the big games and always an exciting time with your mates. Running onto the pitch to celebrate a goal or to get a player's autograph was just classed as high spirits, and being thrown around the terraces by the massive crowds was all part of the fun. Now with all the rules and regulations, going to a football match is like being at school and many of the football stadiums are like graveyards. If you shout too loud or if you get up out of your seat for more than five seconds, you are confronted by a charmless, overweight steward in a Hi-Vis coat. And if anyone should dare to run onto the 'playing area' they can be banned for life from every football ground from the Bescot Stadium to Timbuktu! All true football fans should shed a tear over the fact that the corporate world has stolen football from the working man.

I would like to say a big thank you to Angie, my long suffering wife, for all her help and patience while I worked on this book, also thanks to my old mate Sag, who produced the artwork for the book cover. And Banka, if you're still out there? Get in touch!

I hope you will find this book funny, moving and most of all memorable.

MANDY 1958 - 2018 R.I.P.

1970

In the April of 1970, my Mom was expecting her fifth child. Because my Mom was in her mid-thirties, the doctors advised her to go into hospital for the birth so just as she was shipped off to the maternity ward, I was dispatched to Nottingham to stay with my Grandma and GrandDad. Dad drove me to Sutton Coldfield and put me on the X99 bus bound for Nottingham, instructing the driver to show me where the bus stop to Watnall was when we'd arrived at Nottingham Bus Station. Watnall was where my grandparents lived. Then, without a goodbye or a kiss-my-arse, my Dad headed back to his car. At the grand old age of nine-and-three-quarters, I was off on an adventure and wasn't worried or dismayed at the thought of travelling all that way on my own.

Arriving at my grandparents without any major incident, I received the usual warm welcome from my GranDad: 'When are you going home? And while you're here, you can get your hair cut'. GranDad always sat by the fire whenever he was in the house and listened to the radiogram. Usually it was Radio 4 or Nottinghamshire playing cricket but on a Sunday morning he would 'go for it' and put on Family Favourites. Two Way Family Favourites, as it was also known, was a bit jollier than Gardeners Question Time or The Archers and, much to GrandDad's annoyance, they'd play hits from the 60's, such as my old favourite - Freddy and The Dreamers. More often than not, the boring monotone BBC presenters would play records by Doris Day, Dean Martin, Frank Sinatra and Judy Garland, but my No. 1 one was the great Jim

Reeves. *Distant Drums* was played every week without fail, but my all-time favourite from Jim was *He'll Have To Go.* Even today whenever I hear *'put your sweet lips a little closer to the phone'* it takes me back to my grandparents front room and the smell of Sunday dinner cooking.

Two Way Family Favourites came about at the end of World War 2 and was designed to link families at home in the UK with British Forces serving in Germany or elsewhere overseas. It was a request programme and poor old Johnny based out in Kuala Lumpur or Cyril waiting to be de-mobbed in Italy would send heartfelt messages across the airwaves to their nearest and dearest back home in Blighty. Most of the messages were generic, *'Bill based in France would like to wish his wife Hilda a very happy birthday'* or *'Charlie stuck out in Burma wants to say hello to all friends and family back home'* – that sort of thing, but one particular request really made me sit up and take notice. No doubt wearing his bow tie and dinner jacket and using his very best Queen's English the stuffy radio presenter read out a list of hellos from a serviceman overseas - *'Harry would like to send his best wishes to his wife and family in Kendal and his mother and father in Barrow and his best friend serving in the RAF'*. On and on it went. The presenter's voice remained constant throughout and, in a very matter of fact manner, the message ended with *'and not forgetting the three Arabs at number 18'*. Arabs at number 18! Arabs in England were as rare as rocking-horse shite! What the dickens was going on? The only Arabs I'd ever known were those in the Arabian Nights tales! My imagination went into overdrive. Had Aladdin, Sinbad and Ali Baba moved to our green and pleasant land and, if so, where the bleeding hell were the forty thieves? More to the point, did we need to keep an eye out for them? Were these Arabs keeping dirty oil lamps or a herd of spitting camels in the back yard? If the latter, No.16 and No.20 better beware when hanging out the washing!

My grandparents didn't have a phone, neither did any of their neighbours or anyone else in Watnall as far as I could make out. So once a day, with a penny in my hand, I'd make my way to the local public phone box and call home to see if I'd got a new brother yet.

In those days, there was always a queue outside most public phone boxes. The great British public would wait in frustrated silence as Mrs. Jones or Mr. Smith chatted at length to a sister in Ramsgate, rambling on about how the cat was off its food and isn't the language on TV shocking after 9:00 pm. Hearts would sink as the next in line went into the phone box, closed the door only to line up a pile of pennies, indicating this was going to be a long job! This never happened in Watnall, where no-one ever seemed to use the phone. I even wondered if they actually knew what the Big Red Box was.

On my first ever visit to a phone box I was a bit overwhelmed by the black gloss-and-chrome back panel, with its black monolithic Bakelite phone and large square 'money box' displaying the bold white 'A' & 'B' symbols. The thing that caught my attention was the list of area codes, shown in three separate chrome frames above the telephone. There were hundreds of towns and cities listed: Ipswich, Cardiff, Oxford, Brighton – the list was endless. My excitement grew when I spotted 'Manchester 061' and I couldn't resist dialing '061', hoping that George Best might answer or even a random Man United fan so I could chat about the Red Devils. To my disappointment just dialing '061' didn't get any response!

Anyhow, on this occasion, after reading the instructions several times, I dialed my parents' telephone number. The phone rang for ages but no-one answered so I put down the receiver and pressed the 'B' button to retrieve my unused penny. Much to my delight not one, but three pennies dropped into the slot at the bottom of the 'money box'. Result!

With my newly acquired pennies, I headed off to the local shop to buy a few sweets. The 'shop' was originally someone's front room and the family who ran it lived on the premises. As I entered, a bell on the door rang and a woman appeared as if by magic, to serve me. No words were spoken as she watched me scrutinizing the rows of jars containing sweets. As she let out an impatient sigh, a voice from the back room called for her assistance. She sighed once again and disappeared, leaving the counter unattended. I looked to make sure no one else was around, then stuffed my pockets with Mojo's & Black Jacks. When the woman returned I gave her a big smile and casually asked for a Wagon Wheel. Before I could finish the sentence, a voice from behind the counter whispered *'Mam that boy has put a lot of sweets in his pocket'*. I was totally shocked – where the bleeding hell had that little sod been hiding? *'Have you stolen some sweets?'* the woman barked at me. *'No'* I timidly replied. *'Yes you have'* came the squeaky response from the hidden accuser. This covert security guard tried to carry on the debate but 'He' was all he managed to say before the woman gave him an almighty kick. There was a thud, a slight whimper and a few seconds silence before the shopkeeper handed me a Wagon Wheel and said sharply *'Tuppence!'*. I nervously handed over my two pennies, half expecting her to grab my arm, pull me over the counter and chain me up next to her beaten gimp. Fortunately for me I only got an angry, knowing glare as she snatched the money out of my hand and handed over the Wagon Wheel. Only in Watnall! Bleeding inbreds! I'd put money on the fact that the writers of 'League of Gentlemen' have visited that shop at some time – *'Hello what's going on, we'll have no trouble here, you know this is a Local Shop for Local People'*.

After several more unsuccessful trips to the telephone box, I finally got The Pips! Let me explain… After putting your penny into the 'money box', if you were lucky enough to connect with the person you were calling, you'd hear a loud, rapid pipping noise, indicating you must press button 'A' to continue with the call. Once you had pressed button 'A' your penny would then clunk and bang its way down into the bowels of the 'money box' and you could start your conversation. The Pips were always a give- away, that you were calling from a public phone. After only a few minutes conversation, the Pips would sound again, alerting you to the fact that you needed to put in another penny or you would be CUT OFF! All very, very Hi – Tech stuff!!

So, back to my telephone conversation. Dad answered the phone, informing me *'You've got another sister'*. I can't remember my reply, but I can recall the disappointment at not getting a brother. After the phone call I headed back to my grandparents' house and gave them the news. Both made absolutely no comment about the fact that they now had a new granddaughter and the next day I was packed off on the X99 bus back to Sutton Coldfield!

The big '1- 0' birthday was the first I'd spent away from home and it turned out a big disappointment. We were on a family holiday down on the South Coast, where Mom and Dad had rented a two-bedroomed house miles from anywhere. Remembering, that on all my previous birthdays, I'd always had a party and that it was the only day in the year that I felt special and got some attention, I was very excited during the days leading up to it. I imagined what special treat I'd be receiving for this *Milestone Birthday* and, on the morning of said birthday, I came downstairs into the living room. Expecting balloons, a pile of neatly wrapped presents, a stack of birthday cards and a big cake, I was sorely disappointed. Dad was sitting with his head in a newspaper and Mom was nursing the baby. I wasn't even acknowledged as I entered the room and sat down on the sofa. I sat in silence, getting more and more upset and disheartened. My sisters came downstairs and Mom jumped up and made them breakfast. Next came Big Bro asking for his breakfast and I just sat there, waiting for the attention to turn to me - but it didn't.

I know my Mom had her hands full. With four kids (one of them, a right little bleeder – mentioning no names!) and a four-month-old baby to contend with, not to mention a husband with Victorian views on children! My Dad did a good job *Bringing Home the Bacon,* but when it came to helping out with his kids, forget it! That was 100% left to Mom. But on this particular day, I didn't care about Mom's other commitments. This was the birthday when I hit double figures! This was the big 1 – 0. This was a coming of age birthday and the one day in the year when I could expect to be treated as if I mattered. With tear-filled eyes I eventfully asked Mom where my birthday presents were. She flashed a look, as if to say 'haven't I got enough to do?' then went upstairs, returning with two birthday cards and one single present. My heart sank '*Is this, all I've got?*' I asked, to which she snapped back, '*You ungrateful little sod. You're only happy when people are turning up to the front door with presents in their hands*'.

On my birthday – too bleedin' right I was! And was that too much to expect? Mom then went into a bit of a rant, ending with one of her favourite sayings '*If I scratched my eyes out for you, they'd be the wrong bloody colour*'. Then, to top it off, Dad piped up '*You should be grateful, we've bought you on holiday!*'

Big brother found it most amusing that I was crying, which obviously made me more angry and soon Dad was stepping in to stop us from fighting. That just about set the tone for the rest of the day!

Our special treat for the day was to visit a glorified tin shack – a poor excuse for a Village Hall. Much to Dad's delight and Mom's annoyance, the local history society were showing a collection of slides relating to bygone days in their boring little village. I really had one on me and from the moment we entered the makeshift cinema, I sat on my own and sulked, refusing requests from Mom and Dad to sit with them. I was a stubborn little sod at the best of times and, when I was upset, it could take hours for me to come round! The only fun part about the whole sorry affair was when some doddering old git bumped into the noisy old knackered projector and sent it crashing to the ground. That bought a smile to my tear-stained face!

And so it came to pass that, for the rest of my childhood, my birthdays would follow the same pattern – just another day in the Grainger household as far as my parents and siblings were concerned.

After school one of my regular play areas was at the shops at the top of my road. One evening the boys and me were up to no good at the back of the shops when we came across a discarded fishing net, the type a young boy would ponce about with on the beach, not the sort that you'd find on a sea-going fishing trawler, that would just be barmy! After initially using it as a spear and throwing it at each other, generally messing about, I suddenly thought how we could put the net to good use.

We went round to the front of the shops and made our way to the Post Office at the end of the row. As well as being a post office it was also a general stores and to the right of the front door, which just happened to have a large letter box, were boxes and boxes of crisps. The shop was closed so, huddling around the door, we steadily pushed the fishing net through the letter box. After dropping the first few bags of crisps on the floor, we eventually managed to liberate a packet of cheese & onion crisps. We soon mastered the art of lifting the bags out of the boxes, gently bringing back the cane through the letterbox, with Ant (the one with the smallest hands) lifting the crisps from the net.

It was a great example of team work and great fun as we stuffed ourselves with crisps for almost an hour, pushing the empty packets back through the letter box. No doubt this would cause maximum confusion and bafflement to the shop owner. Imagine the look on his face when he opened the shop the next morning to find scores of empty and several full bags of crisps littered across the floor. Was it the crisp fairies? Was it a hungry ghost? Was it rats? After that feed, they would be bloody big rats! Or was it them pesky kids?

We went back to the Post Office the next night and after successfully lifting several bags of crisps we got adventurous and tried to tackle the packets of biscuits on the shelf above. I managed to hook the biscuits into the nylon net, but as soon as I lifted the packet off the shelf, the weight pulled the cane out of my hand and both fishing net and biscuits crashed onto the floor. The Game Was Up – *what a schoolboy error!* A simple physics calculation would have told us that the operation was doomed to fail!

I walked past the Post Office the next evening and the letter box had been boarded up and on it was a hand written sign: '**BUGGER OFF, YOU LITTLE BLEEDERS**'.

So we were then back to loitering behind the shops and the main reason for being at the back of the shops was – empty bottles! Whenever you purchased a bottled of pop or beer, you got charged a small deposit of two or three pennies. When you took the bottles back the shop, your deposit would be returned. Returned bottles were usually stacked in a secure yard at the back until the van came with new supplies and took away the old bottles. Our devious little scam was to get a 'volunteer' (usually the youngest or smallest of the gang) to scramble over the wall at the back of said shops and pass the empties onto us. We would get anything up to a dozen bottles at a time and then take it in turns to front the shopkeeper with two or three empties and claim the deposit. It was always a bit risky being the last kid to take the empties back, because, by then, the shopkeeper could get a bit suspicious and there were a few occasions when he would simply take the bottles off the kid then smack him around the head and kick him up his arse, throwing the little toe-rag out of his shop! There wasn't any come-back for the shopkeeper acting in this manner as Little Johnny was hardly likely to complain to his parents!

Probably having nothing else better to do, one cold and wet Saturday I travelled with my uncle Bill, my brother and Dad to the Potteries to see Villa play at Port Vale. Much to the annoyance of my Dad and brother, I had my red & white United scarf hidden under my green parka. Arriving at Vale Park a few hours before kick-off, we were all surprised to see hundreds of Villa fans already at the ground and queuing at the turnstiles. There was so many Villa fans waiting to get on the covered terrace (The Home End!) that it was decided we would go in the seats and as we took our seats we could view the steady stream of Villa fans pouring into the terrace to our left and congregating at the back of the stand in line with the goals - in the late 60's/early 70's it was the 'done thing' for travelling football hooligans to try and 'take' the home supporters end, so getting onto the home terrace first was a big coup for the hordes of away fans.

After a short time, a small gang clad in black & white scarfs appeared on the far side of the terrace. Slowly and surely the gang grew in size and as I was watching the players warming up on the pitch, I heard a loud roar! Looking over to the covered terrace, I saw the Port Vale mob had charged into the chanting Villa fans who had occupied their territory. For the next ten minutes there was chaos and mayhem as rival fans did battle on the terraces. This was the first time I'd ever witnessed football violence and, even though I was only ten years old, I was totally intoxicated by the experience and couldn't keep my eyes off the hostile fans. The police finally managed to separate the rival fans and restored order of a sort. The coppers had their work cut out keeping the two mobs apart and it seemed every five minutes or so a new fight would break out on the terraces. Fuck the poxy 3rd division match, I spent the entire afternoon observing the warring tribes on the action-packed terraces! After the match, the fun and games continued outside the ground. I watched wide-eyed as Villa fans turned over cars and Port Vale fans threw bricks at Villa coaches. My Dad and Uncle Bill were disgusted by the behavior of the football hooligans but I was shocked, frightened and enthralled by it all. Come Monday morning, in the school playground the violence at the Port Vale was all I could talk about and to get a pair of Doc Martins and visit Old Trafford became my greatest desire.

On 16th December 1970, my wish to go to Old Trafford came true. United had drawn Villa in the semi-final of the League Cup. The icing on the cake was that, because it was a night game and we had to travel to Manchester, I got to get the afternoon off school. Sadly only half my dream came true as this precocious wannabe football hooligan wasn't sporting a pair of Doctor Martin Boots, but a brand new pair of Monkey Boots. After days & days of pester power, my Mom finally agreed to let me wear the Monkey Boots to the game, a special treat as they were meant as a Christmas present. For a ten-year-old, Monkey Boots were ok! For those of you who are not familiar with monkey boots, let me enlighten you. The Monkey Boot was an ankle-high boot, most popular in brown, with heavy yellow stitching and yellow laces. It was first worn by the Skinheads in the late 1960's but soon became the poor relation to the Doctor Martin boot so that by the early 70's, no self-respecting teenage hooligan would have been seen dead in a pair of Monkey Boots and they were only really worn by Skinhead girls and young wannabes like me.

Back to Old Trafford and the League Cup semi-final. Travelling up, I was relegated to the boot of my Dad's estate car while my brother and two elder cousins teased me from the back seat. All the way up the M6 I waved my red & white scarf at other fans in passing cars. What worried me was that most of the passing cars and coaches were full of claret & blue scarfs. I certainly got my fair share of 'V' signs as I waved my United scarf up against the back window of the car.

Old Trafford's floodlights were visible from a few miles away and they acted as a beacon as we approached the hallowed ground where my hero George Best worked his magic. We parked up near the cricket ground and joined thousands of United fans walking up Warwick Road, (now Sir Matt Busby Way). I was thrilled to hear many of the fans singing 'We All Live in a George Best World' or 'Denis Law is Our King' and it seemed every one of the United fans had at least one red and white scarf wrapped around their neck, tied around their wrist or hanging off their trouser belts.

As we got to the ground there were massive queues at the turnstiles for the terraces, so once again it was decided that we should go into the seats. Our seats were right at the back of the main stand with the TV gantry just above us and the players entrance right below. The infamous

Stretford End, was a sea of red & white to our left, the half-built Cantilever Stand was the opposite side of the pitch and the open Scoreboard End was to our right.

The Stretford End was packed to the rafters and the noise coming from there was fantastic, I was absolutely spellbound and couldn't take my eyes off it. Well that's not strictly true, the other thing that fascinated me was the large TV cameras that were on the gantry and the strange stretching exercises all the cameramen did at half time! Half time also brought refreshments in the shape of a young teenage boy dressed in a white jacket and carrying a wooden tray, supported by a thick strap around his shoulders and neck. He marched up and down the steps shouting, 'Pies, Crisps, Chocolate!' When he told us the price of his wares, even my Uncle Bill, usually a very generous man, winced. 'I'm not a bleeding millionaire' he told the young boy. So it was pies for my Dad and Uncle Bill and a packet of crisps for the kids.

Even though Old Trafford dwarfed the only other ground I'd been to (3rd division Vale Park) I can remember being disappointed to discover that the great Man United had the same old-style, wood-slat seating in the main stand. I'd been expecting comfy armchairs at least! My eyes lit-up when Uncle Bill paid a tanner (2 1/2p) for the hire of a small red leather cushion, for me to sit on. The cushion had the Man United crest embroidered on one side and to this day I could kick myself for not taking that cushion home with me! I'd even got the bloody thing stuffed inside my parka, but when the steward came to collect the cushions just before the final whistle my Dad insisted that I gave it back!

Unfortunately, my beloved Man United, who had won the European Cup two years before, could only draw 1 – 1 with Aston Villa (who at the time were in the 3rd division). In front of my eyes 'Young' Brian Kidd scored a wonderful volley for United and then some old, bald git scored for Villa! Sadly it would be four long years before I would get to visit Old Trafford again and stand at the Stretford End.

The return leg of the semi-final was played at Villa Park a week later and all in all that game was to turn out far worse than the Old Trafford match. I'd already broken up from school for Christmas and on the day of the match I'd been given a few bob by my Mom to go a get a few Christmas presents. As Walsall market was on that day I'd gone into Walsall to try and bag a few bargains. While I was looking around the shops for a little something for my Mom and Dad's Christmas present I noticed a Manchester United pennant in the window of the sports shop in the market square. It cost half the money that I'd got to buy presents with, but I couldn't resist! The pennant displayed the United club crest and read 'European Champions' and the gold tassels made it look so classy. I imagined how great I'd look waving it around at the match and thought 'Sod it - I'm having it'. This left me short so, when buying a small present for Dad in another shop, I nicked a tacky ashtray for Mom's present. Neither my Mom nor Dad smoked!

Arriving home, I suffered a bad migraine attack, blinding headache - blurred vision – throwing up – the lot! So instead of off to the match it was off to bed. Divine retribution!!

When I found out the result the next morning I was gutted, Brian Kidd had once again scored for United, but we'd lost 2 – 1. There'd been almost 49,000 at Old Trafford for the first leg of the semi-final and 63,000 at Villa Park for the return leg - double Villa's usual home gate.

I must add that in the Final, two goals from Tottenham's Martin Chivers were enough to see off Villa. Come on you Spurs!

At this stage, I was still cowboy crazy and, alongside my monkey boots, top of my Christmas list was anything to do with the Wild West. I loved all kind of Westerns and couldn't get enough of Champion the Wonder Horse, John Wayne, Randolph Scott, James Stewart, James Garner and Roy Rogers. Alan Ladd in the tearjerker 'Shane', with Little Joe crying out at the end of the film 'Shane – Shane Come Back' was just the best! You would have to be a black-hearted beast with no soul, not to shed a tear when a heartbroken Little Joe looks on as the diminutive Shane rides into the night!

My very favourite cowboy film star was a young, fresh-faced actor by the name of Audie Murphy. Audie was born in Texas and had a hard childhood, losing both parents at an early age. Even though he had angelic looks and a small build, he had a fearsome reputation and a very explosive temper. Audie fought in Europe in the 2nd World War and was the most decorated American combat soldier, receiving every military combat medal for valor that the U.S. Army could award.

Audie started his film career playing himself in the autobiography film 'To Hell and Back' which was based on his memoirs of the same name. After starring in the film, he made a string of Westerns usually playing the down-trodden or wronged good guy and he would often ride a stunning Palomino or Pinto horse. By today's standards his acting and the quality of filming was a bit cheesy but Audie Murphy was definitely one of my childhood heroes.

In the late '70's I got talking to a bloke in a pub in Aldridge and he informed me that he'd come from Halesowen (approx. twenty-five miles away) just to visit a few pubs in the area. 'Wow, that's a good old journey – have you come in a car? I asked. 'No, I rode over on Audie Murphy's horse' he replied. Well, I'll gew to the foot of our stairs!

Christmas Day washed away any bad memories of my uneventful 10th birthday. I came down stairs to find a massive pile of presents and was overjoyed with what I'd got. To add to the 'Bonanza Chuck Wagon' received the previous Christmas, I got two Bonanza action figures - Little Joe on his black-and-white Pinto horse and old man Cartwright - Ben - along with his Buckskin horse. However, the best present was a double leather gun belt and holsters with two sliver Colt 45's with deer-horn handles. It wasn't just a thin belt that looped through separate holsters; the belt and holsters were integral and at the back of the belt there were a dozen or so 'loops' to house spare bullets. It was simply The Dogs Bollocks!

Micky Gibbs came up trumps again, buying me a twelve-inch record of the radio commentary of Manchester United's European Cup victory – nice!

1971

One afternoon after school I called round to Little Ant's house and knocked on his front door. It was opened by his mother who invited me in whilst Little Ant was finishing off his tea. I'd only taken a few steps into the living room when I was stopped in my tracks, eyes bulging and mouth wide open! In the corner of the room Scooby Doo and Shaggy were jumping around a TV screen. It was only a small screen (14 ' perhaps) but it was in full glorious colour! The first colour TV I'd ever seen!

That's actually not strictly true as just down the road was a gully leading to Walsall Wood Rd and the house at the end of the gully boasted a colour TV. Much to the frustration of the owner, the TV regularly attracted an audience of young kids peering spellbound into his living-room window. Passing adults also stopped and gawped at the modern wonder. Every ten minutes or so, the owner of the TV would jump up from his armchair and bang the window, telling us kids to 'Sod off '. This nightly ritual went on for a few weeks, until one evening we wandered up to the end of the gully to discover the old git had bricked up the window! Even at my tender age I thought this was a bit over the top - why didn't the barmy sod just buy a pair of curtains?

When Little Ant eventually got me away from his colour TV he said, 'I'm surprised my Mom let you in as she's told me to keep that TV a secret '. Apparently they'd only had the telly a week or so and were fed up of the steady flow of neighbours knocking with all types of excuses to get into the living room, intent on marvelling at the magic coloured goggle-box.

A few months later Dad took delivery of a 22" colour TV. It took four men to carry it into the house! By today's standards the TV screen was minute but the surrounding cabinet must have been 3' cubed. It was a monster - but a coloured monster! During the first weeks we had the TV I stayed in every night watching the stuffy BBC2 – the only one of the *three* channels available to broadcast all programs in colour. It was a while before BBC 1 and ITV caught up! Dad had 100% say over what was on TV, but initially I'd sit and watch The Test Card if it was in colour (a surreal image filling the screen when no programs were being broadcast).

All was fine and dandy until the bloody thing started to breakdown every other week. We'd have to wait a day or so for the repairman to turn up and every time the he would say 'Bloody valves'' and proceed to replace one of the large glass valves in the back of the TV. Valves were the size of demi-johns and once the back of the TV had been removed, the internal workings resembled something from a Doctor Who spaceship. When the repairman had worked his magic and the colour was back in our lives, we gave a loud sigh of relief and thanked him profusely.

Probably the most memorable things in colour in those days were the scary Hammer House of Horror films shown on Friday nights. After football, the late night horror films were the main topic of conversation at school on Monday mornings and it was a badge of honour to say that your parents had let you stay up until almost midnight to watch. Parental control in the 70's was a bit hit-and-miss in my home. 'Mom can I stay up and watch the horror film? ' I'd ask. 'No, it's on too late,' she'd reply. 'But it's Friday; I don't have to get up tomorrow,' I'd answer back. 'Ok then, but if you come crying to me in the middle of the night because you're frightened, I'll give you something to bloody cry about,' was Mom's tender response.

Usually starring Christopher Lee as The Baddy and Peter Cushion as The Goody, I watched some classic movies. The Curse of the Werewolf, The Mummy and The Curse of Frankenstein were second rate to me because Dracula and his sexy vampires were my favourites. I was always very frightened by the sudden appearance of fangs and theatrical blood but was comforted by the fact that, after many close calls, the Vampire Hunter always managed to destroy Dracula and his band of vampire beauties. The other appealing thing about the Dracula films was that the scary but erotic vampires would often flash their tits!!

The ghost stories, also screened on Friday nights, weren't as glamorous as the Dracula films and were in black-and-white but, in my opinion, were more frightening. The grainy film, along with the use of sudden loud music and the inevitable twisting door knob really put the willies up me! In the Dracula films the fear was tangible and always dealt with, but the ghost films always left uncertainty - was the ghost still free to haunt and scare me? More often than not, you wouldn't even see a ghost, it was just the anticipation. A dark room, a full moon and the quickening beat of the background music - then CRASH! I'd jump out of my seat and was always too scared to go up to bed. After watching one such film, I lay in bed shaking with fear and thinking the ghost would appear out of the darkness at any minute. A sudden noise, was enough to make me jump out of bed and seek refuge in my brother's bed, crying, 'I'm frightened.

Can I sleep with you?' 'No. fuck off ya cunt' he would snap
back, elbowing me in the face at the same time, catching
me smack on the nose and causing me to have a nose bleed.
At least it took my mind off the ghost!

Staying up late meant I got to hear the National Anthem.
As the TV station was about to stop broadcasting for the
night, the presenter would say in a hushed tone 'Goodnight
and don't forget to switch off your TV set.' *God Save the
Queen* would immediately follow.

The other horror in my life was when, every night after
tea, Dad insisted me and my brother washed and dried the
dishes and put away. We always kicked up a fuss, but Dad
was adamant. The first week of us doing our daily chores
was a nightmare. Both of us hated drying and putting away.
So the first night we were in the kitchen we started arguing
over who would do what. The war of words soon turned into
a fist fight which Dad soon broke up, solving the problem
by insisting that we take it in turns. Unfortunately, when it
was my turn to wash, my brother kept throwing the dishes
and pans back into the washing-up bowl and snarling, 'It's
still fuckin' dirty - do it again!' He threw one saucepan back
into the bowl with such force that water splashed up and
soaked me – that was the cue for the second fight in two
days. The following night resulted in our third fight in as
many days. Dad solved this one by laying down the law –
and only allowing one of us in the kitchen at a time. For
the next five years segregation was in operation and never
the twain did meet!

Even though I did my daily kitchen chores and would
often tidy up around the house, Mom and Dad refused
to give me any pocket money. This meant I had to be

inventive… Every evening there was always a steady queue of people waiting to use the public telephone box opposite our house. They'd be on the phone for ages, feeding two and five pence coins into the slot, which dropped into a cashbox below. On the way home from school me and my mates made a few unsuccessful attempts to get into the cashbox.

Success required me to 'think out of the box': if we couldn't get into the cashbox, maybe we could intercept the coins before they fell into it? The top section of the metal casing was only secured by a small lock and with the help of a serrated fishing knife, I managed to open the top and observe the internal mechanism. I noticed that as the coins were pushed into the slot, they dropped into an angled metal shute. This delivered the coins into a small hole in the top of the cashbox. All we needed to do was to cover the hole and we were in business! I fetched a piece of cardboard from a cornflake box from home and ripped it to size, placing it over the hole and then put the cashbox back together.

Retreating a distance away, we monitored the flow of callers into the phone box. As soon as it got dark and there were no more callers about we dived in to see if the plan had worked. Opening the lock again, loads of coins spilled out, falling on the floor. Bingo! I can't remember how much we got, but it was enough cash to fill both my trouser pockets and we went into the woods to share out the takings. The same drill was repeated every night for a couple of weeks and we were all very much in the money! All good things come to an end (just like the M6) and soon, much to our dismay, a new stronger lock was fitted to the cashbox casing. Try as we might, we just couldn't open the new lock so it was time to look for a different way to make money.

Struggling to come up with an easy (illegal) money-making scheme, me and a couple of mates reluctantly went to 'Snot Rags' farm. The old git agreed to give us some work, but we soon discovered what a tight-fisted bastard he was. After working all weekend he gave us £1.00 - between three of us! At the Easter break a few lads told us they'd been guz-gog (gooseberry) picking at a farm in Stonnall, a village less than half-an-hour walk from my house. So early one Saturday morning me and my mates headed off to the farm. Just as we arrived two coach loads of Indian workers pulled up. We'd never seen anything like it and looked on in amazement as scores of sari-clad women and a few scruffy Asian kids trooped off the coaches. Beside Vernon, a mixed race boy who lived nearby with his elderly foster parents, Aldridge was 100% white, so such a sight was completely alien to us in those days. As we leisurely picked guz-gog's, the Indian women worked like things possessed, chatting alongside us. I felt a bit uneasy but also fascinated by their mother tongue and by the sight of them squatting with legs wide apart, their long gangly arms going ten to the dozen. For every bucket we filled, it seemed the Indian women were filling at least two each. By dinnertime we were worn out and starving. None of us had thought to bring any sarnies and we stared wide-eyed at the Asians eating some kind of thick gravy with white flaky stuff (we'd never seen curry and rice before). Shattered, we decided to call it a day and weighed in our sack of guz-gogs. The farmer handed us a few bob - not a fortune but certainly more than Snot Rag would have paid us. We'd each got enough to buy scallops, chips, mushy peas and a bottle of fizzy pop. The scallops sold by chippies in the 70's weren't the seafood found in posh restaurants today, costing *an arm and a leg*. These scallops were large pieces of flat potato about ¼ inch think (6mm), fried in batter and costing less than a bag of chips!

One of the main reasons for wanting money was to buy sweets and cigarettes. I had left the candy cigarettes behind and along with my mates now puffed on the real thing. Usually choosing Players Number 10 or Sovereign fags because they were sold in packs of five. If you went to the tobacco shop near Walsall train station, regardless of your age you could buy a single cigarette for a penny. It wasn't really a shop; it was a stylish Edwardian cabin made from dark wood and, with its' classy, curved roof it looked quite grand. Tobacco and related products would be passed through a small arched serving hatch at the front. The hatch was so small that you couldn't really see the man sat inside and only his hand would appear to pass you your ciggies and to take your dosh. Our local newsagents Redgates sold cigarettes, but they rarely questioned young kids as to who they were for. My mates and me would pool our meager resources and have no problem purchasing a pack of five.

The safest place to smoke and hide the fags was in the woods but hiding matches in a damp tree trunk wasn't a good idea and more often than not our attempts to light up ended in failure. Another reason for mooching in the woods was to search for hidden porn. You'd be amazed at the number of rolled up 'Girly Mags' we discovered in bushes. After getting our fill of enormous tits and big hairy fannies we'd rip out pages of nude ladies and fix them as best we could to branches and bushes. Large areas of the woods looked like Hugh Hefner's back garden on a windy day! Another place for a quick puff on our fags was the small wooded area that separated the new Coppy Hall estate from the rough Castlefort estate. Kids from Castlefort were usually from coal-mining families and had a reputation for being a tough bunch. One evening three or four of us were in the woods trying to light a fag when suddenly a gang of about ten turned up. Most of them were our age but a couple, the leaders, looked more like teenagers. One of the older boys asked 'Where you from and how old are you?' Nervously we told him, then he asked us for a cigarette. As Little Ant produced a packet of fags, the older boy grabbed them and, lighting up, he enquired 'Who's the best fighter out of you lot?' I was the leader of our little gang and probably deemed by the others to be the best fighter but, taking into account the ages and numbers in the opposition, I was in no mood to be a hero. As far as I was concerned it was every *shit scared* boy for himself! Straight away I turned to my mate Paul and said 'You're the best fighter.' He snapped back, 'No I'm not, you are' and, much to my alarm, my other mates quickly agreed with him. The two older boys were amused that we were disagreeing about who was the best fighter and the one who'd taken the ciggies looked straight at me and said 'I think you're the best fighter.' The bastard then produced a Gat-Gun air pistol and, from close range, shot me in the ear. The sound of the gun going off, coupled with the blood dripping from my ear, made most of the Castlefort gang turn and run. As I fell to the ground, the one who'd fired said, 'It's a good job I haven't got any more pellets or I'd shoot your other ear as well! '. Then, just like a wild west gunslinger, he turned and slowly walked into the sunset. It was a very, very long time before I ventured back into those woods!

Another school holiday meant another trip on the X99 Bus – shipped off to Nottingham once again. This time I had the good fortune to be staying with Aunty Gladys, Uncle Andrew and their spoilt, obnoxious son. Aunty and Uncle really looked after me. Uncle took me to the bakery where he worked and introduced me to his mates, on the way taking me to a derelict house that he was proud to say was the house he lived in when he married my Aunty Gladys. He also took me to meet extended members of his family, generally making me feel wanted and part of the family. My cousin on the other hand was a different story. Six years older than me, he reminded me of my brother. On my first day there, he named several contemporary pop groups, asking me if I like them. I answered, 'They're ok.' Then he said, 'Do you like The Partridge Family?' Thinking he liked them, I replied, 'Yes' to which my delightful cousin snapped, 'They're fuckin' shit and you're a cunt for liking them!' What a charmer! Even back then I thought what a shame we can't choose our family. I wanted nothing more than to have a close and loving relationship with my Dad but, at best, he was cold and indifferent towards me. On the other hand, Uncle Andrew was kind and warm-hearted yet had a selfish, arrogant twat of a son (and they were his better attributes!).

When I found out my cousin was going to watch Nottingham Forest v Arsenal at Trent Bridge, I said I'd like to go along too. Initially he shouted 'No Way!' – a reaction that caused his parents to have a massive barney with him. Then, after lots of raised voices and swearing from my cousin, he finally agreed to take me to the game. He did, however, draw the line at letting me wear my Man United silk scarf to the game! When we got on the bus to Nottingham, I noticed that my cousin and his mates were all dressed identically. They had on brogues or loafers and wore smart Crombie overcoats with matching Trilby hats. The main topic of conversation was about the sixty or so Forest fans who had travelled to Derby County a few weeks earlier in the back of a furniture removal van and caused carnage and severe damage at several pubs used by Derby County fans. Long before West Ham's ICF boys came on the scene with their little white *calling cards*, the Forest boys were leaving their *you've been visited by Forest Mafia!* cards all over the country.

I was soon informed that my cousin intended to off-load me at the ground early so that him and his mates could go and look for Arsenal fans to do over. We reached the ground about ninety minutes before kick-off and, walking towards the Trent End turnstiles, my cousin suddenly stopped in his tracks, 'Fuckin' Cheeky Twats,' he said to himself and stared in disbelief as three men casually walked past us. Later that night, I heard him telling his mates that the men in question were none other than Frank McLintock, the Arsenal captain and two of his fellow team mates, Ray Kennedy and, as Alf Garnett would have said, 'the long haired puff' Charlie George. Can you imagine today's overpaid, over-protected Premiership prima donna's taking a quick stroll around the oppositions ground before kick-off? I think not!

Returning home from my little stay in Nottingham I was excited to see that Mom had received a new Kays Catalogue. Whenever I was alone in the living room I would pick up the 2"-thick catalogue and go straight to the lingerie pages KNICKERS – KNACKERS – KNOCKERS as Les Dawson would later say! I had yet to discover wanking, but I certainly got a few tingles in the groin area as I flicked through the pages and got an eye full of beautiful women wearing only their underwear and skimpy nighties. In search of titillation, I would always go a page too far and come to the more mature models wearing girdles and surgical tights. In a flash I'd flick back to the busty beauties and study their mesmerizing cleavages. I wasn't a total little perv – I'd also drool over George Best football boots and Raleigh Chopper bikes.

I also found entertainment in those days watching The High Chaparral. Manolito in his leather bell-bottom trousers, waist-length jacket and fancy black hat was the coolest cowboy ever (sorry, Audie, but it's true). Manolito fucked around with the ladies a bit too much for my liking so, despite his sartorial elegance, he wasn't my favourite character. Blue Boy, the fresh faced, blond-haired, blue-eyed son of Big John (the owner of the High Chaparral) was number one for me. He only looked about sixteen and rode a beautiful palomino horse and I often fantasied about having one of my own and riding off into the desert with Blue Boy to go and round up some stray cattle. As you will read later, my Dad would soon throw cold water over my dreams of riding off into the sunset.

Mexican Pedro, 'smiling' Sam and Buck were also great characters but I couldn't stand Big John, what a pompous, arrogant tosser! How the fuck he managed to pull the sexy Victoria, I will never know. But, like her brother Manolito, Victoria had an eye for the opposite sex and Buck and Blue Boy both came close to shagging her on a couple of occasions. On the QT she must have pulled out more than her fair share of cactus needles from her arse as she frolicked in the desert!

During the summer holidays my main playground was the Ash Mound and pools surrounding it. The biggest of the pools, the Atlas, was always great to swim in and I heard lots of bullshit stories about 'the one that got away' from kids fishing in the Atlas. There would always be someone who had just got the legendry 'Hercules' on the end of their line. Hercules was a mythical pike said to be five-foot long and weighing 100 lbs (50kg) Fishermen would tell tales of seeing Hercules swallow ducks whole, or biting the leg off a paddling toddler! Dave Mortlock even told me that he'd wrestled with the giant fish, just like Tarzan fighting a crocodile. You could guarantee that every time you went swimming in the Atlas someone would pretend to spot the monster fish and scream out. There would then be a mad dash to get out of the water and, when we were all safely on dry land, we'd all claim to have seen the killer fish and agree we'd just had a near death experience.

Other life forms that were in abundance around the Ash Mounds were grass snakes and newts. The newts had the most amazing colours on their bodies and were very collectable, almost on a par with footie cards. Kids would sneak newts into the school playground and swap them for all sorts of things. Dave Mortlock, who had the biggest and best collection of newts, even got to see a girls *front bottom* in exchange for peak at a prize newt in an old jam jar! The strangest collection of reptiles belonged to a bloke living in a council flat not far from us. He had a fair collection of newts and toads, which he kept in various plastic containers in his hallway and living room. But the *pièce de résistance* was his bath full of grass snakes. A few of my friends had told me of *The Snake Man* but I didn't believe them, so one

1871

evening I was taken to his flat. We knocked on the front door and a half-dressed man answered and, before we could say anything, with a big smile on his face, he said , 'Come to see the snakes boys?' Nervously I followed my friends into the dark hallway and then, one by one, we entered the bathroom. What an amazing sight greeted us! The bathtub was full of wriggling snakes. Even at my tender age I thought the bloke was off his head and wondered for days how him, his wife and young kids managed to have a bath. As we were staring at the snakes, the Snake Man said 'If any of you boys want to sit in with the snakes, just strip off and jump in with them, they don't bite.' Time for a quick exit!! The Snake Man is probably sharing a cell with Rolf Harris now.

One of the 'play areas' we would usually use in the evening was the brick factory. We progressed from climbing on the large piles of bricks to venturing into the factory itself and carrying out the fun, but dangerous, pastime of riding on the conveyor belt. The part of the factory that we played in had a wide conveyor belt that ran almost the length of the building and about ten yards before the end of the building the conveyor belt ran up quite a steep angle and disappeared into another part of the brickworks. At its highest point the conveyor belt must have been about fifteen feet high, so the exciting thing to do was to stay on the moving belt for as long as you dared. It was great fun and we'd play there for hours without being disturbed by any of the workers, who were probably playing cards in the canteen or looking at porn in the bog. No one ever rode the conveyor belt to the top, I think about six feet off the ground was my record. Every time I'd return home after playing

29

in the brick factory my Mom would go barmy, because I would be covered from head to toe in a thick layer of brick dust. 'More bleedin' washin' for me,' she'd complain as she belted me around the head.

During the summer holidays, and just three or four days after my eleventh birthday, me and a friend decided to explore a different part of the brick factory. We came across a row of ten or so small yellow electric trucks neatly lined up in a row being charged through wall-mounted electrical sockets. There were no workers to be seen and my mate and I plucked up the courage to sit inside a couple of the trucks and start pressing buttons and pulling levers. We jumped from truck to truck hoping to get a bit of life out of one of them, turning the handles bars and banging and pulling any button or lever we could find. We were just starting to think that we wouldn't be having any fairground fun on the trucks, when the truck we were sitting on came to life. It jumped forward a few inches then stopped. After hitting the buttons a few more times the truck jerked forward about ten feet, pulling the charging cable out of the wall socket, which resulted in a big flash and a few sparks. Undeterred we continued with our quest for mischief and fun and with the charging cable still fixed to the rear end of the truck I slowly edged it forward. As I got familiar with the controls, I cautiously drove around the area where the trucks were stored. As soon as I thought I'd mastered the machine, I was off like a bat out of hell and drove straight through the heavy plastic curtain that led to the outside yard where the bricks were stored. I was having a great time driving around the brick yard like a young Sterling Moss, with my mate clinging to the truck for dear life, whilst still shouting 'faster,

faster!' Unfortunately, I got over confident, took a bend a bit too fast and ending up having a 'head on' with a wall. My mate got thrown from the truck and, cutting his head open, he was the lucky one! As the truck hit the wall, the front of it caved in and my leg was trapped between truck and wall. The metal panelling on the truck cut straight through my jeans and into my leg. As I struggled in vain to free the leg, I could feel warm blood trickling towards my feet. Once my mate had stopped screaming and he'd wiped most of his blood from his forehead he came to my assistance and tried pull me free. We pushed and tugged my blooded leg but there was no getting it free. Panic started to set in and I told my mate he would have to go and find help. He wasn't happy about going back into the brick factory on his own but finally went in search of someone. After what seemed like ages and, with tears rolling down my face, I eventually heard people approaching. My mate appeared with one of the factory workers and the look on the mans' face as he spotted me trapped in the crashed truck, was a picture. He ran towards me and attempted to free my leg. After a lot of huffing and puffing, and with a very red face he said, gasping for breath 'I'll have to go and get some assistance '. He soon returned with another man, both of them running to my rescue carrying long metal poles. Using the metal poles the crushed panels were quickly separated and my leg was freed. I fell out of the truck and let out a massive sigh of relief but my delight at being released was short lived. I looked down at my leg and to my horror I saw the large tear in my jeans. This was my first pair of fashionable jeans, I'd pestered Mom for weeks to get a pair of Levi jeans for my birthday. When she'd checked out the price of the Levi's, she nearly had a heart attack. I didn't want anything else, just the Levi's, and even suggested she asked my nan and aunties to pay towards it. I don't know who paid what, or how much they actually cost, all I know is, come my birthday, I was over the moon to get a pair of Levis. Now, only a few days after my birthday looking at a six inch rip in my pride and joy! I was in shock as the two factory workers repeatedly asked me if I was ok. I simply couldn't answer for a minute or so, I wasn't in shock because of the cut and bruising to my leg, but because my Levis were ruined. They helped me to my feet and I hobbled about a bit and told them I would be ok and then limped off with my mate in tow, nursing his bleeding head.

Even by the standards of the early 70's I think it was pretty shocking: I was trespassing on private property, had probably caused hundreds of pounds of damage to the truck and charging socket; I'd caused injury to myself and my mate and then we were allowed to just wonder away from the scene as if nothing had happened. No police nor ambulance were called, no company safety officer appeared, no one even asked for our name or address and no doubt the two factory workers went straight back to the canteen and had a nice cuppa. Those were the days my friend – *I feel a song coming on!*

I may have got off lightly as far as the two factory workers were concerned but Mom hit the roof. She couldn't give a stuff about the six-inch long cut to my leg or how I'd managed to cause such injury, she was just fuming about the fact that a pair of jeans that cost a small fortune and were only a few days old, would now end up in the bin. I don't think she spoke to me for the rest of the summer holidays.

I can categorically tell you though, she wasn't as upset as I was over ruining my Levis and I was mad that I hadn't even had time to show off them off to my cousins. Their Dad, my Uncle Bill, spoilt his kids and they always had fashionable clothes and were given regular pocket money. The day after my birthday I'd missed a great opportunity to show them off. I'd headed off to my cousins in Redhouse with my brother, proudly wearing my Levi's, I couldn't wait to show my cousins what I'd got for my birthday. Less than halfway there, a big van pulled up alongside and a fairly young bloke asked us for directions to the T.I. factory. After telling the van driver the directions a couple of times, he was still not sure of the route so I offered to jump in and show him the way, providing he then gave me a lift to my cousins. He nodded in agreement and, without any warning from big brother, I jumped into the van and off we went. Arriving at the T.I. factory the van driver asked me if I wanted to help him with the delivery and go into the offices. I was quick to agree and helped carry boxes from the back of the van, dropping them in the reception area. All the women made a fuss of me and gave me sweets and drinks and when one asked the van driver if I was his younger brother, nobody batted an eyelid when he informed them he'd just picked me up off the street and had only known me for five minutes!

Upon finishing the delivery, the bloke told me to direct him to my cousins' and I quickly replied, 'Where you going next?' 'Wolverhampton,' was the reply and the van driver looked a bit surprised when I asked if I could go with him. Anyhow, he replied 'I suppose so ' so off we went to sunny Wolverhampton. I ending up spending the whole day travelling around with him and he even bought me a bag chips and an ice cream, I had a great time, being treated like a minor celebrity by the ladies at most of the drop offs. Much to my delight, one or two of the ladies commented on my 'posh Levis' and I was quick to tell them that I'd got them for my birthday, which was yesterday! At each new delivery the van driver was asked who I was and his reply was always, *'I don't really know, I picked him up off the streets,'* and just like at our first port of call, this never received any criticism or raised voices of alarm. By 5 o'clock we had finished delivering and the van driver dropped me back home. My exciting adventure as a drivers mate had sadly come to an end! All the time I was travelling about in the van with the young driver, he never once asked me if I wanted to go and look at some puppies or to feel the hole in his trouser pocket. Earlier that afternoon my brother had told Mom that I'd gone off in a van with a stranger and the action she took was to make up one less meal for tea. When I did get home my Mom said *'I didn't think we'd be seeing you again!'*

Every August-bank-holiday weekend the Moorgreen County Show was held near my grandparents' house in Watnall and most years the family attended to see Granddad winning rosettes each year for his prize canaries and other caged birds. The Moorgreen was a real festival for all country-living folk. Amongst the usual attractions were horticultural shows, every type of cow, pig and sheep you could imagine. Bulls the size of a transit van and some truly massive shire horses. There were dog agility displays and even pig racing and, if that wasn't enough, there was farm machinery and classic cars. But the number one attraction for me was *the Fair*, which must have taken up several acres on its own.

The day before the fair opened I had taken the short walk from Grandma's house to the site of the Moorgreen Show just to have a mooch and watch the big tents go up and see the various fairground rides set up by frightening-looking men covered in tattoos. Back in the early 70's tattoos were still very much taboo and only men from the armed forces, criminals, hardmen and, of course, fairground workers had tattoos and never, ever women. As I was wondering around, I got talking to a woman setting up the toffee-apple and candy-floss trailer. I helped pass a few boxes to her and she asked me if I was any good at maths. After telling her I was, she immediately threw some multiplication at me. Luckily, she didn't make the sums too difficult and I got most correct. After the unexpected maths test, she said 'Would you like to help me tomorrow? ' Would I – bleedin' right I would! I promised to be back at the fairground at 9 o'clock next morning. Full of enthusiasm for the next day, I made my way back to my grandparents' house to tell everyone my exciting news. I wasn't surprised, or even that bothered that neither my parents nor grandparents shared my delight that the next day I would be working at the fairground.

The following morning, I made sure I was up bright and early and was sitting waiting on the step of the trailer when the woman turned up. My first job was to help her make toffee, Then I had to push the sticks into loads of apples and finally I got to dip the apples into the toffee. Within an hour, I was a toffee-apple maker and by midday I was given lessons in spinning candy floss! I took to it like a duck to water! My favourite job was wrapping the toffee apples in coloured wrapping paper and placing them on the

sloping display shelf at the front of the trailer. I had great
fun with this and let my imagination run wild. What I'd
experience at Port Vale and Notts Forest gave me an idea –
I made the toffee-apple display resemble a football terrace,
full of rival fans and coppers. Half the display was the Reds
(Man United supporters, of course), the other half were the
Oranges (Blackpool I suppose) and dividing the two sets
of warring fans was a single line of blue (the police) toffee
apples. The Blues were also placed across the front, to stop
the Reds and Oranges invading my imaginary football pitch.
On the few occasions the woman left me on my own I would
throw a few of the Reds into the Orange section and knock
over the weedy Orange boys and then the police would come
into play and restore order. If anybody had noticed what I
was up to, they would have probably called for the men in
the white coats and had me taken away! During the day I
was allowed to eat and drink anything I wanted. Heaven! I
also got a couple of hotdogs from the woman's sister, who
had her own trailer serving burgers, hotdogs and peas with
mint sauce – philistines! We were very busy and the hours
flew by and by late afternoon I was shattered. When the
boss lady thanked me for my help and told me I could get
off I wasn't expecting to be paid, considering the amount
of toffee apples, candy floss and fizzy drinks I'd consumed.
So when she handed me, what I thought was a one pound
note, I nearly fainted. Putting the money into my pocket, I
must have thanked her a dozen times. She kindly said that
I had worked hard and I deserved it. As soon as I left her I
went round the back of the fairground trucks to look at my
pound note and check that I wasn't dreaming. As I pulled
out the money from my pocket I couldn't believe my eyes.

There was not one pound note but THREE! Three pounds, three fuckin' pounds! I felt like I'd won the pools and just couldn't believe my luck. It didn't take long to think what I'd do with the money. Man United had just introduced a new kit, the shirt had a very trendy white collar and the usual red socks had been replaced with the1950's-style black socks with a thin red-and-white stripe at the top. The sports shop next to Harpers bus garage in Aldridge sold the new United kit (boys' size) for the princely sum of £2.50. Fuck Me! I could buy the new United kit and still have ten bob left over! Holding the three-pound notes in my hand as tightly I could, I ran back to my grandparents house to show my Mom and Dad my little fortune. To avoid the crowds that were still milling about, I dodged around the livestock trucks sited on the perimeter of the showground. As I ran past one particular truck I saw out the corner of my eye, four men sitting in a circle, laughing and joking. Tied to the side of the truck was something that looked like a palomino pony. My gallop immediately turned into a trot and then a very slow walking pace. I must have gone past another half a dozen trucks before I finally came to a stand still. I stood rooted to the ground for a while, thinking to myself 'did I really just see a palomino pony?' I slowly turned round and made my way back to where I thought I'd seen it, pushing my pound notes deep into my pocket. Approaching the truck, the noise of the high spirited men made me a bit nervous, but I had to see if I had seen it there. I stood in the gap between the trucks and gazed wide-eyed at the pony. It probably wasn't a thoroughbred palomino but, with its sandy-coloured coat and off-white tail and mane, it was certainly good enough for me! In a daze, I wondered past the group of men and headed straight for the pony, patting it for a few minutes before one of the men called out, 'Do you like it?' I replied. 'Yes, it's fantastic.' The bloke came over and started to list details about the pony - how many hands it was, its age, its name (Quickstep). I had butterflies in my stomach as I listened because it was the most stunning thing I'd ever seen. The bloke must have sensed how much I liked the pony and said, 'I bet you'd like to take him home with you.' I nodded and he said 'You can have him for thirty bob.' (£1.50). Instantly I replied 'I got more than thirty bob and I could afford to buy him.' Excitedly I produced three-pound notes from my pocket to prove I meant business. He was taken aback and said with a surprised look on his face 'Don't you think you should ask your Mom and Dad first?' I told him that my Mom and Dad were staying just a short distance away and I would go and check with them and come back and collect the pony. I ran so fast back to my grandparents' house, I don't think Road Runner would have caught me. I burst in through the back door and, wildly excited, informed Mom and Dad that I'd been given three pounds for working at the fair and I had met a man who would sell me his pony for thirty bob. I was really out of breath, very animated and over excited. Mom kept telling me to calm down and I had to go through my story three or four times before they understood what was going on. When the penny did drop, so did my heart - Dad simply burst out laughing and called me an idiot. He continued to ridicule me by saying 'Are you going to take the pony back home on the bus or ride it home?' and 'Are you going to let it sleep at the end of your bed?' all the time laughing at me and taking the piss. He never stopped once to consider my feelings. Couldn't he see how much this pony meant to me? Mom told him how upset I was and asked him to stop but it didn't cut any ice with him and he continued to poke fun at me. Surely he must have recognised how passionate I felt? Well, whether he did or not, he made me feel worthless and that my feelings meant nothing to him. The way I felt at that moment was by far the worst I had ever felt in my life. If I added up all the humiliation that I received from my old school teacher Mr. Lowe and all the other previous rejections and cold-hearted abuse I'd had from Dad in the past, it still didn't come close to how I felt at that moment. It may have been an unrealistic dream but surely I deserved praise, or at least acknowledgement, for the fact that, at eleven years old, I had gone out and found myself a job at a fairground and earned myself three pounds. Instead all I got was ridicule.

All in all, this was the most hurtful and upsetting day of my childhood. With Dad still laughing at me, I left the house in tears and ran back to the fair. I was still crying when I got to the pony. The group of men who were hanging around the truck tried their best to console me and pointed out all the impracticalities of owning a pony and let me stay with it until it was almost dark. I gave the pony one last hug and said my goodbyes. As I walked back to my grandparents' house, I thought to myself, well my little ride around The High Chaparral with Blue Boy and Manolito would just have to wait.

It had been almost a year to the day since I'd first seen Man United play and just like the previous year, I got an early Christmas present. In the middle of December Mickey

Gibbs and Alfie took to me watch United at Stoke City. Alfie lived not far from me in Aldridge and was the oldest of the Poole family and the father of the infamous Bimbo Poole. Alfie often worked cash-in-hand for my Dad and had a reputation for being a big drinker and a fighter, but I always found him to be a kind-hearted man and he always had a smile for me. Arriving in Stoke, I spent an hour or so standing outside a pub, while Mick and Alfie had a few pints. There was little or no chance of kids being allowed in then, especially on a Saturday afternoon. Most men went to the pub to get away from their wife and kids, so the last thing the average working class man would want was kids running around the local boozer. I enjoyed watching the comings and goings outside the pub and I had a bottle of pop and a couple of bags of crisps, so was happy enough. When we finally left and started to walk towards the Victoria ground, Mick treated me to a Man United rosette and a poster of my hero, Georgie Best. When we got into the ground, we stood in a small terrace alongside the pitch with the Boothen End to our right. Just like in my toffee-apple display, a thin blue line separated the Man United fans from the home supporters and, once again, I was totally captivated by the hostile atmosphere on the terraces. So engrossed was I that Mick had to point out that players were running onto the pitch! Standing almost in line with the penalty area, we could clearly see the United players at the goal nearest to us as they started to warm up. I immediately spotted George Best taking shots at the United keeper, Alex Stepney, and couldn't believe I was so near to my hero. With a sudden rush of blood to the head I said to Mick, 'Can I go on to the pitch and get George's autograph?' He readily agreed and after he had failed to find a pen, a man standing behind us in the packed terrace offered me his and helped Mick and Alfie lift me over the wall onto the side of the pitch.

I ran into the middle of the goal area and said to Georgie, 'Excuse me Mr. Best can I have your autograph please?' Without a word he duly took the pen off me, signed my poster and wandered off to continue with his shots at goal. I stood in the middle of the United players like a rabbit in the headlights, frozen to the spot and caught in two minds whether I should be concentrating on the players' warm-up or on the rowdy United fans behind the goal. After what seemed an age, Bobby Charlton came over to me and said 'You've got George's autograph now, so you'll have to get off the pitch.'

Slowly I walked to the side of the goal and soon realized I was totally disorientated – where the bleedin' hell were Mick and Alf? As I was looking into the crowd behind the goal, a few people were pointing over towards the left, so I turned my head and saw Mick, Alf and several other members of the crowd waving at me. I ran along the touchline and as I clambered back into the terraces I was greeted like a returning gallant soldier. I lost count the amounts of times strangers in the crowd congratulated me for going on the pitch and getting my poster signed! The next day while watching Start Soccer on TV, I got the shock of my life. Just for a fleeting second I spotted myself on the TV screen. There I was in my scruffy old duffle coat running across the football field, heading towards the goalmouth with my poster in hand. What a claim to fame for an eleven- year-old kid, not only getting George Bests' autograph, but also appearing on Star Scorer whilst doing so. Years later, I still have the signed poster - now framed and hanging on the wall.

The next Saturday I was on a totally different field, with my mate Rob picking beetroot at Snot Rags farm. I was desperate to get money to buy my first seven-inch (45) record - the wonderful Ernie (the fastest milkman in the west) by Benny Hill. I'd pleaded with my Mom to buy me the record but, it being so close to Christmas, she flatly refused. I tried several ways to get the 40p that I needed to buy the record – attempting to open the telephone cashbox again and stealing empty pop bottles to claim money back on them. By now most of the shopkeepers were marking the labels of the empty bottles. So, in an act of desperation, I had asked Snot Rag if I could do some work for him. It was a bitterly cold day, and sleet and rain fell on whilst we were picking the beetroots in the muddy field. Snot Rag had his usual drink - tea in a sterilized milk bottle. The tea was kept warm by putting the bottle into two pairs of smelly socks. After picking beets for four or five hours, it was getting really cold and our little hands were red raw. I told Snot Rag that we were going home and waited for him to cross our hands with silver. After searching about first in his jacket pocket and then in his trousers he handed me 10p. I looked at the 10p for a while and said in disgust 'Is that it? After all the work we have done today that's it?' Snot Rag mumbled something about that being all he could afford so begrudgingly I asked where Rob's 10p was. I was astonished when he told me the 10p was between us! If I'd have been a little older and a little bolder, I'd have kicked him in the bollocks! 5p each for working all afternoon – that worked out at a penny an hour. Young Dickensian chimney sweeps got more than that! In a fit of temper I threw the 10p in the muddy field, pushed over the sacks of beetroot and called Snot Rag 'a Bastard'. 'Never darken my door again,' Snot Rag shouted after us as we stormed off! And that, I'm glad to say, was the last I ever saw of Snot Rag.

Come Christmas time the thought of owning a palomino pony and rounding up stray cattle with Audie Murphy or Blue Boy was very much a fading dream. Being a fickle eleven-year-old, my desires were on a new prize. There was one thing above all others that I wanted for Christmas - the stunning Chopper Bike. Its unique design made it a cultural icon, and Raleigh, the manufacturer of The Chopper, marketed the bike as THE HOT ONE. It was by far the coolest thing on the street and it was the *must have* item for all kids who's parents could afford the £35.00 for the standard model or an eye-watering £55.00 for the deluxe model. £55.00 wasn't far off an average man's weekly wage! I must have entered at least a dozen competitions trying to win THE HOT ONE and I was always scouring newspapers and magazines in the hope of finding and winning a competition. When Mom unpacked the groceries I would immediately look on the back of the cereal boxes to see if there was a new chance of winning my dream bike. Sadly it was all in vain. Mom constantly told me the Chopper was far too expensive every time I'd ask for one for Christmas. Ever the optimist, I hoped that pester power would win the day and, going to bed on Christmas Eve, I recited the mantra 'chopper bike, chopper bike ' and when I woke up on Christmas Day I prayed 'chopper bike, chopper bike, chopper bike!' Running downstairs I found the

living room full of presents and soon identified my own pile
but it was pretty obvious a chopper bike was not amongst
them. Downhearted I started to open my presents, feeling
really upset that my parents hadn't met my high aspirations.
Luckily, one present did bring a smile to my face - a pair
of white football boots. Today, with all the multi-coloured
football boots on display, white football boots wouldn't
get a second glance, but in the early seventies only Alan
Hinton of Derby County and Alan Ball of Arsenal had the
nerve to wear white boots. Besides being 'Wow – White'
my new football boots had a unique feature: instead of the
traditional fixed stud, the manufactures Tufspin (it must
have taken all of five minutes for the Ad men to come
up with that name) introduced a rotating studded disc at
the front of the boot. In theory, the moving circular plate
was supposed to allow you to swivel without the studs
moving. The reality was, as I soon found out, when the
studs got stuck in the turf and you tried to move sharply
left or right, your ankle might turn but your hips wouldn't,
thus twisting your ankle at best and breaking the sodding
thing at worst. If these were about in todays 'where-there's-
blame-there's-a-claim' society, Tufspin would be up in court
every five minutes. Anyway, when Mom eventually got
up and came into the living room, she asked if I liked my
presents. Reluctantly I nodded and said thanks. Then, to my
utter delight she said 'Your main present is in the garage.'
Wearing my Tufspin football boots I raced out of the house
and headed across our back garden towards the garage, all
the time thinking 'chopper bike, chopper bike, chopper
bike, chopper bike.' I should have been thinking 'Stupid
Boots!' When I was halfway across the lawn, I noticed my

prized 'Wembley' football and couldn't resist christening my new jazzy boots by taking a kick. The boot studs fixed firmly in the grass and I discovered the design flaw. I did a neat little pirouette then, ripping up a massive piece of turf with the studs, landed flat on my back. Luckily for me I only gave my ankle a tweak and immediately got up and continued towards the garage. Excitedly I flung open the garage door and, with eyes as wide as saucers, looked around for my dream bike. The sight that greeted me brought me down to earth with a bump – just like my stupid Tufspin football boots had! Instead of feasting my eyes on the coolest bike in the world, I was devastated to see a second-hand racing bike. Rust was starting to appear on the pedals, the big leather saddle looked like it was pre-war and the tape that was wrapped around the handle bars had started to come loose. What a rollercoaster of emotions! I felt like I'd been kicked in the stomach and the ungrateful sod in me thought 'I'd rather have no bike than this tatty looking thing.' My face must have been a picture as I walked back into the house and Mom instantly knew I wasn't happy with the bike. Mom and Dad had scrimped and saved and were doing their best to buy Christmas presents for us five kids so, understandably, both were angry with me and, amongst other things, called me an 'ungrateful little bleeder'. As it turned out, that would be the last Christmas I got a pile of presents from my parents. Thereafter my Mom and Dad cut out the Middle Man (aka Santa Claus) and I was given the cash to buy my own Christmas presents. I had no problem with having the cash and was happy to help Santa reduce his carbon footprint.

1972

I was still mad keen to obtain a copy of 'Ernie' so, in desperation, straight after the new year I took on a morning paper-round, which meant getting up at the God-unearthly hour of 05:45. My first day was a Saturday and as soon as I arrived at the paper shop at 06:30 it was a baptism of fire.

The owner of the paper shop was a big, grumpy and curt middle-aged man. He greeted me by thrusting a piece of thin card at me, the card displayed the addresses and what newspaper should be delivered to each particular house. He then pointed to the stacks of various newspapers lying on the shop floor and told me to 'mark up my papers'. Luckily there was a couple of older and experienced lads in the shop, they had already started marking up their papers for the morning delivery and they gave me some much-needed assistance on that first morning.

When I had finished marking up my papers, I put them into my heavy canvas paper-bag and told the shop owner I was ready to go out on my rounds. He barked at me *'are you sure you know where you're going?'* Because of his aggressive nature, I was too nervous to ask him to talk me through my route, so I just nodded and wandered out into the cold dark morning. I had about thirty newspapers to deliver and the first twenty or so deliveries went like clockwork, but when I pulled the newspaper out that had 'Stonnall Road' written on it, I suddenly thought 'where the bleedin' hell is Stonnall Road?'

I was standing at one end of Lazy Hill Road and I knew if I carried on walking down the hill towards the busy Chester Road, then crossed the Chester Road, Stonnall village would be in front of me. Logic suggested that the road leading into the village, must be Stonnall Road. Stone the crows, what a bleeding long walk every morning, just to drop off one poxy newspaper. But being the little trooper that I was, I soldiered on and marched down the hill and into Stonnall. I marched up-and-down a street, which I later found out was Stonnall High Street and not the illusive Stonnall Road. After asking several bemused locals, where 'number 2' was, I came to the conclusion the house/number just didn't exist and the newsagent had given me the wrong address.

Defeated and dejected I made my way back up the long and steep hill and finally delivered my last few newspapers, all except No. 2 Stonnall Road of course! I was completely knackered and as I made my way back to the paper shop, I couldn't help thinking *'if I've got to do this every morning, I'll miss my first two lessons at school. I'll have to ask my Mom to write me a note!'* By the time I got back to the paper shop it was 09:30, the owner of the shop spotted my approach and he came out of a shop to meet me. *'Where the bleedin' have you been'?'* he snapped at me. Before I had time to explain he shouted that 'the person who lived at No. 2 Stonnall Road had phoned up three times and was very angry that he hadn't received his newspaper!'

I told the miserable old sod that I'd spent a long time looking for the fabled No.2 Stonnall Road but I simply couldn't find it. I added I'd asked a few people in Stonnall Road, if they knew where number 2 was, but no-one knew where it was! Without reply the shop owner grabbed me by the arm and marched me over to his car, he then bundled me inside and drove us off. Within less than a minute we were sitting outside No. 2 Stonnall Road. Pointing at the large

detached house he said 'How the hell could you miss that?'.
I blushed with embarrassment as I explained to the shop
owner, I had walked all the way down into Stonnall Village
and didn't realize that Stonnall Road ran parallel to Lazy
Hill Road, I thought it was a continuation of it. He looked
at me as if to say 'you thick twat' then shouted *'well are you
going to delivery the bloody paper or just sit in my sodding car
all morning?'* I'd barely got out of the car, before the horrible
git sped off in his car, leaving me to walk back to the paper-
shop. The next day I did my paper round in less than an hour,
even though I had the heavy Sunday papers to carry around.

By the time payday came around on Friday, I thought the
paper round was a doddle. Knowing that I was going to get
my 70p wages, I arrived at the paper-shop full of excitement
on my first Friday morning. I had already planned my visit
to Kings, the local record store and I intended to buy my
very first single, a copy of 'Ernie' on my way home from
school that very afternoon.

I bounced into the paper-shop and wasted no time in
asking for my 70p wages. As the shop owner gave me my
70p he also handed me, not one but two cards, my usually
mark-up card and an extra 'Walsall Observer' mark-up card.
I looked at the extra card, then looked back at the shop-
owner and said 'what's this one for' *'it's bleedin' Friday isn't
it?'* he said sarcastically. I nodded in agreement and then
he added *'well, Friday is Walsall Observer day.'* He pointed
me to a paper bag next to the Counter and said *'there's your
extra bag!'* 'What Extra Bag?' I thought.

This was all news to me (pardon the pun); when I'd read
about the vacancy at the paper shop in *The Times*, I was
sure it never mentioned anything about double deliveries on

Friday – I was shocked! And if it was bad enough that I had to deliver an extra twenty-five newspapers, the fact that the *Walsall Observer* was over twice as thick as the normal daily paper, was just taking the piss. The extra news paper-bag was so heavy, I had to remove it and have a rest after only a hundred yards. I was starting to think that the shop owner must have gone to the same business and charm school as my farmer friend, Snot Rag. I had to resort to dragging my bags along the pavement to give my shoulders a rest, then I would put the bags back over my shoulders and walk a short way before having to stop due the ridiculous weight - talk about a beast of burden. By the time I'd finished my first Friday round, my back and shoulders were in bits and all for 10p per day. 'Ernie' better have a bloody good 'B' side I thought to myself as I hobbled off home. The child exploitation would have made a Dickensian blush!

After my third 'Observer Friday' I'd had enough and didn't bother doing my paper round that weekend, oh the joy of a *lie in*. But on the Monday the other paperboys told me that's the grumpy old sod had left and a young funny man had taken over and the new owner had asked if I would go back and carry on with my paper round. Being curious about the new owner, I decided to give the paper round another go.

When I arrived at the paper shop the next morning the large bundles of newspapers were still sitting on the footpath outside the shop and a couple of the other paper boys were knocking on the locked door of the shop. There was no lights on in the shop or the flat above, but after a few minutes of banging on the door and shouting, a head appeared from the upstairs flat window. It was the new owner. '*Sorry boys*

I've overslept. Can you open up?' with this he threw down a large bunch of keys. The new owner added *'Oh and drag the papers in for me.'* We opened the shop door and entered the cold, dark and unoccupied shop. The small group of young paperboys all stood like statues as they all eyed-up the lovely unguarded sweets and chocolates on display. A little switch must have gone off in our heads, as there was a suddenly mad flurry of action as we all dived towards the counter and filled pockets with chocolate bars and sweets.

We had pulled in the bundles of newspapers from outside and I had almost finished marking up my newspapers before the new young owner made an appearance. *'Everything ok boys?'* the scruffy young man asked as he slurped on his cup of tea, rubbed the sleep out of his eyes and tried to tidy up the bird's nest on top of his head. What a two-and-eight. It was the same drill for the rest of the week: the paperboys would bang on the shop door; the new owner would stick his sleepy head out of the window and throw us his keys; we would open up and drag the bundles of newspapers into the shop and then fill our pockets with sweets and by the end of the week we had progressed to nicking the fags that were at the back of the counter.

The previous few days had gone really well for me and my fellow thieving paperboys, but there is always something that upsets the applecart. Our applecart was tipped over when on 'Observer Friday' the new owner told us, 'he hadn't got enough change to pay us.' He promised he would be going to the bank later that day and that he would pay us the next day. But when I went to the shop on the Saturday morning, instead of giving us 70p each, the bastard only gave us 50p each and promised he'd make the difference up the following week. Was this young scruffy bleeder 'Son of Snot Rag?' or what? As soon as I was given the 50p, I immediately threw a paddy and with a face like thunder I stormed out of the shop, never to return.

Obviously I wasn't as cute (streetwise) as I thought I was. So all right the incompetent shop owner might have diddled me out of 20p, but I must have been stealing almost that amount every day while the lazy good-for-nothing sod was lying in his pit, instead of taking his place behind the counter where he could keep an eye on his tea-leaf paperboys. If I'd had my thinking cap on, I would have carried on doing my paper round and just stolen more of the stock. But we live and learn.

Politics was almost tangible at the start the year as Joe Gormley and the NUM took on Edward Heath and his conservative government. Because the demands of the miners hadn't been meet by the Tories, for the first time since 1926 the miners voted to go on strike. They wanted an extra £9.00 on top of their weekly wage of £25.00 It very quickly became a bitter and violent dispute and the strike was characterised by the use of flying pickets, who were sent to various industrial sites to persuade other workers to strike in solidarity with the miners. One of the most important of these other friendly groups of workers was the railway workers who refused to transport coal. The miners were also aided by power-station workers refusing to handle coal.

These actions, along with the pickets blocking mines and coal yards, soon led to power cuts for both domestic and industrial users. Different areas of the country had different times when their power was cut off. From memory, the good folks of Aldridge lost their electricity for approximately four hours in the morning and then again from 4:00 pm – 8:00 pm. It was a strange old time, the whole family huddled round the table and eat our tea by candle light. Fortunately we had a gas fire, so we still had heat in the house, but if we moved from room to room we would take a torch to light our way. Candle power also dominated in all the shops and in the few pubs that stayed open - most pubs remained closed toward the end of the power strike.

The first few days of the power cuts were a bit of a pain and there was plenty of moans and groans in the Grainger household, but after that things settled down and losing our electricity every evening soon became normal. In fact it was probably the closest my family had ever been. Because of our circumstances we were compelled to get on with each other and, having nothing else to do, my family interacted at home like never before. We happily played card games and monopoly and very short-lived games of 'I Spy': *I spy with my little eye - something beginning 'C' !* 'CANDLE!! Game over. Previously we had only done this sort of thing on holiday and only when it was raining. But with the flick of a switch in the local Power Station, we were transported from the 19th century back to the 20th century. As much as we enjoyed our card games, as soon as the lights and, more important, the colour TV came on, there was a nightly round of applause, cheering and clapping. There is nothing like *going without,* to make you appreciate what you have!

In all, the strike had lasted for almost two months; it came to an end after miners agreed to a pay offer at the end of February. The offer came from the government after the infamous Battle of Saltley Gate - around two thousand NUM pickets descended on a giant coal yard in

Birmingham and were joined by thousands of workers from non-related industries from in and around Birmingham. I think we were one step away from having the Red Flag flown over Birmingham Town Hall.

God knows how the Villa pulled it off, but while still a third division team they managed to persuade the Brazilian team Santos to play a friendly at Villa Park. Any schoolboy could have told you at the time, that Santos's star player was the one and only Pele, who was probably the best and most famous footballer (after George Best) in the world.

Getting Santos to agree to play at Villa park was one thing, actually being able to stage the game was another thing. Because of the miners strike, Birmingham, like the rest of the UK, was still suffering from power cuts, this effected both domestic and work life. So to ensure the game went ahead, Villa staff had to pay out over £5,000.00 for the hire of a generator to run the flood lights for the friendly game. I'm sure Villa got the money back on their investments as a crowd of 55,000 turned up to witness the great Pele run onto the Villa Park pitch.

I was part of the crowd that night and as Pele stood talking to his team mates in the center circle, I jumped out of the terraces and, chased by a fat and ageing copper, I ran onto the pitch, determined to get Pele to sign my match programme. I easily out-ran the old copper and I got to within a few feet of Pele, then I suddenly froze - it wasn't that I was frightened of asking the great man for his autograph, it was because I'd just realized I didn't have a bleedin' pen with me. What a Thicko! I was almost in touching distance of the man but because of 'lack of planning' I had failed. I could have kicked my self. I turned round so I could run back to the terraces and as I did, I saw the old copper puffing and panting and stumbling towards me. I ran past the knackered old sod and he made a vain attempt to grab hold of me. I was straight past him and nearly back in the stand as the poor bleeder then had to turn round and start chasing me all over again. I think he was one step away from joining the Keystone Cops. As I jumped back into the terraces, I looked round to see how far away the fat copper was but there was no danger of him catching me, he looked like he was about to have a heart attack as he struggled across the goal area.

Aston villa may have captured the local headlines by playing a Brazilian team, but probably the biggest football story of the season was little old Hereford United beating FA Cup giants Newcastle United. The Geordies were a strong first division team and they had the legendary, toothless *Supermac* in their side. Hereford United on the other hand were a struggling non-league team and had no fulltime professional players. But with the help of Ronnie Radford and his 'goal of the season', Hereford United beat Newcastle 2 − 1. As Ronnie Radford's screamer hit the back of the net, hundreds of Parka-clad teenagers invaded the muddy pitch. Along with Charlie George's prostrate goal celebration in the 1971 FA Cup final and Bob Stokoe running all over the Wembley pitch when Sunderland won the FA Cup, Ronnie Radford's super goal and subsequent pitch invasion has to be the one of most memorable images of the early 70's for a vast majority of football fans.

And while on the subject of '*Parka clad teenagers*' no '70's book would be complete without mentioning the ubiquitous green Parka. In the early 70's it seemed almost every kid had a green parka with orange padded lining. Our Parkas were not like the stylish 'Fishtail Parkers' that the Mods wore in the 60's, our Parkas were functional and cheap-looking and although most kids from ten to thirteen years old wore them; they were not considered fashionable at all. We only wore Parkas because our parents couldn't afford the ultimate fashion statement, a Crombie overcoat. If your parents were really struggling for money and they couldn't afford to buy you a Parka, you might have had the misfortune to end up with a coat from the Army and Navy Stores. In the mid 1960s, U.S. Army chic became popular among hippies as they felt they were making ironic statements about peace, by wearing Army surplus. But by the early '70's the ex-army jackets and coats were looked down on and despised by fashion-conscious teenagers. The thick woolen ex-British Army waist-length jackets and three-quarter length overcoats may not have been popular, but another one of the Army & Navy stores products was. The early skinheads were more than happy to visit the un-fashionable stores to purchase 'Black Eleven Hole, Hob-Nailed, Steel-Toe Capped Boots. If you got a kick in the bollocks from a skinhead wearing them, your wedding tackle was mashed.

Are you going to the Comm?' was the most asked question on a Tuesday afternoon. 'The Comm' was a teenagers disco held every Tuesday evening at the Aldridge Community Center and it was strictly ticket only. Such was the popularity of the disco that when the tickets went on sale on a Saturday morning, within an hour or so they had sold out. If you were under age (not a teenager) like me and my mates, it was a big deal to get into The Comm. The DJ was the usual '70's cheesy tosser who thought himself to be super cool and a bit of a comedian, but he did play some great music, besides playing all the hits of the day from the likes of local band Slade, plus T-Rex, The Sweet, Gary Glitter, Alice Cooper and Bowie, he always played the Motown greats and Reggae classics like Monkey Spanner, The Liquidator and Johnny Reggae by The Piglets. And no 70's disco would be complete without Judge Dread's Big 7 and football anthem Hi Ho Silver Lining. I hated it when each week, mine and Ade's cry of 'Man United' was drowned out by Villa fans. For the ones who can't remember the infamous disco lyrics of Jeff Becks song. *Hi Ho Man United, Everywhere you go there's agro, I see your toecaps shinning, And the razor in your Crombie lining, It's so obvious.*

The Comm. was the place to be and the place to be seen, everyone wore their best glad rags. One Johnny Come Lately from down south, had recently joined our class and on his first visit to The Comm, the flash little bleeder only turned up wearing a powder-blue silk jacket – as worn by Marc Bolan and the TV character Budgie (played by Adam faith). Budgie's more popular black-and-white casual jacket, colloquial know as *The Budgie Jacket,* was worn by teenagers up and down the country and there were always a few on show at The Comm. - but a silk jacket, that was avant-garde. And as if his silk jacket had caused enough of a stir, the snazzy sod had only gone and had the feather-cut that very afternoon!

Only the most flamboyant and confident boys had the *feather-cut* style and blow-dried their hair and the puffs would parade about like strutting peacocks. I admired them and loathed them in equal measure. Secretly I always wanted to have the *feather-cut* but none of the local men's' barbers were up to the task of cutting your hair in the latest style. So if you wanted a *feather-cut it* meant a trip to a ladies Hair Salon – and that was never going to happen. Besides my mates taking the piss out of me for weeks, the cost of going to a ladies Hair Salon was three or four times more expensive than a trip to 'Hacker Mullers' my regular barber.

The must-have fashion accessory for the super-cool older boys at The Comm. was an L.P. It was the height of sophistication to walk around the disco with an album cover tucked under your arm. I really couldn't see the point of carrying round an album sleeve even if the artwork on the cover was pretty stunning. There was certainly no chance of me being seen in public with an album cover under my arm, even if I'd wanted to; I simply couldn't afford to splash out £2.00 to buy one. My record collection consisted of my one and only single 'Ernie'.

One kid in my year got slaughtered for turning up at The Comm. carrying an album cover, but instead of a trendy album by Pink Floyd, Cream or Cat Stevens, he had a Top of the Pops LP. The T.O.T.P. LP's were less than half the price of an 'original' chart album and universally despised by a vast majority of teenagers. Both sides of a Top of the Pops album contained anonymous cover versions of recent and current hit singles. The recordings were intended to replicate the sound of the original hits as closely as possible, but they didn't! The albums were recorded by a studio group comprising session musicians and singers who remained unaccredited, although that included my musical hero Elton John. The only redeeming feature about the Top of the Pops albums was the sexy half-dressed girls on the front cover.

Several of the models who appeared on the album covers became Page 3 Girls, these included Ruth Gordon, Sam Fox and my all-time favourite Linda Lusadi. Most mornings before I went off to school I'd have a sneaky peek at The Sun's Page 3 hoping to get an eye-full of Linda's lovely knockers, then just like the Ready-Brek kid, I'd go to off to school with a warm glow, although my warm glow was only confined to one specific area.

Back to the Top of the Pops LP at The Comm. The offending album was spotted as soon as the poor innocent kid entered the disco, he was immediately jostled by the older lads and no doubt called a puff and a bummer. The album was taken from him and slung around the disco and stamped on for the rest of the night. After being roughed-up, the young owner of the Top of the Pops album left The Comm. shell shocked and in tears. I never saw him at The Comm. again, but I was told he went on to become a very successful DJ for saga radio.

The Comm. was the place where I first kissed a girl in public. The girl in question was called Caroline. She was the same age as me and rarely spoke to me at school. Caroline was a precocious siren and one of those girls that all the boys fancied, but were also nervous about when she was around. This particular evening she had fallen out with her boyfriend, but she got jealous as soon as she saw her ex-boyfriend talking to another girl. I just happened to be standing near to the ex-boyfriend and the girl he was chatting to, so I was either in the wrong or right place depending on your point of view. Caroline strolled past her Ex and in full view of him, took me by the hand and lead me to an adjacent alcove.

Still holding my hand she leant back against the wall and said 'you can kiss me now'. As I stood there hesitating, she pulled me towards her and started kissing me. I soon got over excited and pressed my lips hard against her and at the same time my head was swinging side to side in semi-circle motion. Caroline abruptly pulled away from me and with a look of disgust she snapped *'what was that? Have you ever kissed a girl before?'* Feeling totally embarrassed I froze for a few seconds and then whimpered *'Yes, I've kissed lots of girls.' 'Well you're the worst kisser I have ever known'* she replied. Then with the Tams 'hey girl don't bother me' playing in the background she pushed me to one side and returned to the dance floor.

That little minx really knocked my confidence with the girls and it was almost a year before I attempted to kiss a girl again. As I walked home alone from The Comm. I thought *'sod girls, I'll concentrate on my stamp collection.'* My collection wasn't your usual nerd's stamp collection. I wasn't looking for a 'penny blue' from Malta or ten-cents Singapore limited editions or even a King George birthday special.

My passion, bordering on obsession, was for football stamps from the *Sun* newspapers. As well as looking at Threepenny Bits on Page 3 every day, I religiously collected the tokens that were printed in the sports section of the *Sun*. I also pestered family and friends for their 'Soccerstamp Tokens' Following on from the success of the Swap Cards, the *Sun* had issued a football stamps collection the previous year. It was a very ambitious collection and, as the name suggests, the *Soccerstamps* were, well, stamps, rather than traditional cards. There were over five hundred in the complete set and the stamps came in a wide variety of sizes, shapes and colours. Beside the contemporary teams and star players there were also special sections included in the stamp collection: there was Goalkeeping Greats, International Legends, Star Forwards, Wizards of the Wing, and All Time Greats.

All of the stamps were mounted into a 165-page Football Encyclopedia that you had to purchase from a newsagent's for the princely sum of 10p. At the end of every week I would collect up all of my tokens and along with a self addressed envelope, post them off to the *Sun*. Then from Wednesday onwards, I would check the post every morning in anticipation that I would have new stamps to stick it into my Football Encyclopedia. There was nothing more disappointing, after I had eagerly opened the envelope from the *Sun* which contained my new Soccerstamps, than to discover that I'd already got every bleeding one of them!

Luckily, I had a 'Swap Angel' who must have given me almost a dozen stamps each week. I can't remember for the life of me how I got to know about my 'Swap Angel'. This man only lived about a hundred yards from me and he must have been in his forties at the time. Two or three times a week I would knock on his door and he would kindly invite me into his house. He would sort through his spare stamps and happily give me the stamps that were missing out of my collection. And when the *Sun* went and excelled themselves and introduced the avant-garde 3D Actionpix Starcards or, as they were called in the playground, 3D Football Stars, my 'Swap Angel' also gave me a few of them.

Whenever I visited my 'Swap Angel' his teenage daughter was always sitting in the living room watching TV and it seemed she never took any notice of me. But a couple of years after I had stopped collecting the Soccerstamps, I was hanging around the shops at the top of my road when a girl approach me and said '*you don't remember me, do you?* I didn't recognize her so I just shook my head. She informed me, that she was the daughter of the man that gave me all those stamps so I made out that I recognized her and enquired about her father. She said '*he was doing fine*' and after we had exchanged a few more pleasantries, she took me behind the chippie and gave me a 'hand job'. What a great family.

When my mates and me had enough of playing football, our favourite pastimes were 'Thunder and Lightning' and 'Hedge Hoping'. When playing 'Thunder and Lightning' we didn't do the traditional knock on doors and run away; we were a little more sophisticated than that. We would strategically choose a house, one where we could hide nearby and view our victims without being spotted. We would hide behind bushes or sometimes behind cars. One of our favourites spots was the row of houses opposite Leighswood School where were lots of bushes only a few yards away from the gardens, an ideal place for us observe the householders going barmy.

We would usually draw straws to decide who had to take the unenviable task of going up to the front door and attaching a line of cotton to the door knocker. If phase one was successful and we didn't get caught tying the cotton to the doorknocker we would then all retreat to the nearby bushes. The honour of pulling on the cotton line was usually given to the person that had crept up the garden path and attached it to the doorknocker. Two or three knocks were usually enough to bring someone to the front door.

On the first knock the householder would usually pop his or her head outside the door, look round for a few seconds then close the door. This was slightly amusing and brought a smile to our faces, but as we continued with our clandestine game the fun got better and better. After the householder had closed the door, we would wait for a couple of minutes and then, safely hidden in our vantage point, we would pull on the cotton line once more. The second time the householder came to the door, they would be a bit more agitated and from their doorway they would scour the streets for 'the horrible bleedin' kids who were disturbing their evening, this gave us a little chuckle. But when we did knock number three, this was when the fun really started. After our third knock, the front door would usually fly open and the householder would rush out into their front garden and their frustration would lead them to look over into their neighbours garden and walk to the end of their path in the vain hope of spotting their tormentors. The fourth knock would always provoke foul-mouthed abuse, neighbours would be calling for the 'men in white coats' as they witnessed their once mild-mannered neighbour, seemingly ranting and raving at thin air. By this stage, my mates and me we killing ourselves laughing.

The most we ever got up to was six knocks. This particular man went crazy. Desperate to catch us knocking on his door, he actually opened his door on spec a couple of times and jumped out onto his path, just like Cato from the *Pink Panther* films and we hadn't even knocked his door! This again set us off into fits of laughter.

We didn't always have it our own way. One time after the second knock the man opened his front door and noticed the cotton. He picked it up and briskly followed the line of cotton and when he was a few yards away from us we broke cover and ran in all directions. A couple of the lads got caught and ended up with thick ears.

We had two types of 'Hedge Hopping'. The first was the 'suicide run' where we would run through people's front gardens while it was still light. As with 'Thunder & Lightening, my mates and me would pick our targets carefully, ensuring that there was at least six gardens to attack and there were no thorn bushes to cause us damage. For shock and awe and maximum impact we would ask school friends outside of our little gang to join us. On a good night there could be a dozen of us rampaging through people's front gardens. With that many kids rampaging through front gardens there were always casualties of one type or another. After racing through the first couple of gardens there always seemed to be a bottleneck as we all seemed to concentrate in the center of the gardens and this gave the householders a chance of catching the stragglers.

You can imagine the shock and horror of people sitting in their front rooms, quietly watching there favourite TV programmes, then out of nowhere a gang on unruly kids comes running through their front garden. Understandably people would be going crazy as we destroyed privet hedges and trampled over prized flowerbeds. The man of the house would often give chase, sometimes accompanied by their family dog and on one occasion one of the 'suicide runners' was bitten by an over excited dog.

My mate Paul was the once bitten and he was the first to be taken to the police station to be charged with criminal damage. Only after he had been charged was he taken to the Manor Hospital for a tetanus injection.

But my favourite by far was the second type of Hedge-Hopping, the 'commando run'. The clandestine operation of the 'commando run' meant going through back gardens under the cover of darkness and we got up to all types of mischief. A regular stunt was to take patio furniture from one house and bundle it over the fence into the next garden or, if our pathway was clear, sometimes we would move the furniture two or three gardens away. We would do pretty much the same thing if we found washing hanging on the line. One dirty 'commando' picked up some dog crap from one garden then when we were there taking washing off one line and moving its to the next house, he put the dog crap into the bra cups, then hung the bra hammock-style off the washing line. Somehow I don't think that particular brassier would have been worn again, then again, the owner may have been one of the *dirty brigade* and into golden showers; there are a lot of strange people out there.

But by far the funniest incident was when Ade tried to scale a six-foot fence. The fence in question was formed of concrete posts and timber fencing/infill panels. Ade jumped up and grabbed the top of the fencing panel with the intention of scrambling up and over, but the concrete posts either side of the fencing panel must have been positioned a little too far from each other, thus making this particular fencing panel loose. As Ade grabbed the top of the fence panel and put it his weight against it, it immediately fell forward and, along with Ade, crashed into next door's greenhouse. The noise of the greenhouse collapsing was deafening and stopped all the 'commando's' in their tracks but, after the initial shock, we all burst out laughing then assisted Ade to get out of the broken greenhouse. Fortunately Ade wasn't injured and we soon had him back on his feet.

The other person that was soon on their feet was the bloke that owned the house. He must of heard the crash of his greenhouse falling to pieces and quickly rushed to his kitchen window to see what all the noise was about. We spotted him looking through the window and immediately decided to abandon our mission. Our escape route was aided by the fact that there was a row of garages at the bottom of the garden.

We scrambled onto the roof of the garages and made a get-away. The roof of the garages was covered in corrugated asbestos sheeting, well most of it was. Some smart garage owner had decided to remove part of the corrugated asbestos sheeting and had replaced it with plastic sheeting. First I heard a loud crack, then a bang, then a whimper. I looked round and noticed something wasn't quite right - I could only see the top half of Ade's body; the other half had fallen through the plastic sheeting and he was standing on the roof of a car that was locked in the garage below. With tears of laughter rolling down my cheeks and hardly able to walk because I was laughing so much, for the second time in less than a minute I went to assist Ade. Just one of those nights, Ade.

Another August bank holiday and another Moorgreen show and working back on the fair. I went up to the fairground the day before the fair opened to make sure that I was still needed. I was amazed and delighted by the warm welcome that I received from the candyfloss lady and all of her family. I was greeted like a long-lost son. I stayed at the fairground for a few hours and assisted with setting up the candyfloss trailer and one of the small kids' rides as well. I was fed and watered and given a pound note for my troubles, which I was more than happy with. The next day was just as exciting as the previous year and it seemed liked I'd never been away. Besides having plenty of banter with the general public, I was pleasantly surprised about how much attention I got from the young girls that visited the fair, I was getting a 'semi' every ten minutes. At the end of my working day, once again I was given £3.00 and the candyfloss lady made me blush when she gave me a kiss and said *you have been a great help, see you next year*. £3.00 and a kiss on the cheek was all well and good, but hadn't she heard of inflation? The miners had just received a 25% pay rise.

A week or so before Christmas I was over the moon when my Mom gave me £20.00 and told me I could go and buy my own Christmas presents. I was on the first bus into Walsall and got myself a red-and-black *Budgie Jacket*, a couple of pairs of baggy *Rupert Bear* checked trousers, a few pairs of electric-green socks and my first pair of Docker's. Even back then I was a bit frugal and I must have gone to four or five different shoe shops to see where I could find the cheapest pair of eight-hole cherry-red Dr. Marten boots. As I was wandering in and around Walsall's indoor market, I looked in the window of a small shoe shop and couldn't believe my eyes. There was a pair of eight-hole Doc Marten's on display, but instead of having the usual yellow stitching around the edge of the sole, these had White stitching, something I'd never seen before; they were the ones for me. The Dockers cost me £8.00 and immediately they became my pride and joy. I'm sure I didn't wear anything else except my Dockers for a couple of months. Taking special care not to get any polish, on the white stitching, I religiously polished them every day with 'Tucson Red' well what else would I use? Common ox-blood polish? – I don't think so.

1973

Money must have been tight in the Grainger household, because early in the new year my Mom took on a second part-time job. My Mom's second job was as a cleaner at a set of offices on the Northgate, not far from our home. My Dad kindly volunteered my services to Mom, so every other evening I had an hour or two of hoovering and polishing. Cleaning certainly wasn't anything new to me, I had been tidying up the house ever since I could remember. My dear mother was one of the world's most untidy persons and the thing that would drive me mad was when she took the curlers out of her hair in the morning and threw them on the living room floor. I would often return from school in the afternoon to find the floor littered with plastic curlers. When I returned from my office-cleaning duties there was still the washing or drying up to done. To add insult to injury and much to the amusement of my friends, my Mom was constantly ironing double and sometimes treble creases in my trousers and on my shirt sleeves. To save embarrassment, very reluctantly I had to start ironing my own clothes. If that lot wasn't enough, when the good weather returned, it was gardening time. Besides the usual back and side gardens we also had a large side lawn to contend with. Now if we had had a modern hover-mower or even a petrol mower this wouldn't have been too much of a chore. Unfortunately, me and my brother were presented with a manual lawn mower which didn't even have a bucket at the front of it to catch the grass. This made cutting the lawns very laborious. After the strain of pushing the manual mower up and down, the grass had to be raked up into piles and the grass collected up by hand. When the grass was long this could take all afternoon. Happy days! And after doing all these jobs, Mom and Dad still refused to give me pocket money *'get yourself a job'* was always my Dad's response when I asked for money or even if I asked for an item of fashionable clothing. So apart from money I received for my birthday or Christmas, I had to save up and buy my own clothes. As I had no cunning schemes to get some easy money, so I got myself an evening paper-round at the nearby newsagent. The newspaper round was dead easy: I only had twenty-five newspapers to deliver (twelve *Birmingham Mail* and thirteen *Express and Star*) and after I had been doing my rounds for less than a week, I had memorized which households had what paper and I didn't need to waste time marking up my papers before I went out on my round. Also, during the first week of my paper-round, two blokes asked me if I had any spare newspapers. I hadn't on that occasion but every night after that I made sure to slip two extra *Evening Mails* and two extra *Express & Stars* into my paper bag. I would sell two extra newspapers every night and, depending on timings, I would sometimes meet my two regulars as they got off their bus and then I would usually get rid of all four extra newspapers, pocketing all the proceeds of course. On a good week, I could almost double my legitimate earnings.

In the space of a couple of weeks I had received not one, but two love letters from admiring girls. Neither of the girls lived in houses where I delivered newspapers; they just happened to live in houses that I passed en-route. The first girl had been waving at me from her bedroom window for a few days, so I wasn't totally surprised when she came out of the house, gave me a peck on the cheek and handed me a scented envelope. She was a pretty little thing and looked a little younger than me. Her actions may not have surprised me but the contents of the envelope did. Besides the letter in which she wrote of her undying love for me, she had also included a large lock of her blond hair, which was neatly tied with a small blue bow. Even though I never replied to the letter or even spoke to the girl for as long as I did the paper-round, she sat at her bedroom every evening and waved to me.

The second girl was a completely different kettle of fish. The first time I saw her was when she jumped out from behind a hedge, almost scaring me to death in the process. She was tall and slim with long dark hair, but she had a boat-race that looked liked a Bulldog chewing a Wasp and you could have played dot-to-dot with the spots. While I was staring wide-eyed at her, she gave me a smacker on the lips and dropped something into my paperbag. Then, as quickly as she had appeared, she vanished behind the high hedgerow. I walked off thinking 'did that just happen?' then remembered that she had dropped something into my paperbag. I searched my paperbag as I walked along and pulled out a folded piece of paper, I opened it and the message inside stopped me in my tracks, it read in big, bold capitals '**DO YOU WANT ME TO WANK YOU OFF x**' Blinking heck! I had only just started to grow a few hairs round my little willy; there was no way I was going to embarrass myself and let a girl get into my pants so she could discover a bald cock. The pleasure of a young girl giving me a 'hand job' wouldn't happen until I'd got a 'full beard'. After this frightening experience of the dot-to-dot bird, I made damn sure I was on the opposite side of the road every time I passed her hedgerow.

I walked into the newsagents as usual one afternoon and there was a buzz of excitement from the other paperboys. As I walked to the back of the shop where all the papers were stacked, one of the lads said to me *'go and look in the stockroom'* I did so straight away and I couldn't believe my eyes - you could hardly move in the place because it was rammed from floor to ceiling with all manner of Easter eggs. My paperbag was hanging up in the stockroom and the temptation was just too strong. Without a moment's hesitation I threw a large box of Cadbury's Cream Eggs into it. I returned to the shop and with lightening speed, packed my newspapers into my paperbag and with my heart pumping ten to the dozen, I walked out of the front door of the shop.

I don't remember how many cream eggs were in the box I had stolen, but they were bloody heavy. Along with my usual newspapers my paperbag reminded me of an 'Observer Friday'. I hurriedly finished my paper-round as I was excited about showing off my swag to my mates. Their eyes nearly popped out of their heads when I produced the giant box of Cadbury's Cream Eggs and we all eagerly ripped the cardboard box to get at the much-loved cream eggs. The first half-a-dozen eggs were great, but by the time we were getting into double figures, my mates and me were all feeling sick. After a short break from eating the eggs, we had an impromptu egg fight, throwing the cream eggs at each other from close range. I don't know if you have every been hit by a cream egg, but I can tell you, it bloody hurts when you get one bounces off your nose or ear.

After a few bloody noses we called a truce and looked for other sources of entertainment we could find using the cream eggs. We half heartedly threw a few at passing cars and cyclists, then someone had the idea of dropping the eggs from the top floor of some local flats. The novelty of throwing the eggs down five flights of stairs quickly wore off, but throwing the eggs at the tall ceilings and watching them drip and form into stalagmites was much better fun. Some of the egg formations hung down five or sick inches and were works of art. I'm sure the poor residents would have had a different opinion, as they cleaned up our sticky mess.

Just before the Easter holidays the Great Easter-egg God in the sky decided to play a nice little joke on me. As I was doing my paper-round my number one fan who waved at me from her window, came out of her house and gave me an Easter egg. I thanked her and we chatted for a short while, then I went on my way. When I got back to the newsagents I hung my paperbag in the stockroom, took out my Easter Egg and put it my school bag. Thinking nothing of it, the Easter Egg was sticking out of the top of my school bag and as I made my way out of the shop, the owner noticed the Easter egg in my bag and called me over to him. Taking the Easter egg from my bag he snapped *'what the bloody hell do you think you're doing?'* I told him I had been given the Easter egg as a present but it didn't wash with him and when, on closer scrutiny, the shop owner noticed that the Easter egg had one of his price tags on it, my fate was sealed.

I continued to protest my innocence and told him several times that I'd been given the Easter egg as a present but, the shop owner told me 'to get out of his shop or he would

1973

call the police' I replied '*if he didn't give me back my Easter egg,* I *would call the police!*' With that, he ran from behind his counter and chased me out of the shop. And that was the end of my paper-round career.

The Easter holidays coincided with my Dad having the bright idea of buying a touring caravan. On first inspection it looked a nice little caravan, *little* being the operative word. We were a family of seven and the caravan was only a four-berth. This meant that every time we went away in the caravan Mom, Dad and three sisters slept in the caravan and my brother and I had the dubious pleasure of sleeping in the back of our Dad's estate car. The first few times we went away, we had to sleep on the hard metal floor of the car but, after constant moaning and nagging, my brother and me finally got the luxury of blow-up mattresses to sleep on - but we had to inflate them ourselves, by mouth!

The camping sites my Dad chose were always in the middle of nowhere with nothing to do and nothing to see as far as a twelve- coming on thirteen-year-old boy was concerned. And just like when my brother and me were small kids, our frustrations would often turned into kick fights in the back of the estate car.

Yes caravanning was great fun, I don't think - but camping with my mates was another thing. Telling my Mom and Dad I was stopping at my new friend Baz's house, myself, Baz, Mad Mick and a couple of other mates pitched a tent in the small woods next to the T.I. fields. Putting the tent up was not a problem but trying to start a campfire proved to be a bit more challenging.

Freezing cold and getting very pissed off, one of the lads said he would go home and bring back some petrol

73

from his dad's shed and that would certainly get fire going. It seemed ages before our mate returned with his can of petrol, but as soon as he arrived back, Mick gabbed the can off him and started to throw the petrol all over the wood that we had stacked up for a fire. Mick was really enjoying himself, randomly throwing petrol out of the tin can, unfortunately we were soon to discover that our little bonfire wasn't the only thing that had been doused in petrol. When the petrol tin was well and truly empty, Mick lit a few pieces of rolled-up newspaper and threw it onto the wood. The flames must have jumped up six feet and we danced around the fire like things possessed. Sadly our euphoria was short- lived; a combination of building our bonfire too close to the tent and Mick throwing petrol all over the place soon put a stop to our wild abandonment and we looked on in horror as the tent went up in flames. In a matter of a few seconds the tent was history.

'*What the fuck do we do now?*' I said to the other happy campers. My mates banded about a few stupid suggestions, then, after a long silence, I came up with the most stupid idea of all: I told my mates of the young girl who waved at me from her bedroom everyday, maybe she would let us into her bedroom. My mates all thought it was a great idea and, with our spirits lifted, we made our way out of the woods and headed for the estate where my little window-waver lived.

We didn't have a watch between us, so we didn't know the time, but it must have been the early hours of the morning as the streets were deserted. As we walked through the empty streets, we helped ourselves to a few bottles of milk that had been left out on people's doorsteps and Mick tried almost every car door that we passed, hoping in vain to find an unlocked car that we could sleep in or even take for a joy ride.

When we finally got to the young girl's house I collected up a few small stones and started throwing them at her bedroom window. Several of the stones hit the glass but there was no response, from the sleeping beauty. Then without warning Mick produced a gat-gun and fired a pellets at the window. There was a thud as the pellet struck the window frame. As Mick started to reload his air pistol, the rest of us pleaded with him not to shoot at the window again. The appearance of a cat took Mick's attention away from the house and he took a pot-shot at the moggy instead. We threw a few more stones at the bedroom window, but still no success, so we all decided to look elsewhere for somewhere to sleep.

We had only been walking for five or ten minutes when a police car pulled alongside us. *'Hello - hello – hello, what's going on here then?'* the police officer asked. He didn't really, he probably said *'what the fuck are you lot up to?'* This was the first of my many run-ins with the obnoxious 'Ken the Copper'. Mick had 'previous' with this particular policeman and as soon as Ken the Copper noticed that Mick was part of our little gang, he crammed us all into his police car, Mick claiming the front seat, of course. Mick was quick to tell Ken the Copper that we had been camping and someone had set fire to our tents and we were all making our way home. *'Well, we will have to see what the sergeant has to say,'* was Ken's reply.

When we got to the police station we were taken into an interview room and told to sit down and be quiet. We were all starting to get bored when Ken the Copper reappeared with his sergeant. The sergeant got straight to the point and shouted at us *'stand up and empty all your pockets onto the table!'* Having looked at us for a few seconds, he asked, *'have you been stealing bottles of milk?'* *'No'* we all replied together. *'Why then, have you all got milk stains round your mouths?'* the sergeant asked knowingly. We all immediately wiped our mouth clean and started to put the few bits and pieces that we had onto the large wooden table. The sergeant instructed Ken to search us. Mick was the first person he searched and he quickly discovered that Mick was concealing an air pistol. *'What's this?'* he asked as he pulled the air pistol from inside Mick's jacket. Mick shrugged his shoulders and said *'a bunch of flowers'* which earned him a whack round the head from sergeant. *'Is it loaded?'* the sergeant asked. *'I've no idea,'* Mick replied. With that the sergeant took the air pistol, pointed it at the floor and pulled the trigger. A pellet shot out and stuck into the wooden floor. *'You lot are in a lot of trouble, did you know you could go to prison for carrying a loaded air gun in a public place?'* the sergeant snapped.

As soon as the air gun was discovered we were all taken into separate rooms and I was interviewed by Ken the Copper. *'Your mates have told me that you have been stealing from the shop opposite Tynings Lane school'* was Ken's opening line. When I started to laugh and said *'I'm sure they did'* Ken pulled me out of my seat by my jacket collar and slammed me up the wall. With his face close up he said *'any more of your cheek and I will take you to the cells and give you a fuckin' good hiding.'* There's nothing like good old- fashioned community policing. Dixon of Dock Green would have been proud of him! I don't know about 'Ken the Copper', we should have nicknamed him 'Ken the Cunt'. He was a little man hiding behind a uniform. Basically he was a bully; how could any decent grown man threaten a twelve-year-old? I was thrown back into my chair and Ken stormed out of the room.

Mick had told the sergeant that he had found the air pistol and the pocketful of pellets he had on him in the woods. I'm not sure if the coppers on night duty didn't want to do the paperwork, but we were all told that we were going to get a formal caution from the superintendent and they would be writing to our parents to confirm when we needed to appear back at the police station. Then while it was still dark outside, they sent us on our way.

Of course my Mom and Dad went barmy when they received the letter from the police. But when I returned to the police station and found myself in front of the superintendent, it didn't seem any worse than being in front of the headmaster at school and the lecture from the superintendent certainly didn't make me think 'I must keep out of trouble from now on!' Thinking about it, being in front of my headmaster or more to the point, the feared deputy head Nobby Dawes, was probably worse than being in front of a police superintendent.

Funny thing was the school could hand out corporal punishments but the police weren't allowed to, well not officially although quite obviously they did dish it out. I had experienced several smacks and whacks from rulers when I was in the juniors and infants schools but they all pale into insignificant when it comes to having the cane for the first time.

For some reason, after one lesson Ade and me decided to stay in our classroom instead of going into the playground for our break. The classroom was on the second floor on the main block and opposite the grammar school which was only thirty or forty yards away. Thinking I could see my mate Nick in one of the grammar-school classrooms, I decided to show off a little. With help from Ade, I opened the classroom window and holding onto the large cast iron radiator, feet first I lowered myself out the window and kicked my legs into thin air. Ade suddenly shouted 'the grammar grubs are going crazy' - many of the grammar-school pupils had rushed to the windows to see my daring deed and within seconds grammar-school teachers were running across to our block.

Unaware of the commotion that I'd caused I pulled myself back into the classroom and as I looked across at the grammar school, it seemed all the pupils were looking out their windows and waving at me and seemingly cheering me on. I gave my audience a bit more entertainment, by jumping from desk to desk and banging on the windows. My little stage act came to an abrupt end when the classroom door flew open and in charged Nobby Dawes.

'What the hell do you think you're doing you stupid boy, you could have killed yourself!' Nobby screamed as he pulled me down off the desk. Shouting at Ade to follow us, Nobby dragged me down the many flights of stairs and along the corridor to his office. He pushed me against the wall outside his office, banging my head in the process. 'Stay there!' he barked, then he told Ade to 'get into my office!'

Nobby was boiling with anger, I could hear him interrogating Ade and asking him 'why he hadn't stopped me, from doing such a stupid thing.' I also heard Ade's feeble attempt to defend his actions, then whack – whack – whack – whack! Four! that wasn't bad I thought to myself. Ade came out of Nobby's office all red faced and gave me a look as if to say, 'thanks mate – you're a twat.'

Then Nobby shouted 'Grainger, get in here!' and I walked into his office thinking that four whacks of the cane wouldn't be that bad and it would soon be all over. But before Nobby took the cane to me, he gave me the worst dressing-down I had ever received. The force of his voice almost knocking me off my feet. I was in a daze by the time he shouted, 'put your hand out!' Nervously I lifted my right-hand and put it forward. Whack – whack – whack – whack. 'Bleedin' hell that hurt' I thought to myself as I pulled my hand away. 'What are you doing? Put your hand back' Nobby commanded. 'I thought I was only going to get four, Mr. Dawes,' I said sheepishly 'Well you thought wrong!' he replied. He then gave me another two whacks on my right hand. Now my hand was really stinging. As I lowered my right-hand Nobby said, 'now the other one.' By the time I'd received the twelfth stroke I was shaking and almost in tears, but the ordeal still hadn't ended. Without talking Nobby frog-marched me to a nearby classroom. As he opened the classroom door he looked me straight in the face and said, 'if you want to act like an idiot Grainger, you can't spend a week with this lot!'

He pushed to me down into an empty chair and I felt totally shell-shocked. In the space of a few short minutes, I'd experienced the excitement of hanging out of the window and jumping over desks, the embarrassment of being drag down the stairs and through the school corridors to Nobby's office, and the physical pain of twelve strokes of the cane - and now I found myself in very strange and uncomfortable surroundings.

I was in a small class of what today would be called 'special needs' but back then it was called the 'Thicko Class'. There were only about ten pupils and a few of them were playground friends, but I made no attempt to acknowledge them and avoided eye contact. I was certainly no academic wiz kid, but the level of classroom work was desperate. I could recall a few of the books from my junior school and, after only a few minutes, the uneasy silence of the classroom gave me a very peculiar and unsettled feeling. The teacher spoke to the pupils in a very calm and quiet voice and in turn it seemed that the Thicko's were concentrating really hard and trying to take in what the teacher had told them. The teacher pretty much ignored me and just told me to pick a book and read. I was never a great reader and very soon became bored, the fact that I was reading *Janet & John, Book 16*, certainly didn't help the situation.

When Dinnertime came around and I was let out of the classroom, it felt like I had been released from solitary confinement. I know there were other pupils in the classroom, but they all seemed to be in their own little world. For the moment my mates weren't interested that I was in the Thicko's class, they just wanted to inspect the cane marks on my hands and the fact that I had received twelve strokes made me the talk of the playground that afternoon.

The next few days were torturous, being stuck in the quiet little classroom with virtually nothing to do drove me mad. Then at every break time, my mates would take the piss and ask me why I wasn't playing with my Thicko classmates.

Coming out of my Thicko class on the fourth day of my sentence, I got talking to my friend Rob, who told me that his house was empty and he was going to skive off. I quickly agreed to join him - if I had spent another day in that small box of a classroom, I'm sure I would've gone crazy. On the way back to Rob's house we decided to mooch around the back of the off-licence in the village to see if we could come across any empty bottles but instead of discovering empty bottles, we came across boxes of beer – each holding twelve half-pint cans of Watney's bitter. We pulled out the small cans from the boxes and hid them in our schoolbags, then made our way to Rob's place.

We each opened a can of beer then Rob went over to his record player and asked, 'have you heard Elton johns album *Don't shoot me I'm only the piano player?*' I shook my head but immediately recognized the song *Daniel* that had been released as a single. The next song on the album *Teacher I Need You* was followed by *Elderberry Wine*. As the song ended, I was just finishing my can of beer and *Blues for My Baby and Me* started to drift across the room. Rob handed me a bottle of Johnnie Walker whiskey. I took a swig and thought I never tasted anything so disgusting. Encouraged by Rob, a few minutes later I took another swig and, just as the horn section was getting into full swing on *Midnight Creeper*, I threw-up all over Rob's carpet. As Rob rushed off into the kitchen to find some cleaning materials, I shouted after him 'put that LP back on again!' I may well have been in a bit of a state, but I was hooked by Elton John and for the next ten years or so, Elton John was up there with Manchester United as one of the most important things in my life.

We spent the rest of the day drinking beer, throwing up and playing the *Don't shoot me* album. I'm sure Rob must have used a full bottle of disinfectant cleaning up our sick, the smell of the disinfectant was so overpowering it made us both choke. God knows how he explained the awful stink, when his Mom and Dad arrived home from work.

These days it isn't unusual for school kids to go on holiday to Italy, the south of France, the Swiss Alps, skiing in Austria or even as far afield as China on school trips; the only school trip I went on while in secondary school was a week's stay at the world famous 'Chasewater' sailing camp. It was only a ten-minute bus journey from my home, but seemed like the back end of nowhere.

Formed at the end of the eighteenth century, Chasewater was first known as the Cannock Chase Reservoir and was originally used as a feeder for the many miles of canals in the Black Country and Birmingham, but as the canal system became less important the reservoir was only really used for sailing, water-skiing and the odd bit of scuba-diving. In the early 1960's a sailing club was built on the shores of the reservoir and a small leisure complex, consisting of cafés, paddling pools, fountains and a small fun fair, quickly followed. But by the early 70's when I went there the leisure complex was hardly used and was looking very, very tired.

Myself and another dozen or so lads from my school made the short trip from Tynings Lane to Chasewater in a battered old van that had wooden plank seating. We knew what to expect from the moment we arrived at the bleak and wind-swept camp. The camp commandant ordered us out of the van '*quick pace*' and made us stand to attention outside our accommodation, which was a line of poorly constructed wooden sheds. The commandant inspected our ranks and told me *'you're standing nice and straight.'* The fact that I was trying especially hard to stand upright was down to my Mom. Over the past few months Mom had commented several times that I was getting round shoulders and she said, if I didn't stand upright, she would take me to the doctors and get him to fit the 'metal cage' around my shoulders and back to force me to stand upright. Mom was a kind-hearted soul, always looking out for me! The thought of being made to wear a metal cage and everyone taking the piss out of me, petrified me and I made a conscious effort to stand upright whenever adults were around.

A few of my schoolmates, who were sporting earrings, didn't receive such a warm welcome. *'Get those bloody things out of your ears now, you bunch of puffs'* the commandant barked. Earrings were very fashionable, especially small gold crucifixes, and most boys who wore them had their ears pierced by their mates. This was usually done by getting a frozen piece of food from their mom's freezer box. I saw both pork chops and beef burgers used to freeze the ear lobe. After a few minutes of having a frozen burger slapped to their lug holes, a hot sewing needle would be pushed through the ear to form a hole for the earring. Only a girl would think about going to a salon to have an earring fitted.

After the earrings had been removed the commandant gave us a long list of items that weren't allowed in the camp, which included cigarettes, radios, torches, food and girlie mags. We were told that we should hand in any banned items and get them back when we were about to leave the camp, and if any banned items were found during our weeks stay, they would be thrown into the reservoir. All the afore-mentioned contraband was smuggled into our shed and many of the items ended up at the bottom of the reservoir.

The radio was the most sort-after item, along with football results, the Top Forty was religiously listened to by most young teenagers. The number-one record and chart run-down was announced every Tuesday dinnertime on Radio One. This was as popular as the draw for the FA Cup, especially if local band 'Slade' was at number one. On a Sunday evening Radio One played most of the top forty records; even in the summer months, you wouldn't find many teenagers out and about between 5:00 and 7:00 on a Sunday evening. For most boys of my age, music was a close second to football, and a lot of girls, if their parents could afford a tape recorder, would tape/record their favourite songs every Sunday and play them back throughout the week.

At Chasewater, we managed to listen to the Sunday chart show without being caught but unfortunately we were discovered trying to find out the new Number One on the Tuesday afternoon and the radio was promptly dispatched into the water.

We endured a military style regime: up at 7:00am, cold shower, cold breakfast, then back to the our shed for 'kit inspection', then two or three hours out sailing on the cold reservoir. At dinnertime and teatime we weren't allowed to speak in the dining room. If you were caught talking, you had to leave your meal, remove your shirt and run round the camp until everyone else had finished their meal. I only had to do this twice!

To say our living quarters were basic, would be an understatement. There was no furniture at all and no curtains or blinds to cover the windows. Our bed was a thin mattress that lay directly on the floorboards and we only had one thin tatty blanket each, to keep us warm. Lights-out was at 9:00 pm and once or twice each night a member of staff would come into our shed and make sure none of us were breaking the strict rules. They would march up and down the middle of the shed, stopping at the foot of every boy's 'bed', to ensure all was in order.

Halfway through the week, parents of the kids who were staying at the sailing camp were allowed to visit for an hour and the only parents that didn't show up were mine. I felt very hurt and embarrassed and made up the excuse that 'my Dad was working away and my Mom couldn't drive'. If they had turned up, I would have made the return journey home with them, as did several tearful kids who had had enough of the sadistic commandant and his staff.

After a week of tying knots and pulling in sails, reciting 'the bow, port & starboard' and so, tacking this way and that in our little sailing dinghies with our sailing teachers shouting out 'ready about!' to which us landlubbers had to answer 'aye' and then 'lee ho' and ducking down to avoid the boom smacking us on the side of the head, after all this, us young wannabe, or more like don't-wannabe, sailors were paired up and sent out onto the water unsupervised.

I must have done ok out on the water, because just before we left the sailing camp, I was presented with a certificate of merit. This was the first award that I had ever received and even though I really didn't like sailing I was delighted, even proud, that a teacher thought I was good enough at something to give me a certificate. A great boost to my confidence.

Another August bank holiday and another Moorgreen Show. As per the previous year, I made my way to the fairground the day before the fair was open to the public with the intention of helping setting up the candy-floss and toffee-apple stall, but on arrival I was greeted by the father of the candy floss lady and he asked me to help him set up one of the kids' rides. The ride consisted of fifteen to twenty different small wooden vehicles: cars, a bus, motorbikes, a fire-engine and a few animals. Most of them were already in place; my main job was to help the boss erect a small wooden booth that was positioned in the center of the ride and housed the electrical controls for it.

When all was in place, Boss (he told me to call him 'Boss') slowly pushed the dirty old control lever a half circle and the kids' rides came to life. He repeated in the procedure two or three more times then turned to me and said 'you have a go'. I eagerly took the control lever and after ten minutes or so, I was told by Boss I had got the speed correct and I was slowing down the ride 'just right – nice and gentle'. Me controlling a fairground ride! I was well chuffed with my self, even if it was just a Micky Mouse kids ride. Then, knock me down with a feather, Boss asked me 'would you be able look after this ride for me tomorrow?' With great enthusiasm I immediately agreed.

The next morning Boss ran me through the instructions once more, then handed me a small money-apron that was full of loose change and said 'take it slow and no more than eight spins for each ride - and always tell 'em to HOLD TIGHT. Any problems, I'll be on the Bumpers.'

Luckily things were a bit quiet for the first hour with only a few kids on the ride. This helped me build up a bit of confidence. After all I was just thirteen years old and I had never had such responsibility. Things were going great guns until I got my first full ride. Being inexperienced, I failed to stop the ride where I had started it. This resulted in mayhem for a minute or so as parents bumped into each other, while trying to get round to the other side of the ride to collect their children. And when the little kids couldn't see their Moms and Dads, they started screaming and to add to the confusion some of the kids got off the ride and wandered off in different directions. I was like 'a rabbit caught in the headlights' all I could do was to stand and watch the chaos, sort itself out. After that experience, I made pretty sure that I always stopped the ride where I always started it to ensure parents and kids were reunited.

By late morning, my money apron was bursting at the seams, with coins and pound notes and being on my own I couldn't resist slipping a pound note into my shoe. Not long after I had nicked my first quid, Boss came along to see how things were going. He seemed to be pleased with how I was controlling the ride and he took a large percentage of the money I had taken that morning.

I was having a great time and didn't stop taking loads of money all day, virtually every ride was packed with kids. I was taking so much money that in the afternoon, I helped myself to another three pound notes. Boss called by a couple of more times to collect cash from me, but there was so much cash he would never have missed £4.00. Several times throughout the day while the ride was spinning round, I counted all the cash I had collected and I reckon I took almost £350.00 in a day!

It was early evening before Boss came and relieved me, took my money apron and told me I could go home. He asked me if I had enjoyed the day and would I like to help again in the future? I said '*Yes!*' to both. Boss then asked for my telephone number and handed me a five-pound note. My eyes nearly popped out of my head, 'a fuckin' Bluey – a fuckin' Bluey'. For a second and only a second, I felt a little guilty for stealing the £4.00. I walked away from the fair with £9.00 and I felt like a millionaire. Three years later I only picked up £16.00 for my first week's wages.

When I got back to Aldridge I was quick to show off my newly acquired five-pound note and they were all very impressed and very jealous. I was still on cloud nine from my experience at the fair and as an act of bravado I told my friends I would buy them a drink in the Elms pub. As soon as the pub opened it's doors, me and my thirteen-year-old mates went into the lounge and marched straight up to the bar. I produced my five-pound note and said to the elderly barmaid. '*four halves of bitter please.*' She looked at me and my spotty mates for what seemed an age and said, '*I will serve you, but not your friends, they're never eighteen!*' '*Ok*' I replied, '*just one half a bitter then.*' I was charged the ridiculous sum of 8 1/2p for my first drink in a pub and the barmid was none too pleased that I gave her £5.00 for a half of bitter. When she passed me my drink, my mates and me sat ourselves down in one of lounge booths and passed it around. After we had all had a sip of the Ansell's best bitter, we all agreed it tasted 'bleeding awful' so it was off to the off-licence for a bottle of dandelion and burdock.

No more of my money was wasted on alcohol, instead I went on a shopping spree to Walsall. The French might have had Lacoste, Yves St. Laurent, Pierre Cardin and Givenchy, but we had Nelson House and SMC. My mates and me spent a lot of Saturday afternoons window shopping in SMC. When Oxford-Bags first became popular they displayed five different colours in their shop window: white. electric blue, red, green-and-black. Me and four or five of my mates all purchased lime-green shirts with jumbo collars and double buttons from SMC and dubbed ourselves 'The Lime Green Boot Boys', a name to strike fear and terror into even the fiercest of men.

On this occasion I was searching for a very flashy green-and-gold two-tone suit. Two-Tone was all the rave. Blue-and-maroon was the most popular colour but I thought the green-and-gold was far classier. I visited many shops and fought through the crowds in Walsall market but unfortunately my £8.50 wasn't quite enough to buy me the suit that I wanted so I settled for a pair of two-tone trousers and a pair of oxblood loafers – nice!

I even had a few bob left over to get myself a sterling silver identity bracelet, very popular back then and there was only one place to go for an ID bracelet - the engraver on Walsall market. The engraver was a bit of an institution and took up the same position at Walsall market every week come rain or shine. I'm sure he made a good living, because any time of the day you passed his little workbench, he always had a queue of people, usually teenagers, waiting for his services.

Just a few weeks after I had worked at the Moorgreen Show I got a call from Boss, asking me if I could help him the following weekend at a fair in Leicestershire. After getting the ok from my Mom and Dad, I agreed to work with him on the Saturday and Sunday. Everything went fine on my first day and, as to be expected, I helped myself to a few quid. As it got dark Boss came over and told me to pack up as most of the kids were going home, so I helped him cover the little control booth with a tarpaulin and then I followed him to his large caravan. 'Wait here,' he said as he made his way up the steps to his caravan. He returned a few minutes later carrying a sleeping bag and as he walked down the steps, he indicated that he wanted me to follow. Not far from the caravan was a Land Rover and when we reached it, Boss opened up the back, threw in the sleeping bag and said, or more like told me, 'you'll be alright sleeping here!' It didn't look like I'd got any bleedin' choice. I scrambled into the back of the Land Rover and Boss told me he would be back soon with something to eat and the torch. 'Wow this is just great,' I thought, '- all the fun of the fair!' I wasn't expecting the red carpet to be rolled out for me, but I was certainly expecting something a little better then the back of smelly old Land Rover to sleep in. As I lay looking at the holes in the canvas roof of my boudoir, I suddenly had a thought: had my Dad told Boss that I had to sleep in the back of our estate car, when the family went away in the caravan? I wouldn't have put it past the miserable bleeder.

To be fair, I was that knackered that I soon went off to sleep – until I was woken by a commotion going on just outside the Land Rover. I heard a few angry voices then the Land Rover rocked from side to side as someone was thrown against the side of the vehicle. There were suddenly a few wild screams and war cries as it seemed more people had arrived on the scene. I realized that there was a full scale riot going on, immediately outside the Land Rover. The canvas sides of the Land Rover bulged inwards, as the people outside wrestled against the side of it. Then I heard a few loud thuds and what seemed like a bottle breaking, followed by screams of pain and men shouting 'kill the cunts!' and 'kick their fuckin' head's in!' I was petrified as the screams got louder and the beating continued.

The violent disturbance seemed to go on for ages with ever more people going to join the mêlée and, as the Land Rover continued to be rocked from side to side, the tears ran down my face. My mates and me were obsessed with football violence, but we had never experienced violence on this level, this was a reality-check! I realized that I had been living in a fantasy world. As soon as I experienced real violence, I knew I was just a wannabe young boy and I was shit scared. It took me a good ten to fifteen minutes to gain the courage to venture out of the back of the Land Rover after all the fighting had finally died down.

Outside the Land Rover, I could see two men lying unconscious on the ground. It was too dark to see what sort of a state they were in, but just seeing them sprawled out on the ground filled me with fear. I went to Boss's caravan and banged on the door, but no answer, so I walked between the fairground trucks and caravans until I came to a main road and went in search of a telephone box. When I eventually found one, I called my home number and my Dad answered the phone. Trying hard to hold back the tears, I told him of the fight and that I was sleeping in the back of a Land Rover and I pleaded with him to come and pick me up and take me home - he flatly reused!

My Mom eventually got involved in the conversation and after a few minutes of arguing, between Mom and Dad, Dad reluctantly said he would come and collect me first thing in the morning. Still frightened to death, I made my way back to the fairground, where there were now a few police cars about and most of the rides were packing up for the night. I went back to Boss's caravan, but there was still no sign of life. Very reluctantly I made my way back to the Land Rover and I was extremely relieved to discover that the two men who had been lying at the side of it had now up and gone. I jumped into the back of it and pulled the sleeping bag up over my head.

I was dead to the world when Boss woke me up the next morning. I told him want had happened the previous night and how frightened I was, but he didn't seem to be too concerned at all. 'Just a few of our boys sorting out the local tear-aways,' he said in a very casual manner. We started to open up my ride and once I'd had my hot-dog and a cup of tea, I had all but forgot about the horrors of the previous night.

I had also forgot that I had asked my Dad to come and fetch me! I was happily taken money off my first customers when, to my surprise, I noticed my Dad walking towards me and he didn't look happy. As he approached me I quickly said 'I'm ok now – can you come back later?' 'No I bleedin' can't!' he snapped. 'Get your things together, you're coming home now.' I told him I would get a coach or a train home by myself, later that day. but he said he wasn't going to have a wasted journey and I was coming home with him.

I went and told Boss my Dad was insisting that I had to go home, he was fuming and shouting at me: 'who the fuckin' hell is going to look after the ride?!' He then had a few words with my Dad but my Dad couldn't be persuaded to allow me to stay. When I asked for my day's pay, Boss begrudgingly gave me £3.00, still good money for a thirteen-year-old but £2.00 less than he'd given me a few weeks before. Unsurprisingly, my Dad didn't talk to me during the long drive back home and Boss must have been really pissed off with me as he didn't call me again for well over a year.

Tina Hall was one of the best-looking girls in my year (if not the best-looking) and one morning just after school assembly, her best friend Caroline (the girl who had told me I was a crap kisser) told me that Tina wanted to go out with me. I immediately agreed and that was the start of a six-year, on-and-off relationship.

I gave Caroline my Man United ring to pass on to Tina. At the time football rings were very fashionable with teenage boys. The rings were silver grey stainless-steel with a small team crest on the front face and the common practice at Tynings Lane School was to let your girlfriend wear your football ring. Within a day of 'going out' with Tina, she asked me to spend the evening with her at her house, which was only a short walk from my house.

I was a little shocked when I first walked into Tina's living room. Compared to my home, it was like a show-house. Everything was nice and tidy and Tina's family sat quietly watching the TV. At home I was forever tidying up after my Mom, who would leave clothes, plates, newspapers thrown all over the furniture and when she took her blue plastic hair curlers our her hair in the morning, she threw them straight onto the floor, as I have mentioned. And of course there was always bickering and arguments going on at my house. Mine and Tina's first day out together was to go the pictures in Walsall. We queued for almost two hours in the freezing cold to see the James Bond film *Live & Let Die* and in the dark of the cinema we had our first real snog. The snog went on for at least five minutes, so Tina must have thought I was a better kisser than Caroline did!

After a week or two, snogging progressed to heavy petting. I fumbled around trying to take Tina's bra off a few times then, one evening when her mom and dad had gone out, I finally plucked up the courage to put my hand up her skirt. I had seen plenty of hairy fanny's in porno mags, but to actually have my hand on one was unchartered territory for me and I was pretty nervous. My heart was racing and my hand was shaking as my fingers explored inside her knickers.

All the porno mags in the world couldn't have prepared me for I what I was about to discover in Tina's knickers. I had the shock of my life as I came into contact with her pubic hairs. Her bush was like an over grown privet hedge. For a few seconds I thought she kept a gerbil in her bloomers. Tina must have been very comfortable with what was going on, because while I was playing around with her big hairy bush, she was giving me a massive love-bite. When I got home and looked in the mirror, I nearly died. There was a love-bite on the side of my neck and it was the size of a tennis ball. I was quick to show the love-bite off to my mates at school but when I was at home, I had to wear polo-neck jumpers for a couple of weeks. If my Mom could have seen my giant love-bite, she would have killed me.

Even though Tina and I were both only in our early teens, we spent as much time as we could getting to know each others bodies. This activity would usually take place in the cold and dark scoring hut at the local cricket club. I thought I was the luckiest kid alive - happy days.

Even though I was having great fun Tina at least two or three times a week, being a teenage boy, I still needed to have a *Tommy-Tank* most nights. One night I was lying in my bed, giving myself a hand job and my brother shouts across the bedroom 'stop wanking you cunt!' I snapped back 'fuck off!' No sooner had the words left my lips, than my brother jumped out of his bed and while I still had cock-in-hand the bastard punched me in the face several times. Well it could have been worse – he could have jumped into bed with me and give me a blow-job!

The last time I had enjoyed people reading to me was back in the mid 60's at Kingstanding Library but, as the winter nights drew in, me, Ade and Nick would spend a lot of time in each others bedrooms and I think it was Nick who was given a short Horror Book and one evening he decided to read the story of *The Tattooed Man*. Being a crap reader I really enjoyed the story being read to me and over the next few nights I encouraged Nick and Ade to take turns in reading the rest of the horror stories in the book. As we were reaching the end of the book, Nick said that I should take my turn in reading the book. I reluctantly agreed, but while I was only half way down the second page, Nick gave me a telling look and said 'give it here, I'll read it!'

When the book was finished, I said to my two mates, 'I tell you what, I'll nick some more horror books if you read 'em.' They readily agreed and I soon started on a mammoth shoplifting spree. I nicked that many ghost and horror books from Kings (books & records) that I almost emptied the shelves. I got many Stephen King books and classics by Edgar Allen Poe and Richard Laymon. But my favourite stories were by James Herbert. Being the uneducated lout that I was at the time, I didn't know any of the authors before I nicked the books. If the books were in the Horror Section, I had them away.

When all the books I had stolen from the local shops had been read, we moved onto the book shops in Walsall. I had a couple of successful trips into WH Smiths but then I tried a little newsagent in the Old Square. Me, Ade and Nick mooched about the shop for a few minutes. Once Ade and Nick saw that I'd got a book, they left the shop and I was just about to follow them, when I was stopped by one of the shop assistants as I went to walk out the door with my ill-gotten gains. A woman, who must have been my Mom's age grabbed me by the arm and took me to the till where another shop assistance glared at me. If looks could kill! I was told by the angry looking woman who was behind the cash till to 'give back the book, I had tried to steal.'

'Book - *book*?' I thought, 'not *books*?' I produced a book from inside my jacket and the woman, who still had me by the arm, pulled the book out of my hand. The angry women said 'I should phone your mother and tell her what kind of a son she's got.' 'We haven't got a phone,' I replied. 'What's your name and address then?' she snapped. I gave her a false name and address and she told me never to come back to her shop again. The other shop assistance let go of my arm and I walked out the shop.

As soon as I got outside, I saw Ade and Nick waiting me and the little show-off in me raced to the surface. Their faces were a picture as I stood directly outside the shop and produced two stolen books that the shop assistances hadn't noticed. Ade and Nick nearly wet themselves when I turned round and banged on the shop window and revealed the stolen books to the shocked, and no doubt fuming, shop assistants

1974

The Fair had arrived in Aldridge and this was always a time of excitement for all the local teenagers. The younger boys would fight boys from other areas that had wandered onto their patch. The older boys would fight with the fairground workers. And all the girls hoped, that they would get fingered by one of the rough and tough fairground workers.

I got into a fight with a lad from the grammar school and after a bit of rough and tumble, he went home in tears and told his parents of his terrible ordeal. His parents not only called the police but also went round to my house to inform my parents that I had beat their son up. It was bad enough the kid's parents turning up at my house, but when the police turned up a little later, my Mom and Dad were fuming. I arrived home from the fair late, as usual, and my Dad gave me both barrels as soon as I walked through the front door. He was livid that the police had called to the house because of my behaviour. It was the angriest I'd seen him.

I had to go to the police station the next day with my Dad and, as we approached the police station, he said, 'I hope they lock you up' and, by the look on his face, I'm sure he was serious. My Dad had never had any time for me, but now that I was bringing trouble to the house, he was openly hostile towards me. He sat stony faced as the police inspector read the riot act to me and he must have been gutted when I only received an official caution. To me - no more than a 'slap on the wrist'. Dad grounded me for a month and barely looked at me, let alone spoke to me, during that time.

After two weeks of being stuck In my bedroom, I was going stir crazy. The weekends were the worst they seemed to drag on forever and ever. So in an effort to get a bit of parole, I told my Mom and Dad a little white lie - that I'd got the opportunity to join the RAF cadets. I told them I would have to attend on Tuesday and Thursday evenings and, just to make it sound more convincing, I added I needed 10p for 'subs' (subscription) each time I went. Amazingly they agreed and didn't ask for any proof of me attending the cadets. They didn't even question the 10p for my 'subs'. So for the next few Tuesday and Thursday evenings, I got my 10p off Mom, polished my shoes and marched off to meet Tina up at the Cricket Club where I let her play with my 'middle stump and bails'.

After four long weeks of being grounded, I was eager for a bit of fun. So on the very first night that I had being allowed to go out and hang around with my mates I wandered down to the precinct to see who was out. When I got to the precinct, the only two lads hanging about were a couple of grammar-school boys I knew, Riga and Flet. We were sitting having a chat when I noticed Mad Mick walking towards us. 'Here comes trouble' I thought and I was right. Mick was a year older than me and the other two lads and he'd only lived in Aldridge for a year or so, but he had quickly gained a reputation for fighting and stealing. He was only a small skinny kid but as his nickname suggests he was a 'nutter' and trouble was his middle name. Mick soon got bored sitting round the precincts and led us off in search of excitement! Now Mick didn't force me to follow him, he didn't drag me along kicking and screaming 'leave me alone Mad Mick, I don't want to play with you'. I followed him knowing I might well be walking into trouble and because this was my first night back out on the streets.

After mooching around the back of the shops next to the Croft, we wandered up to Cooper and Jordan school at the back of St. Mary's Church. Just before the main school building there was a small swimming pool covered by a brick and glass structure. There must have been well over a hundred small panes of glass in the side of the building that we were walking towards. I can't remember who threw the first stone and smashed the first window pane, probably Mad Mick, but we were all quick to join in and to paraphrase Nick Lowe 'I loved the sound of breaking windows'. All four of us were eagerly picking up stones and aimed for the windows in the school swimming pool and, in less than a minute of mindless vandalism, more than half of the windowpanes were smashed. With glass flying into the swimming pool, the kids of Cooper and Jordan school wouldn't be having swimming lessons for a few weeks.

After causing hundreds of pounds worth of damage, we casually strolled up to the nearby cricket club and plonked ourselves on the grass near to the clubhouse. We had only been at the cricket club for five or ten minutes when a police car pulled up near to us. And the one and only 'Ken the Copper' got out the car and approached us. 'Have you been anywhere near Cooper and Jordan school tonight?' K.t.C. enquired. 'No!' Mad Mick snapped back immediately. 'Well we've had a report that four lads answering your descriptions have been smashing windows at school,' K.t.C. continued. 'It wasn't fuckin' us' Mick replied. That remark from Mick started a few minutes of barbed exchanges.

K.t.C.'s patience eventually broke and he ordered all four of us to get into his police car and took us the short journey to the police station.

On arrival at the police station, we were questioned by a very aggressive and scary sergeant. After a barrage of abuse and being told exactly what he thought of teenage delinquents like us, the sergeant informed us that the school caretaker had witnessed our act of vandalism and that he was willing to give a statement and testify against us in court. 'You may as well own up now and you will receive a lesser punishment from the magistrates when you appear in court,' the sergeant growled at us and with that he stormed out the room, slamming the door behind him, leaving the four of us unattended in the interview room.

I looked at Riga and Flet and they looked as worried as I was, but Mick sat there with a big grin on his face and said 'fuck 'em' As the three of us looked at Mick with a mixture of admiration and fear, the door opened and in walked Ken the Copper.

It was time for Good Cop – Bad Cop. K.t.C. reiterated what the sergeant had previously told us, but in a much calmer and friendly manner. 'You're definitely going to be found guilty boys,' K.t.C. told us, 'and because of the amount of damage that you've caused, if you don't own up now I'm sure you will get a bigger fine or even a bit of Borstal, when you go to court. Own up now and we can let you go straight away – I'll give you a few minutes to think it over.' With that he left the room.

Doing his best impression of a young James Cagney, Mick said, 'as soon as I get out of this cop-shop I'm doing a bunk, I'm up in court next week for breaking and entering and if I'm going to be charged with criminal damage as well, I will be definitely going down. Then in a moment of madness or panic or bravado all maybe all three, Riga and Flet said they would also go 'on the run' with Mick. Once Riga and Flet had agreed to disappear along with Mick, I knew Mick would make sure that they accompanied him on his little get-away adventure. 'Riga and Flet must be barmy going on the run with Mick,' I thought to myself.

'I'm definitely not running away from home,' I told them as the three of them stared at me for a response. It didn't take Mick long to come up with a plan. He looked at me intensely and said, 'well, if you're not coming with us, why don't you take the blame and say you broke all the windows on your own and met up with us three later? Then, when we've gone, you can tell them that we forced you to say that you caused all the damage on your own. After we have gone you could even say - you didn't break any windows at all and you tried to stop us!'

It seemed like a good idea at the time and I agreed to go along with Mick's plan. When K.t.C. came back into the room he was happy with the storyline that I smashed all the windows on my own and the other three had nothing to do with causing the damage. The fact that both the sergeant and K.t.C. had told us that the police had a witness that saw four lads breaking the windows, didn't seem to matter any more. Hardly the crime of centuries, but K.t.C. had got a confession. Smiling, K.t.C. told us we could leave the police station and said to me: 'he would call round my house tomorrow evening to take a formal statement.' I'm sure he was doing everything by the book – NOT!

I was very relieved to be out of the police station and I soon left the other three to make their plans for life on the run and made my way home. As I walked home I couldn't believe that I had got into so much trouble on the first night I'd been allowed out with my mates for over a month. I tried to convince myself that, once I told my parents and the police the fairy-tale that 'I didn't break any windows, it was the other three and that they forced me to admit that I was alone when I broke all the windows', they would believe me. The fact that the Aldridge Three had ran away from home would surely back up my story.

As I walked through my front door my Mom immediately shouted 'you're early; have you got the police with you?' I didn't reply but thought 'if only you knew'. I can remember the next evening as if it was yesterday: it was lovely and sunny and I was sitting in our living room with the rest of the family watching the World Cup which was being beamed live from Germany. My Mom, being oblivious to the impending bombshell, asked me 'aren't you going out tonight?' I didn't reply and just shook my head. I was keeping one eye on the TV and one nervous eye on the road, hoping and praying the police would have forgotten all about the previous evening's mischiefs, but my heart sank when I saw the police car drive slowly past our house and pull into the entrance to 'The Grove' at the side.

'Oh Fuck' I thought, then announced to my Mom and Dad 'I think the police are here to see you.' There was a look of astonishment on both their faces, but before they could say anything there was a bang-bang-bang on the door. My Dad gave me a look that would kill, then got up to answer. He came back into the living room followed by Ken the Copper and a another policemen.

'Do you know why we're here Mr. Grainger?' K.t.C. asked my Dad, looking at me. My Dad replied through gritted teeth, 'because of him I suppose.' Dad told my siblings to leave the room, then K.t.C. started to inform my Mom and Dad of what I'd been up to the night before. Both Mom and Dad sat there in silence, occasionally shaking their heads in disgust as K.t.C. explained how I'd admitted causing hundreds of pounds of damage to a school swimming pool.

After K.t.C. had finished I was asked to make a statement and I immediately claimed that I had been forced to make a confession by Mad Mick and the other two and added that the three of them had proven their guilt by running away from home, which was news to K.t.C. Up to that time, none of my three accomplices had been reported missing. But I was still required to give a statement and I stuck to my story that I was the innocent party and I was bullied into my confession. I was then told by K.t.C. that he would visit the homes of my friends and see if my story about them running away from home was true.

As soon as the police had left the house my Dad snapped at me, 'the first night we let you out and you get into all this trouble; you'd better get out of my sight before I kill you.' I hurried off to my bedroom in quick time.

A few hours later the police returned and stated it did seem that my three friends were indeed missing from home. This news seemed to back up my story of me being innocent and that I tried in vain to stop them breaking the windows, and Mom and Dad were a little more easy-going on me. I couldn't articulate it at the time, but what I tried to say to them was: 'I was at the wrong place, at the wrong time, with the wrong people; it won't happen again' - even though I knew only to well, it was all lies!

For the next few days at school, I was continually questioned by teachers and classmates about the damage to the swimming pool and the whereabouts of the Aldridge Three. I also had a couple more visits from the police and each time they said the same thing: 'my friends' parents were really worried and upset and if I knew where they were I should tell them straightaway.'

I continued to maintain my innocence regarding smashing the windows and I genuinely had no idea where Mad Mick, Riga and Flet were hiding. Riga and Flet were not in the same league as Mad Mick. Mick always seemed fearless and had a total disregard for authority and at the age of fourteen Mick had already been to court several times and had spent time at a young offenders' establishment. Riga and Flet were like me, a couple of 'wanna be Jack the Lads who liked to mess around a bit and usually knew how far to go.

While the Aldridge Three were 'on the lamb' Mick insisted that Riga and Flet join him in various criminal activities such as shoplifting and burglary. While Mick was doing his first bit of time, he'd made several criminal contacts and one of them lived in Handsworth. I later found out that this is where the Aldridge Three hid out.

Both Riga and Flet knew they were out of their depth and, after being away from home for three or four nights, Flet made an excuse to go to the local shops but instead of picking up a pint of milk and a loaf of bread he jumped on the nearest bus and made his way back home. When Mick discovered Flet had 'done one' apparently he went crazy, thinking that Flet would give away his hiding place. Mick thought Riga would soon be having the same idea as Flet, so he took evasive action and threw Riga down the cellar steps and locked him in. Over a couple of days Mick and his Handsworth mates would regularly open the locked cellar door and throw various missiles at Riga as he cowered in the corner of the dark cellar. Nuts, bolts screwdrivers and even a few bottles were thrown at Riga and the one time Riga threw something back at his captures and Mick and a couple of his mates flew straight down the cellar steps and gave Riga a good kicking.

While Riga was locked in the cellar, he had time to come up with a 'cunning plan'. He eventually persuaded Mick to let him out of the cellar, and he told Mick that he didn't want to go back home, but was happy to stop with Mick and his mates and, as an act of allegiance, he would set up a burglary. Riga said he knew where his parents hid their money back at his house, and there was probably a hundred quid to be nicked. Mick's eyes lit up straightaway and when Riga said 'every Thursday afternoon, the house is always empty' Mick was sold on the idea. Riga was welcomed back into the circle of thieves.

Riga had few days, before Thursday afternoon came along, to put Part Two of his 'cunning plan' into action. On the Thursday morning Mick and one of his housemates went off to 'borrow a car' to take them to Aldridge and back and Riga used the opportunity of Mick's absence to tell the remaining housemates that he was going to the shops to buy some cigarettes. He purchased his fags then went to a nearby phone box and called his parents.

It was the first time he had spoken to his mom and dad in almost three weeks. Full of tears and sobs, Riga told his mom and dad that he was desperate to come home and

Mick had kept him as a prisoner. He went on to tell them of the planned burglary and asked them to contact the police so they could arrest Mick and his friends and get himself freed.

When Riga got back to the house he 'crashed the ash' to endorse the fact that he had actually bought some fags and tried his best to make out all was well. When Mick returned in his 'borrowed car', he didn't even know that Riga had left the house.

So Mick, Riga and two of the housemates, jumped into the car and headed out to Aldridge and, when they arrived in Aldridge, they parked the car in a pub car park near to Riga's house and made their way through a small alley which lead to the street where Riga's house was. Once all four of the would-be burglars were in the alley, the 'Sting' went into full operation and the police blocked off the entrances to the alley and several Bobbies who had been lying in wait behind garden walls and hedges, pounced out and apprehended the four fugitives.

Riga was re-united with his loving family and Mad Mick and his accomplices were dragged kicking and screaming into custody. But now that Riga and Flet was back, there was a black cloud hanging over my innocence regarding breaking any windows. I'd made a statement to the police that Mick, Riga and Flet caused all the damage; I wondered if they would backup my story. Before I'd had a chance to talk to Riga and Flet I got a visit from Mick's elder brother who said, 'Mick's already in enough trouble. He doesn't need a charge of criminal damage piled on top of his existing charges – so you tell your other mates to say that Mick wasn't involved with breaking the windows.' He stopped for a moment to gauge my reaction. I just nodded, then he added, 'Mick knows that Riga set him up, but if he sticks to this story, Mick won't put him in hospital when he gets out.'

To quote Walter Scott, 'Oh, what a tangled web we weave, when first we practice to deceive.' So now I was supposed to change my statement and tell the police and my Mom and Dad that I'd been lying all along and Mad Mick was the innocent party in all of this. Not wanting a wild and vengeful Mad Mick on the warpath when he came out of Borstal, me, Riga and Flet agreed to go along with the line that Mick was a wronged blue-eyed angel.

When the day arrived when we had to appear in court my Dad was fuming that he had to lose a morning's work to accompany me. It was my first appearance in a magistrates court and it was all a bit daunting. But as we sat in court waiting for the judges to appear Mad Mick was brought into the court handcuffed to a prison officer. Mick still had his usual swagger and 'couldn't care less' attitude and gave us a big cheeky grin as he sat down next to us. Mick's dad addressed the judges and was at pains to point out that Mick had always pleaded guilty to his crimes in the past and stressed that the apple of his eye was totally innocent of causing any damage to the swimming pool. I'm sure the judges had no way of checking whether Mick had always pleaded guilty to his previous crimes but, no matter - he got away with it. He was found not guilty and he gave the three of us another big smile as he was lead out of court and returned to his incarceration. Me, Riga and Flet were all fined £10.00 each after apologizing for our actions and grovelling to the judges. Dad paid my fine as soon as we left the court room, then told me 'you'll pay it back'. I ended up paying it back by working for my Dad for four weekends in a row without pay.

§

On the 27th April Manchester United had a do-or-die game against their City neighbours, simply if United lost they would be relegated down to the 'old' Second Division for the first time since the mid-1930's. They did and they were! It's a myth that the goal scored by former United's living legend Denis 'the King' Law put United down. Birmingham City won that afternoon, so even if United had beat Manchester City, United would still have been relegated.

On the same day as the Manchester Derby, I was working in Burton-upon-Trent with my uncle Bill. As we drove through the town centre we stopped at some road-works and in a car park opposite to where we had stopped were a large group of Man United supporters boarding a couple of coaches, no doubt on their way to Old Trafford.

Most of the lads were mid–late teens and they created a very colourful spectacle; they all had two or three red-and-white scarfs tied around their wrists or hanging off their belts, most of them wore the ubiquitous Skinner Jeans – at 'half mast' of course - and with four-inch turn-ups. A couple of the lads were dressed up like Christmas trees, they wore white butchers' coats and had a red-and-whites scarf hanging off each wrist a scarf around their neck and one of them had a scarf wrapped around his head, Geronimo style. But the super-cool kid who really stood out from the crowd and fascinated me wore white Skinners, a blue denim jacket with a red silk United scarf wrapped round his neck and *pièce de résistance* a pair of highly polished 'eleven hole' black Dockers (high, eleven-eyelet Doctor Marten Boots).

99% of football fans my age and of a certain disposition in the Walsall/Birmingham area wore 'eight-hole – cherry red dockers'. Black eleven-hole Dockers were as rare as rocking-horse poo. I stared at him open-mouthed as he boarded the coach and I would have sold my soul to the devil to be going up to Old Trafford with him and the rest of his Man. U. mates I was still only thirteen and had never seen a mob of young United fans like this before. I couldn't stop thinking about them all-day and even when I heard the fateful news on the radio that United had been relegated, I wondered how the super cool kid in his white Skinners and black Dockers had reacted and whether or not he was scuffing his shiny Dockers while kicking some city fan's head in – I was wishing he was!

A month or so before the end of the school year, my third year at Tynings Lane, all the pupils in my year had to decide what lessons they were going to concentrate on in our fourth and fifth years. (Much to my dismay the government had just announced that all secondary pupils would now had to stay on and do a fifth year in secondary education. Before this children could leave school as young as 14 years old.) Basically this meant I had to choose between taking up the sciences or general studies. I had little or no aptitude for any of the science disciplines but all my best mates wanted to take the science route. General studies included geography, which I enjoyed and I was quiet good at, and history, which I loved. I would often get 8 or 9/10 for my history work and I really had a passion for the subject.

I anguished in silence over which path I should take for a few week and during this time my form teacher would be pressuring me for a decision. What to do? My mates were very important to me and I felt comfortable and even safe in their company, but the thought of regular science lessons churned my stomach. I knew kids that were going into general studies but they weren't mates that I would knock around the playground with or meet out of school, at best they were acquaintances. I might have had the outward appearance of being a confident, even a cocky little sod, but it was a thin veneer and the thought of making a new set of friends filled me with dread.

But all that wonderful, spell-binding history was a really big pull. One Friday I was told by my form teacher, 'I need to know whether, you or choosing science or general first thing Monday morning.' Maybe because I could be a bit disruptive in class, many of the teachers didn't really want me in their classrooms, so I got no guidance from any of the school staff regarding the most importance two years of my educational life.

I wrestled with the quandary until the Sunday morning and I had got myself very worked up and, as Monday morning was fast approaching, I desperately needed advice on what I should do. So as my Mom was preparing Sunday dinner in the kitchen I approached her and told her of my dilemma. I explained how much I hated science but all my friends were going into the science group and the fact that I loved history but I had no friends in that group and I did something that I don't think I'd ever done before, I opened up to my Mom and told her in detail how worried I was that I would really struggle if I stayed with my friends and took science and that the teachers had told me that it was the most important decision of my school life.

All the time I was talking to Mom, I noticed she had a strange perplexed, even nervous and look on her face. I ended my little speech by asking, 'well, Mom, what do you think I should do?' Before she replied she stared at me for a few seconds, then spluttered out, 'how the bleedin' hell do I know?!' Then without another word, she turned around and continued peeling the spuds.

As usual, I was on my own and I finally decided to go with the lesser of two evils and took the option of staying with my friends and going to the science group. This was a decisive moment for me and the first real 'crossroads' in my life. Unfortunately when I returned to school after the summer holidays, I very quickly realized I'd definitely chosen the wrong path. So started two years of turmoil, truancy and trouble.

Millwall fans had long had a reputation for violence and whereas most football teams' hooligans were teenagers, Millwall's boot boys were often grown men. So United's visit to Millwall's ground, the infamous 'Den' in south London, was seen as the Clash of the Giants as far as football hooliganism was concerned. In an attempt to cut down on crowd trouble, the game was played on a Monday evening (a school day) so it would have been extremely difficult for me and Ade or even Decca to get to the game. On the day of the game me and Ade couldn't think about anything else but how United's mob would cope with the fearsome Millwall thugs. We got so worked up that we agreed we must show the rest of Aldridge that we were United fans and display some true solidarity for our Man

United brothers who were literally going into the Lions Den. Me and Ade had arranged to meet in the village, after we'd gone home and had tea - even wannabe football hooligans can't go on the rampage on an empty stomach! On the way home 'spray paint' popped into my head. 'Wouldn't it be great, if I could get a spray can and me and Ade could spray MUFC & United Agro all over Aldridge,' I thought to myself.

There was a row of shops at the top of my street, Luckily for me, one of them was an ironmongers and they stocked cans of spray paint. And fortunately the naïve shopkeeper kept his cans of spray paint in a tall metal merchandiser right next to the door that was not visible from behind the counter where the shopkeeper usually stood. As the shopkeeper was serving a customer, I opened my schoolbag and threw half-a-dozen cans of spray paint into it. When I got home I tipped the cans of paint out of my bag and onto my bed. One of the cans contained silver paint. This was the time when Glam Rock was at its peak and everything glittery, shiny and silver was fashionable. I held the can of silver paint in my hand while I considered my options for using the paint as a fashion statement. My old Dockers caught my eye. The very first pair of Doc Martens that I owned were worn-out, the sole was almost bare and the wonderful white stitching was splitting and falling apart. Even though I had recently had a new pair of Dockers for my birthday, I still loved the old ones and I just couldn't bring myself to get rid of my original boots. I was like a boy reluctant to throw away a favourite battered old toy. I stared at my old boots for a minute or so then said out loud, 'fuck it, I'm going to spray 'em silver.'

And while we're on the subject of Doctor Marten boots, a few days before I sprayed my old Docca's, United played West Brom at the Hawthorns. Half a dozen of us had made the short trip from Aldridge and it was as good as a home game for us. When we arrived at the ground, there was a sea of red and white with the ubiquitous Football Jumpers well in attendance. The Brummie Road End had already closed its turnstiles but not before several hundred United fans had planted themselves in with the home fans. So we were guaranteed entertainments on and off the pitch!

As we queued up to get into the Smethwick Road End, I was horrified to see the local constabulary forcing United supporters to remove the laces from their boots and if the coppers got 'too much back-chat' or if they saw 'steel-toecaps or 'hobnail' boots they insisted the unfortunate hooligan remove their boots and collect them after the game. As I approached the turnstiles I gazed wide eyed at the large pile of shinny Docca's and black hobnailed boots stacked against the wall.

It was certainly a strange sight to see thousands of football hooligans on the concrete terracing with laceless boots or even bare-footed. Five minutes before the end of the game, the gates opened and hundreds of United fans spilled out of the Smethwick End and headed for a battle with the Albion fans. It was a comical sight to see hardened hooligans charging at opposing fans while still trying to pull their boots on and tie their laces. I'm sure I heard one old lady shout out to the charging mob 'do your laces up, or you'll fall over and hurt yourself!'

Pancho Pearson scored for us to give United a 1–1 draw. Any road up – back to the spray cans! I ran downstairs and got some old newspaper and took it back up into my bedroom. With the newspaper pages spread across half the bedroom floor I started the task of turning my old Dockers into a work of art. After a few minutes of spraying, I stood back and thought 'WOW – Elton John would be proud of 'em!' I hurriedly put on the boots and checked them out in the wardrobe mirror. 'Fuckin' Bostin' was my reaction. I tied a few United scarfs around my wrists, shoved a few cans of spray paint in my jacket pockets and headed off to meet Ade.

Unfortunately the paint job didn't work, in the fifteen minutes it took me to walk to the village the paint had all cracked and had started to peel off in places - but I still got a few pedestrians and drivers stare at me in amazement. Ade was overjoyed with the fact that I'd managed to get hold of a few cans of paint but he wasn't very diplomatic about my silver boots and said 'Grange they look crap'. The saving grace was I'd got the can of silver paint with me, so every few hundred yards, in-between spraying UNITED AGRO and I HATE VILLA on various walls around Aldridge, I stopped to re-spray my boots.

When we had exhausted the spray cans and expressed to the citizens of Aldridge our love for Manchester United, Ade and me made our way to his home to tune in to his radio and try to find the United result. We were both ecstatic to learn that a Gerry Daly penalty had given United a 1–0 victory and we were top of the league (where we remained for the rest of the season). As I was getting ready for school next morning I took the fateful decision to throw the remaining spray cans into my schoolbag and during the dinner-break me and a few wannabe graffiti artists headed into the village. Because of the number of shoppers around we decided to head for the nearby cricket club and practice our 'art form' on their walls. Full of teenage bravado and playing to the crowd (and being a twat), en-route to the cricket club in full view of passing cars and local residents I sprayed 'Man United Rule Ok' on the sidewall of a private block of flats.

My brazen behaviour would cost me dear. After we had emptied the remaining spray cans by daubing witty one-liners such as 'Nobby Dawes is a cunt' and 'Winters is a cock sucking poof' and 'Sims is a spastic' (Nobby Dawes. Winters and Sims were all teachers at our school), we boldly marched back to school with spray paint on our hands and clothes and totally oblivious to the chain of events we had set in motion. Not surprisingly several members of the public had contacted both the school and the police and reported seeing a group of teenagers spraying graffiti on walls. Me and Ade would have been immediately 'in the frame' as far as the school was concerned, but when it was mentioned that part of the offending graffiti read 'Man United Rule Ok' CASE SOLVED! Our Head of House was waiting outside our classroom as we returned from our dinner break, a quick inspection of our paint-covered hands and we were frog-marched to the headmaster's office. Our mild mannered headmaster was not available so we were dragged in front of the frightening Mrs Wilkins, the Deputy Head; she was a cross between Maggie Thatcher and the character Frau Blucher from the comedy film Young Frankenstein but much more frightening. She read us the riot act and screamed at us 'you will all go to Borstal for causing such damage to private property and disgracing the school.' She continued, 'we are passing all your names and addresses on to the police and they will be visiting your parents this evening!' 'Oh fuck,' I thought. It had only been a few months since I had appeared in court for smashing windows, my Mom and Dad would go crazy.

The old battle-axe didn't paint a rosy picture for our future and on our walk home after school, me and my little band of terrified schoolboys discussed our options. Being young, stupid, naïve and scared to death, by the time I approached my house my mind was made up. Me and one of my mates, Rob H. had decided that rather than risk the wrath of our parents and a potential trip to Borstal we were going to run away from home. The rest of our merry bunch had decided they would stop at home and face the music. I went straight into my bedroom and emptied my old suitcase where I kept all my football and music souvenirs and threw most of my clothes into the case. I then looked out of my bedroom window to make sure Rob was waiting in the back garden and threw the suitcase down to him. Amusingly as Rob tried to catch the flying suitcase it knocked him to the ground, which was quite fortuitous as it's made us both laugh and forget just how serious our actions were.

I had less than a quid to take with me but Rob said he'd got quite a few quid stashed away at home. So we took the short walk from my house to Rob's place and I waited outside while he went in to collect his cash. I was delighted when Rob returned and told me he had almost £9.00 - not far off a kings ransom for a fourteen-year-old in 1974. We spent no time hanging around in Aldridge and jumped on a Harpers bus heading to New Street Station in Birmingham.

While on the bus, Rob and me discussed a next move and I came up with a bold and daring plan. During my summer holidays in Devon, I'd met a girl approximately the same age as me and she came from Wallasey (the other side of the Mersey to Liverpool). I got on really well with this girl and had exchanged a few love letters with her. I convinced Rob that if we headed to Wallasey, she would look after us and find somewhere for us to stay. So when we got to New Street station we boarded the first train we could find that was heading to Liverpool. We had the time of riley on the train with Rob continually visiting the buffet car and buying us loads of snacks and drinks. We acted as though we didn't have a care in the world and I casually made up some cock-and-bull story for the ticket collector, telling him that we were going to Liverpool to stay with my auntie'.

Our mood soon changed when we got to a dirty, noisy and frightening Lime Street station in Liverpool. We gingerly wandered out of the front entrance of the station and felt completely over whelmed by our alien surroundings. As we walked away from the railway station, we soon came across the Adelphi hotel, the old hotel looked grand and very inviting and I suggested to Rob, that we might be able to sneak into one of the empty rooms and sleep there for the night, but in a port city like Liverpool, they must have seen little toe-rags like me and Rob every day of the week. I told the doormen, that we were meeting our parents inside but they had no doubt heard it all before and told us 'to come back with our parents'. When I tried to convince them that our parents were already inside, one of the doormen said in a strong Liverpudlian accent 'fuck

off you little bleeder's before you get my toe up your arse!'
Charming! Little did they know, I was carrying my Gold
American Express Card.

After walking the streets for quite sometime, we
eventually found ourselves at the dock side and found
ourselves staring up at a big white ship. It must have
been the first ship that I'd seen up close and my sense of
adventure soon kicked in. I asked one of the young men
who was loading boxes onto the ship, 'where did the ship
come from?' 'Ireland' he casually replied and then added,
'it will be heading back there in the next couple of hours.'

'Fuckin Hell - Ireland!' I thought Wow, that would be a
tale to tell to my mates back home. We tried every which
way to get onto the ship: the passengers' gangplanks, the
crew gangplanks, the service gangplanks. I would have had
a go at climbing the anchor rope, but thought it might be
a bit tricky with my suitcase in tow.

Reluctantly we had to admit defeat and said goodbye to our
pipe dream of a trip to the Emerald Isle and went in search
of somewhere else to sleep the night. For a couple of hours
we must have tried a hundred doors of all shapes and sizes, all
of them locked. Getting tired and cold we eventually decided
we would have to stay the night in the only building that
we found was open – a dark, smelly, public toilet. For extra
warmth we put on extra layers of clothes from my suitcase and,
locking ourselves in a cubicle, we tried to get comfortable for
the night. We continually swapped positions from the floor
to sitting on the well-worn wooden toilet seat and asked each
other, 'what do you think your parents are doing now?' And I
wondered if we would be able to find my summer girlfriend
in Wallasey and what sort of reception we might expect.

When it started to get light Rob and I had quite a shock, the walls of the toilets cubicle was covered in homosexual graffiti. There was things like 'Colin sucked my dick here' and a date 'if you want to see a big dick come here at 8:00pm' and 'I want a sailor to fuck me hard.' There was also various crude drawings of men receiving blow-jobs and being rogered up the dirt box. But the most concerning item was a small hole in the cubicle wall and written around the circumference it read 'stick your cock through here if you want it sucked'. We slowly opened the cubicle doors hoping that's no one would be outside and were even more shocked and frightened to discover all the toilets was covered in the same type of graffiti. Fortunately there was no Bumbandits about, but just out of childish curiosity (honestly!) we couldn't help but read the graffiti and we kept saying to each other 'look at this one – just look at this, dirty bastard' But the longer we stayed there the more frightened we became, and by the time we left the toilets we were convinced that Liverpool must be full of poofs.

Leaving home in such a hurry, I hadn't thought to take the Wallasey girl's address or phone number so my thought was to try and find her school in Wallasey and hopefully see her coming out of the gates. After asking several locals for directions we found a bus that would take us through the Mersey Tunnel to Wallasey. When we finally find the senior school in Wallasey it was mid-morning, so we had to hang around until dinnertime and hope my girlfriend would appear. No such luck, the school dinnertime came and went and only a trickle of school kids came through the gate.

We would have to wait until the school closed later that afternoon, in the meantime we went for a look round and while wandering around we came across another public toilet, so we popped in for a jimmy riddle and we were horrified to discover the walls of the toilet were covered in same graffiti as the toilets we had slept in the previous night! We soon convinced ourselves and each other that we had come to the Land of OMO's and we were both scared to death.

We got back to the school just as the kids were coming out of the gate, but much to our disappointment my holiday sweetheart was nowhere to be seen. 'What are we going to do now?' Rob asked. 'I really don't know,' I replied in a dejected manner and we sat in silence for an age contemplating what we had done and, 'what now!' We were lost in every sense of the word and home seemed a very long way away. We wandered around aimlessly for quite awhile until we came across a small transport café where we had a sandwich and a cup of tea and where stayed for at least an hour, until the frustrated owner finally kicked us out. So we continued walking around, drifting in and outs of various shops and more often than not being asked to leave by the shop owners.

As night fell we were getting very nervous in case we were kidnapped by Liverpool poofs and bummed to death. Borstal no longer seemed such a bad option. But our luck was about to change; we came across a building-site and right at the entrance to the site was the show-house. We stared through the window and the carpeted and fully furnished house looked very, very inviting. We made our way to the back of it and looked for a way in, delighted to discover a small window on the ground floor that hadn't been closed properly from the inside. Steadied by Rob I stood on my old suitcase and, after banging on the frame a few times, the window burst open. Rob gave me a leg up and I was in through the window in no time. I then opened the larger window and dragged Rob into the house.

Our mood was immediately lifted and we danced with joy, thinking we didn't have to spend another night in a public toilet with the fear of being bummed to death – what a way to go! As we explored we couldn't believe our luck: we found tea, milk, sugar, bread, butter and jam in the kitchen cupboards and up in the bedrooms - made-up beds with fluffy pillows. The Only thing we were missing was a TV. It had been a long and tiring day, mainly because we had carried that bloody suitcase everywhere, and it wasn't long before we decided it was time for some sleep. So off we went up the wooden hill and made ourselves comfortable on the big double bed.

I was sleeping fine but Rob kept waking me up and saying 'he couldn't sleep' or 'I can hear noises.' Then in the middle of the night he came up with a crazy suggestion: 'shall we go and sleep in the loft?' 'Are you fuckin' mad?' I replied. Rob continued, 'but I'm scared and keep thinking someone will come into the house and find us. If we go into the loft we will be safe and no one will know that we are here.' So I went downstairs and got a side chair to help get us up to the loft. I climbed up first then after several attempts and lots of laughter and more than a few bruises of Rob's arse, I finally helped drag Rob up into the loft. I wasn't happy, I'd given up a comfortable bed to lay across timber joists.

Then, just as I was nodding off, Rob announced, 'I need a shit.' 'Well go down to the bleedin' toilet,' I snapped. But Rob kept moaning on about how frightened he was about going out of the loft on his own and that he might not be able to get back up into the loft. 'But I really need a shit,' he kept repeating, so just to shut him up, I said, 'well go over to the far end of the loft and do it over there.' So off Rob shuffled. He got as far as the sloping roof joists would let him then dropped his trousers and crouched down and then he started to groan and moan as he was pushing his kak out. This really amused me and soon I was in fits of laughter and Rob also got the giggles. I then discovered bits of leftover building material near by me in the loft and I started throwing them at Rob. My aim was all very much pot luck, because it was so dark in the loft I could only just about see where Rob was but the combination of laughter and dodging missiles made Rob lose his balance and he fell back through the timber joists. Fortunately for Rob he managed to grab onto the joists to stop himself falling completely through.

Imagine the scene, Rob hanging on for dear life, with his skinny arms and legs gripping the timber joists and his shitty arse hanging out the broken plasterboard ceiling and the pair of us in hysterics. Through tears of laughter I managed to get over to pull him back up into the loft. After a few minutes we finally stopped laughing, but then we looked through the hole in the ceiling and saw the broken plasterboard and bits of Rob's kak all over the bedroom floor below. We cracked up even more this time and we must have been crying with laughter for a good ten minutes. God only knows what the sales person must have thought when they opened the bedroom door to discover the broken ceiling and plasterboard and kak all over the floor, I only hope they had a potential customers with them. Even today when I think of Rob and me in that loft, it always makes me laugh. Without doubt one of the funniest moments of my teenage years.

Deciding that Liverpool was not the place for us, we headed back to Lime Street Station and without thinking to buy a ticket jumped on the first train to Birmingham. The plan was to get nearer to home so hopefully our friends would be able to help us. We had only been on the train for ten minutes or so when the ticket inspector came into our small first-class six-seater carriage. 'What the bloody hell are you little sods doin' in here?' He snapped at us. 'If you haven't got first-class tickets then you're off the train.'

Rob messed around with his money, but the regimental Clippy wasn't impressed. 'Guard's van for you two, follow me,' he instructed us. We had only been in the guard's van for a few minutes when we pulled into Runcorn station. The Clippy opened the train door and ordered us off the train. 'If I see you again, you'll get a couple of smacks around your earholes, one from me and one from the copper I hand you over to, now sod off,' was the farewell dispatch from the no-nonsense Clippy.

We left the station and walked through the small town, wondering what to do next. Two young lads with a suitcase went completely unnoticed in the busy port city of Liverpool, but in a little town like Runcorn it seems everyone we passed stopped and looked us up and down; it made us very nervous.

The aggressive Clippy had certainly put us off trains for a while, so Rob suggested that we hitchhiked and we soon came across a road sign stating 'M6 Birmingham and the South'. It was a busy dual carriageway and, like a couple of pratts, we started walking along the side of the road, taking it in turns to hold the suitcase or stick our thumbs out.

We had been walking along for about fifteen minutes when a police car pulled up alongside us. Our first reaction was to run up the steep bank at the side of the road. The young copper got out of his car and simply shouted to us 'you'll never get over that fence get back down here!' Rob and me looked at the high fence which was situated at the top of the bank and thought, 'the copper is right.' Heads bowed we made our way back down the bank and the copper started to ask us what we were up to. After two or three replies from me, the copper shook his head and said, ' get in the back of the car you two, I'm taking you down the nick.'

On the way to the police station we admitted that we had ran away from home and the young copper duly informed the desk sergeant when we arrived, and we were shown into a small office and given tea and biscuits. A sergeant asked us a few questions about how we got to Runcorn and where we had slept. I told him that we had slept in public toilets and certainly didn't mention anything about the show house in Wallasey! He told us that our parents had been informed that we were in custody and they were on their way to collect us. With that he left us alone in the office. Both of us were dreading facing our parents and we knew we would be in major trouble and that we would be facing severe punishment. Our fate was sealed, I thought, then I noticed that the window in the office was open and left my chair for a closer inspection. To my surprise the open window faced out onto the pavement and as I stuck my head out of the window I could see there was about a five-foot drop down to the pavement. I told Rob to come over and look for himself. 'What do you think Rob? We could easily jump out of this window and get away.' The expression on Rob's face gave me his initial answer. 'Yes, go on then, but you first,' Rob said quietly as if he thought one of the police officers would overhear us.

I went through the window legs first and slid down the external wall onto the pavement. 'Right, come on Rob, your turn,' I said but just as Rob started to climb out of the window he stopped and pulled himself back into the office. He then poked his head through the open window and, almost whispering, said 'I haven't got any money, the policeman took it off me – I'm staying here!' Fuckin' great! I was a fugitive for all of ten seconds; no way did I fancy going on my own.

I asked Rob to help me get back inside. Getting out the window was far bleedin' easier than getting back in, the outside wall was painted in heavy gloss paint and I couldn't get a footing to lift myself up and Rob wasn't strong enough to pull me up. Try as I might, I just couldn't get back through the window. There was no alternative, I had to go round to the front desk and ask the sergeant to let me back in. As you can imagine he was not impressed, he grabbed me by the collar and dragged me up to a second-floor office 'feel free to jump out of that window if you like,' he said as he firmly pushed me onto a chair.

When our parents arrived at the police station our moms were tearful and our dads were fuming and hardly a word was spoken on the journey back home. When we got to our house my Dad told my Mom to get out of the car and we would return shortly. Immediately all types of horrors ran through my mind: where on earth was my Dad taking me – maybe down to the woods to give me a good hiding? or maybe he was going to throw me to pack of dogs? or take me to my school and humiliate me?

As it turned out it wasn't any of the above, but it was very humiliating. Dad took me to the local hairdressers called Müllers, affectionately known as 'Hacker Müllers'. I was sat down in the queue and waited my turn, wondering what more fate had in store for me. When it was my turn to sit in the barber's chair my Dad turned to the barber and said 'cut it all off.' Both me and the barber looked at my Dad in shock. As was the fashion in 1974, most boys had shoulder-length hair and it had taken well over a year to grow it. The barber questioned my Dad's decision but Dad firmly repeated, 'cut it all off' The tears fell down my cheeks as Hacker Müller started to cut my long blond locks and to be fair to H.M. seeing how upset I was, he did stop cutting my hair a couple of times and turned to my Dad and said 'is that enough?' but Dad just kept shaking his head and saying, 'cut it all off'

I didn't end up with a skinhead, but it wasn't far off it and I was totally devastated. As well as the savage haircut, I was grounded for six weeks and the first two weeks I had to spend in my bedroom. To hide my embarrassment, for the next few months I would pull my Parker hood over my bald head on every occasion I could. The one upside to the fall-out of running away from home was that, even though we had only been away from home for a short time, it turned Rob and me into minor celebrities. For a while and I was pleased to receive quite a lot of attention from the girls, especially the ones in the year above me. They were all fascinated about where we went and what we did when we ran away from home, and a few of the older girls also told me that they fancied me with short hair, which was a much-needed confidence boost. Even though I was game for most things and still came across cocky and self assured, it was all just a thin veneer and underneath it all, I'm sure that unconsciously I was very insecure. It wouldn't be until much later in life that the lack of love and guidance in my childhood would really come back to me haunt me and cause me so many problems.

Probably the worst thing about being grounded at the time was not being able to see the wonderfully obliging Tina. When I found out that Mom and Dad were taking my sisters out to visit family for the evening I made arrangements for Tina to come down and see me. We still had the touring caravan and it was locked-up and parked at the back of our house on the side driveway. Luckily for me, I knew where Dad hid the key so Tina and I snuck into the caravan and made ourselves cozy under a pile of sleeping bags.

I was obviously enjoying myself a little too much and didn't keep a watching eye on the time; we were in a deep embrace when my Dad walked alongside the caravan. I whispered to Tina 'keep it quiet and they won't see us.' But my eldest sister decided to look through the caravan window 'Mom, there is someone in the caravan,' she said. 'No there isn't,' my Mom replied, 'come away from the caravan.' But my sister wasn't taking any notice and as Mom walked towards the house my sister cried out, 'there *is* someone in the caravan, come and look!' Huffing and puffing, Mom made her way back to caravan and stood next to my sister and looked inside it. There was silence for a few seconds as they both stared into the darkness of the caravan, then

Mom screeched, 'Steven is that you? And without waiting for a reply she shouted, 'get your bloody clothes on and get into the house!'

I hurriedly got dressed and went to face the music once again. To my amazement as I walked through the front door, Mom calmly enquired, 'was that Tina in the caravan with you?' I nodded. 'Where is she now?' my Mom continued. 'Walking home,' I replied cautiously. 'You had better go after her then and make sure she gets home safely.' Well I'll gew to Cannock – you could have knocked me down with a feather! To say I was surprised at my Mom's reaction was an understatement; I was expecting to be called 'a dirty little bugger' and receive a dozen or so smacks around the head. Consideration and understanding were very much in short supply in the Grainger household.

§

After four long years I finally got back to Old Trafford. United had a top-of-the-table clash with Villa and somehow I'd got the pennies together to go to the game with Ade. We travelled up to Manchester in a small pea-green coach from the Harpers garage in Aldridge and the coach looked as though it was built pre-war. Not surprisingly the rattily old coach was full of Villa fans, most of them adults, but there was also a gang of scary-looking kids, a few years older than me and Ade. So reluctantly we decided to keep our United scarfs hidden until we got to Old Trafford.

As we drove up the M6, there was lots of banter and even a few songs from the Villa fans on the coach, but the mood changed as we approached the ground. Because of heavy traffic we were driving very slowly along the Chester Road and had stopped at a set of red lights, just opposite the Drum pub in Stretford. Outside the pub was a small mob of United fans enjoying a few drinks before the game. Some of the Villa fans on our coach were wearing scarfs and this was quickly noticed by the United mob.

In no time the coach was surrounded by United fans and they were kicking and banging the side of it. A few of the United fans stood on the curb-side railings and were doing a great job of balancing on one foot and kicking the coach windows with the other. The few kids who had been sporting Villa scarfs couldn't remove them quick enough and threw them under their seats. One United fan started banging on the window next to me and Ade. All the time he was banging the window he was shouting abuse at us. Ade immediately got out his United scarf and put it up to the window. The United fan saw Ade's scarf and stopped banging on our window. As he stared at the red-and-white scarf the United fan had very puzzled expression on his face. He seemed totally thrown for a few seconds. 'United fans on a villa coach? What was going on?' He slowly and silently moved away from us and moved to the next window. The United fan looked through the next window and when no United scarf was produced, he continued his attack on the coach.

At last few coppers came to rescue of the coach and its occupants and we made the rest of the short journey to the ground without further incident. Ade and me were bursting with excitement as we queued to get into the Stretford End but having been on the terraces for only a short while, we were disappointed to discover just how small the Stretford End was. And we were shocked to see seating at the back of the terracing. The United mob wasn't anywhere near as big as we'd imagined, but what we didn't know at the time was that United had mobs all around Old Trafford. Besides the Stretford End, there were big mobs in the Stretford Paddock and Scoreboard Paddock, and there was a loony mob in the Scoreboard End which was at the opposite side of the ground to the Stretford End. Above the Scoreboard End terrace, United's main mob the 'Boys' were in 'K Stand' seats.

Old Trafford was a veritable fortress. Thus the very few away fans that visited Old Trafford, never wore their scarfs around the ground, let alone turned up mob handed. The game wasn't a classic and Ade spent most of the second half trying to persuade a small group of United fans from Birmingham to travel over to the Aldridge and beat up the local villa fans for us. Sadly we never saw them again. Over 55,000 United fans left the ground happy because two goals from Gerry Daly gave United a 2 -1 victory.

On the journey back home Ade and me were delighted to overhear so many stories from the Villa fans on the coach of how they got beat up or had missiles thrown at them. A lot of the older Villa fans had gone in the main-stand seats and throughout the game they said they were constantly being pelted by United fans in the Scoreboard Paddock with coins, batteries and broken glass. And Ade got an hard-on when he heard one man saying, 'he thought he would be safe being in the seats, but he saw at least three darts flying out of the terraces and heading towards the terrified villa fans.'

§

On the morning of 22nd November I was munching on my cornflakes when I heard on the radio that during the previous night two bombs had exploded in Birmingham City Centre. It was reported that hundreds and been injured and there was several fatalities. The IRA were immediately blamed for the atrocities. The first bomb explode at approximately 20:15 in the Mulberry Bush pub, situated at the base of the Rotunda building, and the second bomb exploded ten minutes later in the basement pub, the Tavern in the Town, which was located in New Street and less than a hundred yards from the Mulberry Bush. The police were evacuating the Tavern in the Town when the second explosion occurred. It was later confirmed that twenty-one had died and 182 were injured, making the Birmingham Pub Bombings the worst terrorist atrocity (in terms of number of fatalities) to occur in mainland Britain throughout the 'Troubles'.

Forget who was top of the League, or what group was at number one, or who had the shiniest Dockers, the only subject in the playground for the next few days was the IRA bombings in Birmingham. Unlike the passive reaction of the general public today when there is a terrorist atrocity, the Birmingham Pub Bombings stoked considerable anti-Irish sentiment in Birmingham and the surrounding areas, including first and second generation (like me). It was estimated there were 100,000 Irish in Birmingham alone, but very quickly the Irish community were ostracised from public areas and subject to physical assaults/verbal abuse and even death threats. Irish homes, pubs, businesses and community centres were vandalised and attacked. More than one factory in Birmingham suspended hangman's nooses for Irish work colleagues who they thought were IRA sympathisers. And in Aldridge, Irish hardman Jimmy Joyce had to take his British Army Medals to work to prove to the baying mob that he was loyal to Britain and the Queen.

One of the saddest episodes was when Irishwoman Mrs. Bridget Reilly, the mother of the two Irish brothers who were killed in the Tavern in the Town explosion, was refused service at her local shop. Rightly or wrongly, retribution and reprisals were the order of the day.

My retribution was dished out on an obnoxiousness and mouthy London kid who had joined my school at the beginning of the new school year in September and was in the same year as me. He was always boasting about his imaginary exploits at his former school and about his Irish descent and that his cousin was in the IRA . Nobody took any notice of him, he had few friends if any, and all of the girls gave him a wide berth and thought he was creepy, all – in - all he wasn't a well liked boy. A few days after the Birmingham Pub Bombings, I was at school and running late for my lesson (as usual) I came out of the playground and into an almost empty corridor. I was immediately stopped in my tracks. I couldn't believe my eyes - marching towards me - marching mind, not walking - and dressed in a black paramilitary outfit including black sunglasses and a black beret was the goby cockney twat. I was proud of my Irish roots but first and foremost I am English. As he approached I grabbed him by the throat and pushed him into the cloak room. Luckily for the wannabe terrorist one of the teachers spotted me pushing the horrible bastard into cloakroom and came to his rescue. I had only hit him a few times before the teacher pulled me off him. Usually I would have expected the cane if I was caught fighting, but such was the public anger at the time, I was just told to get to my lessons and only the twat in black was dragged off to the head master's office. I only ever saw the horrible bastard once more, a week or so after I'd tried to shove his sunglasses and beret down his throat; he was spotted entering the school playground, this time wearing civvies. That made no difference; en-mass about thirty or forty boys charged at him as soon as he appeared. He ran for his life and was never seen in Aldridge again.

1975

My life-long fascination with tattoos progressed to 'home-made' Indian-ink tattoos. The Indian ink was sold in a craft shop in Aldridge. You just had to wrap cotton around the end of a needle, so only the point of the needle was visible, then, you had your DIY tattoo kit. The first tattoo I had, I did it myself, it read **'STEVE + MUFC'** and I put it on my left wrist. Sadly I have to admit, it wasn't very good.

Seeing my tattoo Tina said she wanted one so I tattooed a big 'S' on her forearm. It was crap and looked a right fuckin' mess. Fortunately for me, Ade was great at drawing and so was Nick. Ade soon mastered the use of the cotton-wrapped needle and he was tattooing some great images on his arms, Desperate Dan being the pick of the bunch. Ade readily agreed to tattoo me and in a few short weeks, I had some half-decent tattoos on my arms. I had a love-heart with a spider dangling from it, a couple of swords & daggers, a skull-and-cross-bones, a few more Man U's, and of course STEVE + TINA.

I started to put M.U.F.C. on my fingers but the needle hitting my bones on my skinny fingers was so painful, I gave up after only a few jabs. Lucky Escape! One crazy lad in the year below us, covered his hands in awful Indian-ink tattoos, including BCFC on his fingers! After a few trips to see a shrink, he had laser treatment to remove the tattoo's. Unfortunately for him, the scars from the laser machine looked worse than his crap tattoos.

My tattoos were hidden in the house, but at school and out and about, mine and Ade's tattoos got a lot of attention.

Everyone knew we were Man United supporters, how could
they miss the fact? we wore our United scarfs everywhere.
But when older lads, especially the Walsall Wood gang saw
our United tattoos, we got a very negative response. We
got comments like 'think you're hard bastards, now?' and
'what's that shit on your arm?' Luckily, me and Ade had a
few older friends like Decca Bradley and Mad Mick and
our friendship with them stopped the Walsall Wood gang
from battering me and Ade. And I could always use my
cousins name - Paddy McArdle, if I got into any bother.

At the time me and Ade were simply not liked by a
majority of Villa fans in and around Aldridge. Because of
our fear of the Walsall Wood gang, one Sunday afternoon
Ade thought it would be fun to play a dirty little trick on
me. As usual, after my Sunday dinner, I wandered down to
the new park in Leighswood to have a kick about, but as I
approached the small football pitch, Ade turned round and
his face was covered in blood. 'What the fuck happened to
you?' I asked. 'The Walsall Wood gang just came down and
battered me and they said that they would be coming back
a little later, for you!' Ade replied. I was shitting myself, Ade
looked liked he'd been given a right kicking and I didn't
fancy receiving the same treatment.

'I'm going home to phone Paddy McArdle and tell him
to come down with his mates to sort out those Walsall Wood
wankers,' I said. My heart was beating ten to the dozen as I
left the football pitch, and as I walked away I was thinking,
'what if the Walsall Wood gang get me before I get home?'
– 'what if Paddy isn't in when I phone?' – 'oh fuck!'

I'd only walked a short distance, when I heard fits of
laughter behind me. I turned round and saw all the lads

on the pitch were laughing their heads off. Ade was on his knees he was laughing so much. 'You should have seen your face,' Ade spurted out between his hysterical laughter. 'You shit yourself,' he continued then Nick added, 'you went white as a sheet.' I was a bit baffled: what the bleedin' hell was going on? Then Ade shouted out, 'it's fake blood!' All my fears and anxiety immediately disappeared, but I couldn't see the funny side of it for a long while, not until I'd given Ade a few dead-legs anyway.

I cant remember why, but my brother suddenly started to hang around with Walsall Wood gang, a decision he would soon live to regret. One Friday there was a fight in the Elms car park between the Aldridge and Walsall Wood lads and during the fight a skinhead girl (Sue Brookhouse) who knocked about with Aldridge gang got quite badly hurt. The Aldridge lads wanted revenge and they wanted it quickly. Knowing that my brother was now part of the Walsall Wood gang, bright and early the next morning Mark Collins (local hardnut and almost a pro-goalie) and half a dozen of his Albion mates came knocking on our front door. They casually asked my Mom 'to tell Kevin to come to the door.' When Mom said 'he's still in bed,' they told her, it was important, so to go and wake him!. Like a good 'un Mom trots up the stairs to our bedroom and tells her first-born, 'some of your friends are at the door and they want to talk to you.'

Big brother stumbles out of bed and wearing just a pair of shorts goes down to the front door. Looking through the glass panel in the door, he knew that the gang hadn't come round to invite him for a game of footie. He turned to our Mom and said 'the're not my friends! They've come to beat me up!!' Now I know a lot of moms who on hearing a statement like that from one of her children, would have picked up a poker or broom handle and charged outside and seen off the would be attackers. Not our Mom! 'Well - you'd better go out there and get it over with,' was her motherly reply. And with that she opened the front door and pushed her son outside to meet his fate. When big brother came back into the house, all battered and bloody from his beating, Mom simply said 'well – its all over now.' I thought I was still dreaming as I saw my brother come back into our bedroom with a black eye, cut lip and bloody nose. Without a word he got back into his bed and pulled the covers of his head and I turned over and went back to sleep.

Our Mom's loving and caring streak continued. After belting me and my brother for having yet another fight, she announced, 'that's it! I'm sick to death with hurting my hands hitting you two – I'm going to get my self a stick!' Which she duly did. So the next time me and my brother were rolling around the floor kicking and punching lumps out of each other, Mom came running into the room with her new 'stick' and as my brother happened to be on top of me, he received a vast majority of the blows from our Mom's stick. After a dozen or so strokes to his back and legs my brother suddenly broke away from me, stood up and grabbed the stick from Mom. He stared at her for a few seconds then broke the stick over his knee. 'You'd better get a stick with a nail in it next time,' he told her. 'Don't worry, I bleedin' will,' was our Mom's heart-felt reply.

Nail or no nail, even with her stick, Mom wouldn't have been able to stop the worst fight me and my brother had had to date. It was a Bank Holiday and all my family were out the house, I was sitting in our living room, playing records with a couple of mates. My mates and me were having a good time, then my horrible mouthy brother and one of his mates walked into the room. My brother came over to where I was sitting and stood over me and said 'you think you're hard now, don't you? Just because you've got a few shit tattoos' 'Fuck off' I snapped back. 'Look at his shiney Dockers,' my brother snarled and with that, he stamped on each of my boots and kicked me in the shin.

I immediately jumped out of my seat and started to grapple with him. After bouncing off the walls and fireplace a few times my temper was really up. I pushed him away from me and made a dash to the back of the living room, where my parents kept a carving set in the shape of a long wooden fish. If you pulled the head off the fish, it revealed a large carving fork, pull the tail out and you had a long, wide carving knife. I got to the wooden fish, pulled the head and threw the carving fork at my brother. My aim was off and the fork flew past my brother and took a chunk of plaster out of the wall. I then pulled out the big carving knife and ran at him. Him and his mate ran for the door and were out of the room like a shot. I tried to follow them, but they were holding the handle so I couldn't get out.

I blindly stabbed the carving knife straight through the living-room door and the door handle was released pronto. My brother and his mate retreated to the dining room and put a chair against the door handle to stop me from getting in. I was still raging mad and when I couldn't open the dining-room door I not only stabbed the door several times with the carving knife, but I also started kicking a hole in the bottom of the door.

What I didn't know was that while my brother's mate was holding a chair against the dining room door, my brother had ran into our garage to find himself a weapon. After stabbing and kicking at the door, for what seemed an age, the door suddenly flew open and my brother stood in front of me wielding a chain with a padlock on the end of it. I charged into the dining room, which I don't think my brother was expecting, and I ran him straight into the wall behind him. We both grabbed each others wrists trying to avoid each others weapons. After struggling to disarm one another for a minute or so, my mates and by brothers mate, finally broke up the fight.

When I'd calmed down and looked at the damage I'd caused, I thought I would be in major trouble when my parents got home. Mom arrived home first with my sisters and as soon as she saw the damage to the doors she said 'what the hell as been going on here? And my reply was 'I had a tray in my hand and couldn't open the doors, so I tried to kick them open.' My Mom shook here head in disbelief and I thought It was time for me to disappear and I left the house. When I returned later that night, my Dad had taken the damaged doors off their hinges and within a few days, they had been replaced with new ones. The strange thing about the whole episode, was my Dad never said a word about the damage to the doors. I can only imagine, he was so angry with me, that if he'd started having a go at me, he would have probably ended up giving me a bloody good hiding.

Leighswood park had been used for a year or so as a stop-off after we had purchased cider and sherry from the 'offie' at Lazy Hill. We would fool around the park before we made our way down to the weekly Comm Disco. There was always a mix of girls and boys, but Tina never joined us, It was always a 'boys night out' for me. One girl from school had been trying to get off with me for ages, even buying me Christmas presents and bringing me stuff back from her holidays. Every time I saw her in the park or at the Comm. she would tell me what she wanted to do to me and that 'I could do anything I liked to her'. So one warm sunny evening, after drinking too much cider and sherry, she finally persuaded me to go into the woods with her. It was a dirty job – but someone had to do it. As we wandered off into the woods for a bit of privacy, I was thinking, 'what a wonderful, obliging young lady. I fully respect her precocious and liberated approach to sex, girls should be able to enjoy a bit of "how's your father" just as much as boys, without being labelled as a slut or a tart.'

Ade had turned up at the park and had asked about my whereabouts. When he was told I had took a certain girl into the woods, he instantly went in search of us. The girl and me had found a nice little spot. We were both prostrate on the ground and I was having fun playing with her threp'ny bits. I was just thinking of adventuring a little further south, when Ade suddenly came flying out of the bushes, looking like Tarzan running away from the Fuzzy- Wuzzies The difference between my mate Ade and Tarzan was, Ade wasn't wearing a loincloth and I'd never seen Tarzan flying through the jungle with his dick in his hands. Ade was certainly ready for action as he burst onto the scene and without 'an hello or kiss my arse' he dived knees first onto the ground (similar to how a modern footballer would celebrate a goal) and stuck his dick in the girls mouth. I don't know what shocked me the most: the way Ade had crashed my private party or how readily the girl took Ade's cock and how much she seemed to enjoy it! I thought to myself, 'I'm sure that's not the first time, she's had her chops round Ade's cock.' Ade's grunting and groaning soon put me off, the brash and unexpected threesome wasn't for me and I decided to leave them to it.

As Ade eventually wondered back to the park with the girl, you could tell he definitely must have had a good 'happy ending' as he had a smile on his face from ear to ear, the party-crashing cad. After telling him what I thought of him, Ade and me along with the girl started to walk down to the Comm. We had only just strolled out of the woods and onto the footpath that ran along side Northgate Road when the girl announced 'my tits are too small!' Ade and me disagreed with her and we had a bit of 'yes they are' 'no there not' - 'yes they are' 'no there not' banter. Just as it was starting to get boring, the girl suddenly shouted at the top of her voice, 'yes they are – look!' With that she lifted up her top and exposed her (nice sized) tits. As she did this, an on-coming motorist got a right eye-full. The driver slowed down and as he approached us, his eyes were almost popping out of his head. In a vain effort to see more of her tits, he spun his head round 180 degrees. Unfortunately his lack of concentration cost him dear. Even though he was going at a snail's pace, he mounted the curb and knocked over a large wooden sign that belonged to a nearby engineering company. Breast-baring girl pulled down her top and carried on as if nothing had happened but Ade and me were in fits of laughter; we laughed that much it hurt.

Like most teenage boys, girls were constantly on my mind, along with Man United and Elton John of course. And on the last ever holiday I went on with my family, I hit the jackpot where the girls were concerned. As usual when I went on holiday, every boy or girl that I met, I told them I was a lot older than I really was. And during those Easter Holidays I told all new acquaintances that I would be eighteen in the summer, when in fact I was only going to be fifteen . This lie would come back and bite me on the bum.

As we all know most teenage girls are strange and complicated creatures. When they are at home with their friends and classmates, often a girl won't let a boy get to 'second base' because they fear they will gain a reputation for being easy and loose with their sexual favours. But when these same girls go on holiday and there are no prying eyes, the inhibitions very quickly fade away. Most teenage girls want to experience the excitement of being with older and more mature boys and it's amazing how far a bit of the old blarney and a few compliments will get you, when you're hanging around the amusement arcades or camp site disco. Teenage boys on the other hand are a walking wanking machine and will grab a girls tits or put their hands down their knickers at the drop of an hat. At my school the older boys passed down the charming feminist mantra of 'The Five 'F's: find 'em, fondle 'em, finger 'em, fuck 'em, forget 'em. Wordsworth, eat your heart out.

The planets must have been in line for me on that Easter holiday. From a few snogs to some very heavy petting, I must have got into double figures with the amount of different girls I met in the week or so I was at the caravan site. So here is the best bits of *Confessions of a Teenager Camper*.

I was in the amusements arcade, happily shooting little yellow ducks on the electronic rifle range when a young girl came and stood beside. After a few seconds she said 'when you've finished shooting ducks, I'm going to snog you' She was an attractive girl so I took up on the offer and immediately got her tongue in my mouth. A few minutes later we were behind the large rubbish bins at the back of the arcade and I was playing with her tits.

Another girl asked me to join her in the photo booth and have a few snaps. After the photographs had been taken she gave me a hand job while her friend stood on guard in front of the short curtain that covered the photo booth entrance.

On my way back to my parents' caravan one night, I bumped into a girl I had spoken to a few times. We started chatting and soon ended up on the back seat of her parents' car. Unfortunately the family dog was tied up near the car and all the time we were in the car, the dog was scratching at the door and jumping up the window and the dog's poofing and panting reminded me of party-crashing Ade. If the mutt hadn't have been so big, I'd have got out the car and kicked the bleedin' thing but the sodding thing looked like a massive overgrown wolf.

One morning I was at the shop near to the camp and I got talking to a woman in the queue and as I only had a loaf of bread to carry I offered to help carry her bags. While walking back to the caravan she noticed the Man United badges on my denim jackets and told me her daughter also supported Man United. When we got to the caravan she introduced me to her daughter and later that evening I got to 'F3'.

By far the most memorable experience was with a gorgeous sixteen-year-old girl called Julie from Derby. I had chatted to her a few times at the camp disco, but this particular evening I spotted the lovely Julie and her friend having a drink outside a pub. My new Nottingham mate and me sat down alongside them and started to have a natter. Julie and I got on like a house on fire, but our respective friends didn't and after a few sharp words were exchanged my new mate said he was off. I said, 'I'm staying.'

I was very impressed when first Julie then her friend brought me a drink. Then I got excited when Julie asked, 'shall we go for a walk?' I immediately agreed then Julie added 'you haven't got a problem if my friend comes with us, have you?' 'No problem' I replied. So the three of us headed towards the beach and as we were walking, Julie told me that she really fancied me, but she hadn't had much experience with boys and that's why she'd asked her friend to accompany us. We soon found ourselves in the privacy of the sand dunes and Julie and me started to get to know each other, her friend sitting just out of view.

It wasn't until we lay down in the sand that I noticed Julie was wearing tights. 'Oh bollocks,' I thought. I always had a problem with tights. When Tina wore tights, I often found my hand bouncing in and out of her knickers or being trapped by the tight elastic waist. Having received no resistance after fumbling around trying to undo Julie's front-buttoned dress and groping her tits, my hand started to venture up her dress. I had got almost to the top of her leg, then suddenly I stopped (no she didn't have meat & two veg up there) I unexpectedly felt the warmth of her firm thigh. She wasn't wearing tights, she was wearing stockings.

KNICKERS – KNACKERS – KNOCKERS I was as stiff as a broom handle. Excitedly I carried on venturing north, then as I hit her underwear I stopped again. Her knickers seemed awfully thick and they seemed to go on forever. When I finally got to the top of her knickers, I couldn't squeeze my hand inside. As I was struggling to gain entrance to her furry front bottom Julie's friend popped her head up and enquired, 'is everything ok?' Julie replied, 'he's having problems with my panty-girdle.'

Panty-girdle! A bleedin' panty-girdle? Wasn't that what I saw middle-aged women wearing in the Littlewoods catalogue? Julie's friend scrambled over the dunes and quickly gave us the benefit of her experiences. 'First, let the rabbit see the dog,' Julie's friend said as she quickly un-buttoned Julie's dress and exposed Julie's sexy black underwear. She then reached round to Julie's back and un-fastened her bra. A few seconds later the bra was off. Grabbing one side of Julie's panty-girdle Julie's friend said to me 'you pull that side and I'll pull this.' The panty girdle seemed like it was stuck on with glue but we persevered and soon Julie was lying there in all wonderful glory. Julie's friend obviously wanted to stay and watch procedures as she only moved a few yards away from us and made herself comfortable. She shouted over, 'right, get on with it!' Sadly Julie's reaction to my advances was to 'lay back and think of England'. There was quite a few moans and groans from Julie and she seemed to be enjoying my hands all over her body, but she made no attempt to touch me. Out of desperation I finally unzipped my trousers and released my purple–headed soldier.

Julie's eyes suddenly lit up when she saw it, but she refused to touch it. I told her 'the thing will explode if you don't you relieve the pressure,' but she was adamant; she didn't want to touch it. Without a word, Julie's friend suddenly came bounding over and, lying across Julie's midriff, grabbed hold of my broom-handle and started to wank me off. After only a few strokes she got her laughing gear round the business end of the things which was nice of her. Then without looking up she said, 'if you come in my mouth, I will bite the bloody thing off - not so nice!

To my dismay, Julie and her friend went home the following afternoon. Julie did give me her phone number, but I could never get the courage to call her. I didn't know how long I would be able to keep up the pretence of being seventeen, working in a clothes shop and being a semi-professional footballer.

On my last night I was in the amusement arcade with my friend from Nottingham, when a older teenager came over to me and said 'my mate thinks you're a cunt and he's going to batter you!' Without a reply from me he turned round and returned to his little gang that was standing by the entrance doors. I had spoken to the gang several times over the past week and didn't think I had any problems with them. But somehow I had obviously upset them. After five or ten minutes the lad who thought 'I was a cunt' lead his little gang into the arcade. As they approached me I suddenly remembered telling the gang that I was seventeen 'oh shit'. The lad that squared up to me had sideburns a bushy moustache, a deep and gravelly voice and to me, looked like a young man. I couldn't fall back on the fact that I was only fourteen, I'd even told my mate from Nottingham that I was seventeen. Saying I was only fourteen would really make me look like a twat. I initially refused to go outside and fight, using the excuse that I thought his mates would also join in but he told me 'it would be a one-on-one fight' and after exchanging a few insults I nervously went outside.

As I got outside I saw my brother with his girlfriend (who was a bit of a skinhead girl). I told my brother that I was going to have a fight but was worried that other lads might join in and help my opponent and to my great surprise he said, if anyone else joined in, he would get involved. As always the rumour that a fight was about to take place soon drew the crowd. As the crowd got bigger and bigger I started having serious doubts about fighting this older guy – then I thought how embarrassing it would be if I backed out, or if my opponent kicked the fuck out of me. 'What the fuck should I do? There was a Mexican standoff, which seemed to last for ages, but with my brother looking on I knew I would have to fight, or he would never let me live it down. I stared at my opponent, I though 'if he hasn't made a move yet, maybe he's as nervous as me.'

My Nottingham friend was standing by my side as I continued to eye up my challenger. 'Tell him to take is hat off and when he goes to remove it, smack him in the mouth,' my new mate whispered to me. What a bloody ridiculous suggestion I thought, but not having a better idea, I went along with it. I took a few steps nearer to my fight partner and said, in the deepest voice I could, 'take that stupid hat off and I'll fight you.' To my amazement it worked, he immediately took off his hat, then turned round to pass it to one of his mates. as he turned, I punched him on the side of his face and the blow knocked him to the floor. 'Fuck me, I'm fighting a man and winning' I thought to myself. I then threw myself onto my floored opponent.

I was definitely getting the better of him, when suddenly I felt somebody grab my hair and pull my head back. A girl had jumped out of the crowd and joined the fight; in turn, my brother's girlfriend quickly attacked the other girl and like a crazy mixed-doubles tag team, we all rolled round on the ground, with fists, boots and handfuls of hair flying everywhere. My brother's girlfriend was making mincemeat of the other girl and pretty soon he had to step in to stop his girlfriend from doing serious damage to a very shell-shocked and blooded girl. As my brother tried to drag his girlfriend from the fight, she managed to stamp on my opponent a couple of times - what a girl!

My fight was eventually broke up by the campsite staff, but I'm pretty sure I would have soon overcome my opponent if we hadn't been split up - well I would say that, wouldn't I? Nottingham did me good. Win, draw or lose, I was pretty pleased with the fact that I did myself proud and held my own with a lad almost four years older than me. But my biggest sense of pride was meeting all those lovely girls.

The day after returning from holidays, I was shocked when Dad offered me a couple of days' work and, using a bit of kid-ology, said, 'if you can keep the bricklayer going (feed him with bricks and compo) and knock down a chimney breast in two days - instead of paying you £3.00 a day I'll pay you £5.00 a day.'

I knew it was a tall order, but over the next two days I worked liked a Trojan. On the morning of the second day working on the extension of the house, me, my Dad and four or five other workers (one of them being Mickey Gibbs) sat down for breakfast in the front garden. I had just started to tuck it into my spam sandwiches when my Dad said 'that the teenage boy that lived at the house had scaled the nine-foot-high wall that was at the side of the house. He went on to say how amazed he was at the young boys athleticism. I looked at the wall then looked at my Dad and said, 'I could do that.' Dad instantly replied 'you could never climb that wall' Determined to prove him wrong, and hopefully make him proud of me, I put down my sarnie and took a run at the high wall. My right foot hit the wall and helped me catapult myself up it and I just about manage to get a grip on the top course and drag myself up. When I'd scrambled to the top I turned round to face my Dad; Mickey Gibbs and the other workers applauded my triumph but when I looked towards Dad for approval, instead of congratulating me, he just stared up at me for a second and the expression on his face, shouted out to me, 'so fuckin' what?'. While the other men were still applauding me, he stuck his face in a newspaper.

The fact that once again my Dad hadn't shown any interest in me, didn't really bother me at the time but what certainly did bother me, was that I had worked extremely hard for two days with the bricklayers and knock-down and cleared almost all of the chimney breast, only leaving the last five or six courses – so that meant I never got my £5.00 a day.

I looked at my Dad with disgust when he only handed me £6.00 for the two days of hard toil. When I remonstrated, he said 'the deal was to knock all the chimneybreast down - and did you knock all the chimney breast down? No! End of conversation.'

My hard work hadn't gone unnoticed in all quarters however. Mickey Gibbs was impressed with my work ethic and said, 'if you're interested you can come and work with me for a week or two' Mick often did foreigners (small jobs away from your main employment) but he had recently teamed up with his brother and they had a few extensions to go at.

Even though it would mean me missing over a week at school, I readily agreed. I was doing crap at school and I found the science classes extremely difficult, I just had no aptitude for the subjects at all. I was often skiving off, so thought I might as well get paid for the time I was playing truant.

I had arranged to meet Mick at Lichfield bus station the following Monday morning. When Mick turned up, I was shocked to see that he was sporting a shiny black eye. Mick was in his car with three of his friends when they had a little bump with another car and this led to a bit of road rage. In the other car, there was only the driver, but the driver could definitely look after himself. Being aggrieved at the collision Mick and his three mates jumped out of their car and started to verbally abuse the other driver. One thing led to another and the lone driver hit one of Mick's friends knocking him immediately to the ground. With this another one of Mick's friends stepped forward and he received the same fate, falling unconscious onto the car bonnet. Two down – two to go. Mick thought he'd have to have a go and got a black eye and several punches in the ribs and stomach before crashing to the floor. Mick's third friend was apparently dispensed with in similar fashion. Even though Mick and his friends were going down with like nine pins, it never entered their heads that they would gang up on the lone driver. Instead, foolishly as it turned out, they chose to take him on one at a time. I Very much doubt that kind of chivalry would take place today.

The first job Mick took me to was the house of an old lady who wanted her chimney re-pointing. Pennies from heaven as far as Mick was concerned. I thought the world of Mick and thought he was a great character, but that day, I discovered that he was also a bit of a con man. After giving the old lady a bit of old flannel and lots of charm, we took the ladders of his van and went up onto the roof and checked out the chimney stack. The chimney didn't look in too bad condition and for someone of Mick's ability with me assisting him, it would have only been a morning's work to make good. Mick wasted half an hour on the roof by reading the Sporting Post and writing out a bet. When we eventually climbed off the roof and made our way back down the ladder, Mick put on his best poker face, telling the old lady that, not only was her chimney extremely unsafe, but all the internal flue linings needed changing and the double-swivel back-valve which helps to extract the smoke and fumes was out of date and needed to be replaced and to put it right – it would cost her £120.00 (about the average weekly wage for a brickie, back then) Looking worried to death, the old lady said if the chimney was unsafe then he must carry out the work as soon as possible. Mick's response was 'it will have to be cash on completion.' The old lady nodded in agreement and Mick said, 'we'll go off now and get the required parts and materials.'

Instead of driving to a local builder's yard we pulled up near a bookmaker's. Mick was a very successful gambler, so successful that many of local bookies in his native Burton-upon-Trent had barred him from their premises. 'Have you ever put a bet on before, Steve?' Mick asked me. When I shook my head, Mick casually said, 'there is nothing to it, just walk in, hand over my betting slip and the cash to the birds behind the counter, get a receipt and come back out here.' So like a good 'un I got out of the van with Mick's betting slip and £50.00 in cash and walked into the smoked-filled betting shop. After the betting shop we made a stop-off at a greasy spoon, and then a newsagent where Mick brought himself a large packet of cigars.

Then we finally headed back to the old lady's house and started both the actual and the imaginary work. Mick finished the work in a few hours and spent the rest of the day sitting on the roof listening to various horseraces on his small radio. To make it look more convincing, every twenty minutes or so, he made me carry a few bits and pieces up and down the ladders, usually, carrying the same thing back up that I'd just bought back down. So it didn't look too obvious, I would leave my mysterious load in the back of Mick's van for a few minutes, before heading back onto the roof. What a Game.

Just after 5 o'clock, Mick announced to the old lady that we had completed the work and offered to show her the items that we'd replaced that were now in the back of his van. The old lady said that 'wasn't necessary' and with a smile she handed over £120.00, in cash! Just in case you're wondering - there is no such thing as a double-swivel back-valve!

As soon as we had got the ladders back on the van, we were back round to the bookies to collect Mick's winnings.

The next day was very uneventful, digging out the footings ready for the concrete foundation for a house extension, but the day after that was quite memorable, Mick had left me on my own to finish off the footings. I was happily digging away when the teenage girl who lived at the house called over to me. As I looked up, she lifted up her jumper and, to paraphrase the great Norman Stanley Fletcher, revealed a fine pair of un-fettered knockers. Well, I nearly fell off my shovel.

When Mick returned I told him what had happened but he didn't believe me. So the next time I noticed the girl through the kitchen window I waved and beckoned her to come outside. When she opened the back door, I said to her, 'show Mick, what you showed me earlier.' Without hesitation she duly obliged and Mick cried out with joy and launched himself at her, his hands primed in the 'grab 'em' position. Luckily for the girl, she managed to close the door before Mick could reach her. That was the last I saw of that girl.

Mick and his brother must have run up a lot of debt with the local builder's merchants and only one or two of the companies would even allow them to enter their yards. So when it came to the time to order the concrete for the footings I was given a signed cheque from Mick's brother and I had to go into the office of the concrete company and sort out payment. I was very nervous about this, not because I thought I might be doing something illegal, but because I could hardly spell and my handwriting was atrocious. My scribble was no better than a six-year-old's.

Unfortunately, when the ready-mix concrete truck delivered the concrete, it soon became clear that Mick's calculations were incorrect and we needed a bit more- but the ready- mix could not be delivered until the following afternoon. So Mick and his brother said that we needed to go to a builders yard and pick up some gravel and cement and knock up the concrete ourselves. The problem was that Mick and his brother weren't allowed in any of the builder's merchants that sold gravel and cement.

The three of us drove to a builder's yard where Mick and his brother tried to work out a plan how they could get the gravel and cement. After ten minutes or so of debating Mick turned around to me and said, 'Steve, have you ever driven a car before?' I replied, 'no' and Micks brother said, 'you've been on the bumping cars haven't you? I nodded and Micks brother continued, 'well if you can drive a bumper car, you will be able to drive this.' He told me to get into the driver's seat and started to give me my very first driving lesson.

I tried really hard to concentrate on getting the clutch and accelerator right but I just couldn't master it, so Mick came up with a bright idea: him and his brother would push the car right up to the builder's merchants gates, then all I needed to do was to turn into the yard and apply the brake when I got to a parking space. Then when I had paid (with another cheque) and filled the boot and backseat with bags of gravel and cement, I would go to the front gate and give Mick the signal to run in and take the car out of the builder's yard.

Full of excitement and dread I agreed to the plan. To my relief and great surprise it went off without a hitch. I successfully steered the car through the gates of the builders yard and managed to stop safely, without crashing into anything. As with the ready-mix office, the only time I felt nervous or embarrassed was when I had to fill out the details on the blank cheque. When the car was fall of gravel and cement, I waved to Mick and he rushed in and reversed the car straight out of the yard.

On the Friday dinnertime I was taken to the pub by Mick and his brother and while I was sipping on my lager and lime, I heard Mick say to his brother 'when we get the next payments for the extensions, I will give you the cash for the concrete and gravel.' Mick's brother casually replied, 'there's no rush, there's no money in my account anyway.' Mick just laughed but I got to thinking, 'have I been used to pass on dodgy cheques?'

The next week, we started a second extension. While Mick and his brother worked on the brickwork in the footings of the first extension, I was given instructions, then left on my lonesome to break up the concrete in the backyard and dig out the footings for the second extension. I found it really boring working on my own all day, so when Mick dropped me off the following day I asked if I could have his radio to make the day go little quicker. 'Sorry Steve, I've got to listen to the horse racing', was his unsympathetic reply and with that he drove off, leaving me to my own devices again.

In the late morning, the man that lived in the house returned and offered me a much needed cuppa. After an hour or so, the man said he needed to go out again but would leave the back door open, so I could make myself another cuppa when I needed it. Within a minute or so of him leaving, I was in the kitchen brewing up and looking through his cupboards for biscuits. I not only found his biscuits, I also found a radio which I quickly tuned to Radio One and positioned it near to the back door so I could listen to it while I worked.

A few hours later I was singing along to the latest hits on the radio and happily digging out the footings when the man returned. He didn't say anything to me but switched off the radio, then closed and locked the back door. I was a little disappointed, but didn't think much of the incident but later that evening Mick phoned my Dad and told him that he didn't want me to work with him any more. Mick said the man where I had been working had complained that I had used his radio without his permission and he didn't want me back at his house. My Dad informed me in a very patronising manner that my services were no longer required. Then he (a thieving bleeder himself) tried to lecture me on morals. What a two-faced pratt! but I had come to expect that sort of thing from him.

I wasn't surprised by Dad's reaction, but I was appalled and disgusted at Mick's behaviour. What a hypocritical wanker, he was. In just over a week I had witnessed him con an elderly lady, I had illegally driven a car into the builders merchants for him, I had unknowingly passed on moody cheques for him and on several occasions he had left a certain fourteen-year-old boy (namely me) working alone, sometimes all day. I didn't speak to Mick again for almost ten years.

When I eventually returned to school, it was confirmed that not only did all children have to stay on and do a fifth year of secondary education, it was also announced that Tynings Lane Secondary Modern and the Grammar schools would combine to form Aldridge Comprehensive School and me and my peers would be the first fifth formers at the new school. Fuckin' great! I was already struggling at school, so this news was devastating. Now there would be another hundred-plus pupils in my year that were more able than me.

Fortunately, soon after I had heard the news about the two schools joining together, I had a very memorable experience: I actually got to eat in a restaurant for the very first time in my life. I was at Nick's house for the first time in very long time. I hadn't fallen out with him, but a month or so earlier I had accidentally shot Nick's younger sister in the face with a gat gun. A few of us, including Nick's sister, had been sitting in Nick's living room and playing about with the gun for some time. We didn't have any pellets, we just enjoyed the noise that the gun made when you pulled the trigger after compressing the barrel. I was sitting next to Sharon (Nick's sister) when the gun was passed to me. I was playing about with the gun and telling Sharon 'stick 'em up' but I didn't realise that the barrel had been compressed, so when I put it near to Sharon's face and pulled the trigger, the compressed parts of the barrel shot forward and Sharon took the full force of the metal barrel on her jaw. Understandably, she screamed her head off and I thought I'd done some serious damage. Luckily I hadn't and she was just left with bad bruising to the side of her face, although that, for a thirteen-year-old girl, was a very big issue.

I had also upset Nick's dad, Larry. I had agreed with Nick, that Francis Lee was correct to hit Leeds hardman Hunter in the 'Battle of the Baseball Ground' when Francis Lee of Derby County and Norman 'bite-your-leg' Hunter of Leeds went toe to toe on Derby's mud bath of a pitch. After watching the action on Match of the Day, the following Monday it was the talk of our school and probably every other school up and down the country. After school Nick and I were discussing the incident in his living room when

Nick's dad Larry walked in and overheard our conversation. He immediately disagreed with us and told us we were idiots. When Nick and me argued back, Larry got very animated and red in the face. Larry suddenly jumped up out of his chair grabbed his copy of *The Sun* newspaper and pushed it into Nick's face saying repeatedly, 'read this! Read this!' As Nick struggled to get the back page of newspaper out of his face, I went to his aid, which upset Larry even more. In no uncertain terms, Larry told me to get out of his house.

Thankfully those two unfortunate incidents being forgotten, I was back in the 'Inner Circle' and Larry was in an exceptionally good mood after hearing that Sharon had done well in some examination, or something like that. Any road up. Larry said it called for a celebration and they would be going out for their tea, which was unheard of in my house and probably all other households in Aldridge. It was 'time to get me coat' but to my great surprise and joy, Larry only went and said, 'you can come as well, if you want.' 'If I want! Too bleedin' right, I want!'

Larry drove us all down to the *Phoenix* Chinese restaurant in Aldridge. By today's standards, the interior of the Phoenix would be classed as tacky at best but for me it was like a mini-palace and for the first few minutes I couldn't stop looking around. I was amazed by the Chinese lanterns, paintings of rural China and dragons. I even enjoyed the tinny Chinese background music.

But I was bought down to earth with a bump when I was given the menu. Apprehensively I opened the menu and immediately my heart sank. I couldn't read the vast majority of the words in the menu let alone understand what they were and I could feel my face going red with embarrassment. As the others cheerfully looked through the menu and asked Larry to explain the different food items, I was getting more and more anxious about the fact that I couldn't read/understand the menu and to stop me from showing myself up, I even thought of saying I didn't want any food Luckily Larry came to my rescue and suggested that he should order a set meal for all six of us. It was like a weight being lifted off my shoulders.

When the first course of soup arrived, Larry asked the Chinese waiter 'where are the bread rolls?' to which the waiter replied 'bled lowes – no cook yet' and disappeared back into the kitchen. When we were halfway through our soup, another Chinese man entered the restaurant via the front door and he was carrying two large bags of shopping and under each arm he had a pack of bread rolls. When Larry noticed this, he shouted at the top of his voice 'bled lowes – no cook yet' and the Chinese shopper nearly jumped out of his skin. After that, every time the waiter appeared Larry, Nick and me took turns in shouting out 'bled lowes – no cook yet!' In return the waiter gave us the occasional dirty look, as if to say 'White Savages, I piss in your soup next time you come here!'

Besides having great fun and games taking the mick out of the waiter's accent and asking him if he knew Bruce Lee and how many Alsatian dogs did he have in his freezer (well it was 1975 and if it was good enough for Benny Hill it was good enough for us), I thoroughly enjoyed the whole experience of eating in a restaurant and tasting foreign cuisine for the first time. I was so proud that I had actually eaten in a restaurant, that for a week or more I would try and drop the fact into as many conversations as I could. And if

Nick was around, I would ask, 'what was the name of that chicken food we had in the Chinese restaurant?' I became a proper show-off, foodie bore. The Phoenix Restaurant was to become a regular Friday-night haunt in the late 70's for my mates and me. But the poor Chinese waiters got more than good-humoured banter from the late-night customers.

§

On 26th April, Man United paraded the Second Division Championship trophy around Old Trafford and Ade and me were part of the 59,000 crowd. United had clinched the Second Division championship the previous game with a 2–2 draw away to Notts County. There were several pitch invasions at the game and a police officer's helmet was struck by a metal Kung Fu throwing star. And of course, to celebrate United winning the league, hordes of United fans went on the rampage through Nottingham City Centre.

Ade and me had arrived at Old Trafford at 1:30 and there were already massive queues to get in to the Stretford End. Thinking we might not get in, we decided to pay well over double the price of the entrance to the terraces and went into the seats at the back of the Stretford, and we spent most of the match jumping into the packed terraces, then climbing back into the seats for a better view. The whole stadium went wild with delight as the players trotted round the pitch with the small silver trophy, and the Stretford End sang 'hello - hello United are back - United are back' throughout the game - which United comfortably won by beating Blackpool 4-0, following on from the previous season, a fact that I am still proud of today.

Aged just fifteen and still at school, me and Ade went to five of the first six United games of the 1975-76 season. We beat both Wolves and Birmingham City away, then we thrashed Sheffield United 5–1 at Old Trafford. The club was so thrilled and excited with the 5– 1 win, they produced a commemorative mirror headed 'United Are Back'. I've still got my mirror (somewhere).

We then had a trip to Stoke where we won 1–0, and finally we saw United beat Spurs 3-2 at Old Trafford. Loyal Supporters!!! The Spurs game was quite significant for Ade and me because that same day we joined the Birmingham branch of the Manchester United supporters' club and became official Brummie Reds and travelled up by coach to the game with another hundred like-minded souls, from the Birmingham area. They would become my new family.

As my school and the grammar school had amalgamated, it was almost like going back to a new school at the end of the summer holidays. It was all a bit strange and it was about to get stranger. Firstly, along with Ade, I found myself in an all-boys class. In the fifteen years the school had been open, there had never been all-boys or all-girls classes before. Taking into account that most of the boys didn't want to be at school, a class of all fifth-year boys, would surely cause problems for certain teachers.

I tried to stick to my lessons but unfortunately, I just couldn't concentrate and I was having continuing problems trying to cope with the dreaded science lessons. A new school brings a new headmaster and this came in the form of an enlightened and softly spoken man called Mr. Rocket. In less than two weeks, I found myself in front of Mr. Rocket in his impressive office; I had been told by my

new form teacher, Mr. Bailey, that the headmaster wanted
to see me. Mr. Bailey was quick to remind me of what he
told me and Ade the first time we had a class registration
with him: 'I won't stand any nonsense from you two and I
promise you that I will repeat any punishments you receive
from Nobby (Mr. Dawes) or any other of the deputy heads
- you get six-of-the-best from them, then you can expect
to get six of the best from me!' Old School or what!

As I made my way to the new headmaster's office, I
racked my brain to think what mischief I had been up
to in the last week or so, but for the life of me I couldn't
think what I had done wrong. I had to wait in Mr. Rocket's
secretary's office for a few minutes, but soon his the secretary
said, 'I could go in and see the headmaster now' and she
opened his door for me.

I walked into Mr. Rocket's office and to my amazement
he got up off his chair and offered me his hand to shake and
said, 'hello Steven, I've heard a lot about you.' After shaking
my hand he gestured, for me to take a seat. 'What the fuck
is going on here?' I thought to myself. Mr. Rocket then
proceeded to waffle on about how important the image of
the school was and we should all pull together and that his
goal was to make Aldridge comprehensive the best school
in the area and on and on he went. I have to admit, most
of what he told me went in one ear and out the other, but
he ended by telling me that he intended to form a students'
committee which would be made up of fifth-year pupils,
half would be ex-grammar and half would be ex-secondary
modern and he wanted me to be one of the representatives
from the old secondary modern school. Me! On a students
committee? Was he having a laugh?

Mr. Rocket must have noticed how shell-shocked I was because he told me that I was liked by many teachers and that my peers looked up to me and he thought I had a lot to offer the school, and if I worked with him, he was sure it would benefit both parties.

I agreed to give it a go and walked out of his office, I didn't know whether to laugh or cry. When my teacher and mates found out why the new headmaster had wanted to see me, their reactions were all the same - jaw dropping. I stuck with the students committee for four or five weeks, but after our first one or two meetings, I knew I was out of my depth and mainly surrounded by goody-two-shoes. I felt totally inferior to my fellow committee members, as they were definitely more articulate than me and they continually came up with good ideas, things I would not have thought of in a month of Sundays. Basically I felt like the class dunce and I was only too aware of my failings. The Final straw came when one of the committee members had taken notes during our one meeting and then passed her notepad round for the rest of the committee to read through. When the notepad was passed to me I was astounded by how neat the hand writing was and embarrassed by the fact that I struggled to read or understand most of the words that had been written.

I soon went back to my old ways of skiving off lessons and playing the fool. Perhaps the most memorable and funny prank that I pulled at school that year was just after we had a heavy snowfall. Mr. Hendry was the former deputy head of the Grammar School and a very strict disciplinarian. One dinner break I noticed Mr. Hendry walking up and down one of the main corridors and, even though it was very cold outside with snow on the ground, he was telling pupils to go out into the playground. So me and three or four of my mates armed ourselves with snowballs and waited by one of the exit doors to the main corridor. My plan was, when Mr. Hendry walked past us, we would dart into the corridor and throw snowballs at him. We would then run back to the exit door and then, the 'masterstroke', turn around and calmly walk back into the corridor as if we had nothing to do with Mr. Hendry being pummelled with snowballs.

The plan worked like a treat, unfortunately there was collateral damage. Purely by chance, a group of younger boys just happened to be running away from the building, as Mr. Hendry turned round to see who his attackers were. Mr. Henry immediately pursued and apprehended the young boys. My mates and me were in stitches as the young boys proclaimed their innocence and Mr. Hendry man handled them off to his office. After ten minutes or so, the young boys walked back up the main corridor with tears in their eyes and sore hands from Mr. Hendry's leather strap. Being sadistic teenagers, my mates and me couldn't resist throwing snowballs as the young boys approached us. Isn't life cruel?

Three or four weeks before Christmas, out of the blue, Tina chucked me for a seventeen-year-old; I was heartbroken. Even though I missed Tina like mad, I was keen to get another girlfriend as soon as possible: 1. to give Tina a poke in the eye; 2. for a few extra Christmas presents. Just after we had broken up for the Christmas holidays, Ruth, one of the ex-grammar-school girls had invited me and a few of my mates to a party that was being held at her parents' house at the Pheasey Estate. What better place than a house party to pick up a new girlfriend?

Ruth's house was only a few minutes walk from the Cat and Fiddle pub and the pub was right next to our bus stop. Before we went to the party my mates and me decided to have a few drinks in the bar of the Cat and Fiddle. We had no problem getting served in there and after consuming three or four bottles of Skol Special Strength, I felt drunk even before I got to the party. When we got to the party there was more alcohol and Nick was soon throwing up, then sleeping in the bath. The party was in full swing with teenage couples snogging, loud music, beer being spilt everywhere and soggy sandwiches trampled into the living-room carpet. And things were looking up when a girl I knew from Tynings Lane, asked me to join her on the sofa.

We were chatting away nicely and she had touched my knee a few times and given me the old glad eye and I was just about to kiss her when suddenly I felt very sick. I excused myself and made my way out to the front door with the intention of throwing up in the front garden but standing by the front door were two girls who were brain-boxes from the student committee. I told them I needed to go outside for a minute and, fearing that I might be locked out, I told them not to shut the front door after me. They replied that it was too cold to keep the door open and they were going to close it. On hearing this, I stuck out my hand to stop the door closing, unfortunately my hand was still partway inside the hallway and the door was made up of four glass panels, so when the girls tried to slam the door shut, my hand and forearm went straight through one of the glass panels. There were screams, glass, puke and claret everywhere.

I received many cuts to my left hand and forearm, the most concerning being a deep laceration to my wrist, resulting in blood gushing out of me like a fountain. Within a few seconds I was unconscious. I was carried into the living room and when I regained consciousness, I woke to the sound of wailing girls and the sight of chunks of flesh hanging from my arm. Luckily for me there must have been a few ex-boy scouts and girl-guides at the party; a few tourniquets had been applied to my upper and lower arm and most of the blood had stopped flowing. Later I helped to spread the myth, that if the tourniquets hadn't been applied, I would have probably died from loss of blood. Well, you have to milk it – don't you?

Someone had phoned my parents and Mom turned up just as I was being put into the ambulance. As the ambulance men helped me out of the house, I couldn't help but notice the blood all over the sofa and carpets and the damage to the front door. 'I hope I don't end up getting the bill for all this lot,' I thought to myself.

When I arrived at the hospital the nurses asked me if I had been drinking? I admitted I had and then they said, unfortunately, they couldn't give me any painkillers. I had to have twenty-four stitches to my forearm and seven stitches to my finger without anaesthetic. And too add insult to injury, I had ruined my new shirt that was less than a week old and Mom had noticed my home-made tattoos for the first time.

When I went back to the hospital a few weeks later to have the stitches removed, Mom was quick to point out that, written on the top of my notes in half-inch high letters, was my date of birth and next to it, written in inch-high letters and double underlined were the words *VERY DRUNK.* On a positive note, Ruth brought me a new shirt for Christmas to replace the ripped and bloodstained shirt that I wore to her party.

Photographs

Grafting for a Living

Enjoying a pint and a fag with Nick at the infamous
Mackadown pub in Tiles Cross, Brum

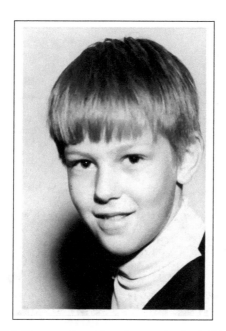

Circa 1970, Fairground tough and wanna be football hooligan.

The finished article or so I thought, until I went away to
the likes of West Ham, Newcastle and Scouseland.

How the Stretford End looked when Ade and I first
started going to Old Trafford in the mid 70's

The Stretford End's finest. Ade wearing his
United scarf round his head as usual

Girls Girls Girls

Top left with Tina, Top right with Anita

Below; a few holiday romances

Enjoying the delights of Great Yarmouth with Eddie R. and Micky C.

Banka, Eddie R and Myself roughing it on a campsite.

Living it up around the Greek Islands with Ged,
Knockers, Wilkie and Clarkie! (inc overleaf)

174

1976

School was still the bane of my life and I was only attending about 25% of my lessons, and by now most of the teachers had given up trying to get me to their lessons. But fortunately not all the teachers had given up on me: two of my science teachers, Mr. Garbett and Mr. Mundey and my math's teacher Miss Baker, all told me that I was welcome to attend lessons as long as I didn't play up and disrupt the class. So the classes I did attend I often found myself sitting at the back of the classroom and when the teacher had instructed the rest of my class on what they should do for the rest of the lesson, the teacher would regularly come to the back of the class and sit with me and have a little heart to heart or lecture me - depending on their mood, although, being young, immature and barely literate, their well-intentioned words and guidance went straight over my head.

One teacher who did get through to Ade and myself was our English teacher Mr. McCloughlin He was only a small slim-built man, but no one - but no one - got out of line in his class. Any backchat or disturbance and Mr. McCloughlin would grab hold of the offending pupil and drag him round the classroom by his ear or ears! The punishment would usually conclude with the unruly pupil having their head bounced off the blackboard.

Ade and me got on very well with Mr. McCloughlin and we would often stay behind after our lessons and tell him of our adventures at the United games. In return, Mr. McCloughlin would give us life lessons and I think, once or twice, he may even have got through to me. Several years after leaving school, I had quite a few younger lads, who attended Aldridge Comp., tell me that Mr. McCloughlin would often talk about Ade and me and use us as an example when he wanted to take down an individual by a 'peg or two'. 'Grainger and Chambers (Ade) thought they were little hard knocks and Jack the Lads, but when they spread their wings and travelled outside of Aldridge, they soon discovered the wider world was a much harder and more dangerous place than little old Aldridge,' he would explain. Which was very true.

The polar-opposite to Mr. McCloughlin was a young French teacher who had the mannerisms of Frank Spencer . This inexperienced teacher was a nice enough bloke and I later found out that he was a good amateur boxer, but there was no way he could handle a classroom full of boisterous fifteen-sixteen-year-olds.

My class had given Frenchy a hard time all year. After only a few weeks of him teaching us, we'd been banned from the language studio where we were supposed to talk French into our own individual tape recorders. But instead of *bonjour* and *au revoir*, we all ended up singing football songs, telling dirty jokes and generally swearing at the microphone. The first time that I used the tape recorder, I was playing around and fast-forwarding and I came across the voice of my mate Riga doing his Bruce Lee impressions. It was extremely amusing and after I had got a few of my mates to listen to the recording we all started to shout out our best Bruce Lee war cries and practice our Kung Fu moves on each other. Our young French teacher did little or nothing to stop us.

We had sensed fear and the scene was set. Throughout the months the general behaviour in our French lessons got gradually worse. Anarchy finally raised it's ugly head when a few of my classmates suddenly decided to start stacking desks on top of each other. Then a few lads climbed up and sat on top of the stacked desks. More classmates decided to join the party and started shaking the desks so the kids sitting on top of the desks, fell off. The stacked desks were then toppled and this got a raucous round of applause from the rest of the class.

Very much out of character, for some strange reason Ade, Baz and me just sat at the back of the classroom observing the shenanigans. Then someone threw the wastepaper bin out of the first-floor window and this was soon followed by several schoolbooks, a few coats and then a chair. *Sacré bleu!* Our French teacher was running around the classroom like an headless chicken. After a chair had been wedged against the handle of the classroom door, there was a full blown uprising; books, coats, school bags and chairs were freely thrown around the classroom; it was chaos.

One of the few classmates who hadn't joined in with the riotous behaviour tried to remove the wedged chair from the door, but by now Ade, Baz and me were in the thick of the things and we stopped him from removing the chair. Of course, these misfits had to be punished for treachery. I had recently watched a film about Genghis Khan and saw the Mongol leader have a traitor torn limb from limb by wild horses. So the four of us grabbed a limb each and did our best to separate one of the misfit's limbs from his body. I'm happy to say, we didn't succeed.

Just like a few years previously when I had hung out of
the top-floor window, teachers and pupils from the adjacent
building were soon off their seats and observing us. When
a desk was pushed out of our classroom window several
teachers ran across the grassed area that divided the two
main buildings and tried to come to Frenchy's rescue. The
teachers shouted and banged on the classroom door but
the chair wedged against the door handle held firm.

The main door to the classroom had been wedged
closed but the adjoining stockroom door had been
overlooked. The stockroom door suddenly burst open
and, lead by the fearsome Mr. Simms, about half-a-dozen
teachers rushed into our classroom and witnessed half of
the class stretching our treacherous classmate; there must
have been three or four kids pulling at each limb and the
poor sod was squealing for mercy. We all instinctively
dropped our torture victim and he hit the floor with a thud.

Mr. Simms went crazy, shouting at the whole class. He
looked like he was going to blow a gasket. In military-like
fashion Mr. Simms and another few teachers supervised us
cleaning up the classroom, while another couple of teachers
escorted our shell-shocked and tearful French teacher off
to the staffroom. Then the whole class was marched off
to the assembly hall and interrogated. Of course Ade, Baz
and me were the prime suspects but after talking with the
headmaster, our French teacher had put a few other names
forward and said 'that they were mainly responsible for the
disturbance'. But Mr. Simms really didn't like my mates
and me and he wasn't going to let us go unpunished. After
our torture victim confirmed that it was Ade, Baz and me
who had instigated the initial attack, Mr. Simms decided

that it would be the leather tawes (a three-thonged leather strap) for my mates and me.

At the start of our new school term, Walsall had become only one of a very small number of education authorities in England that allowed the leather tawes. And after a minor scuffle with an over-zealous music teacher, my mate Chris Selby was the first kid in our school to receive the tawes as his punishment. He said the tawes hurt twice as much as the cane.

Mr. Simms lead Ade, Baz and me off to his classroom where he kept his very own leather strap. He removed the tawes from a draw in his desk and just the sight on the long, thick leather strap was enough frighten me - but when he whacked the tawes on top of his desk with all his force, my legs turned to jelly. He gave us a quick lecture about being mindless hooligans and bullies and then whacked the top of the desk once more and said with real venom in his voice, 'six for each of you'.

For some strange reason Mr. Simms always carried out corporal punishment in the privacy of his stockroom. 'Right come in one at a time,' he told us as he strode towards it. All three of us looked petrified and Ade said 'I'm not going first!' Baz replied, 'nor am I!' Mr. Simms was getting impatient and shouted from inside the stockroom, 'will one of you get in here!'

They say fight or flight. I didn't fancy my chances against Simms so I thought, 'fuck this, it's flight,' and I headed for the door, immediately followed by my two mates. We were down the stairs and into the main corridor before we heard the distant voice of Mr. Simms hurling slanderous insults at us. Mr. Simms gave chase but by the time we got to the main school gate he had given up.

Baz and me didn't go back to school for over a week and spent most school days skiving in Baz's flat in Redhouse. During this time Mr. Simms told some of our friends to inform Baz and me that when we did come back to school, we were going to be punished not only by him but also the headmaster and I would also have to answer to my form teacher, Mr. Bailey.

Well if Mr. Simms was going to get other people involved, so was Baz. Time to call in the big guns; Baz had a brother who was almost ten years older than him. Big Brother had quite a reputation and readily agreed to assist Baz with his problems at school. Just before the morning break, Baz and his brother marched into Mr. Simm's classroom and big brother immediately pushed Mr. Simms up against the wall then in no uncertain terms told Mr. Simms what would happen to him if he, or any other teacher, were to hit Baz with a leather strap. Mr. Simms went white and nodded in agreement as Baz's big brother held him by his jacket lapels. Case dismissed.

Even though Ade and myself was still getting into bits of bother and sailing very close to the wind, our headmaster was still taking a liberal approach and cutting us lots of slack. That said, Ade and me were amazed when Mr. Rocket readily agreed that we could finish school early one afternoon, so we could travel up to Old Trafford to see United take on Liverpool. Ade and me were marching down the school corridor with United scarfs hanging off our wrists and belts, when we were stopped by Mr .Hendry 'and where the hell do you to think you're going?' enquired Mr. Hendry. When I produced the letter that Mr. Rocket had given me, Mr. Hendry shook his head in disbelief and as he passed the letter back to me under his breath he muttered, 'the lunatics have taken over the asylum.'

As the Brummie Red coach neared the ground, we parked up and were met by a few souvenir sellers, besides offering the usual rosettes, metal pin badges and scarfs but one man was also selling what the Sunday papers would later call 'BADGES OF HATE'. These were approximately two-inch diameter white badges with various slogans like, 'Fuck Off City', 'I Hate Leeds', 'All Cockneys Are Cunts' and, of course, 'I Hate Scousers'. Not all the badges were hateful one-liners. There was also the poetic, 'Ashes to Ashes Dust to Dust, if The Stretford doesn't get you The Scoreboard must' I had the set!

After pinning my new 'I Hate Scousers' badge to my denim jacket, Ade and me made our way to the Stretford End. Once inside the ground Ade and me were surprised to see a section of the Scoreboard End was full of Liverpool fans. We had never seen away fans in numbers at Old Trafford before. But As Tony O'Neill (the so called Red Army General) said 'Liverpool always turned up, they had to, they had the number one firm'.

Now a lot has been said about the abuse that the black players received from football fans in the 1970's. Without doubt a certain amount of the football fans hurling abuse at black players were racist, but for me it was all 70's 'terrace banter', and by no stretch of imagination can anyone say that it was only black players that received abuse from the terraces. Any weak link would be used to try and throw a player off his game: 'don't bend around when Summerbee is around, or you'll get a penis up your arse,' 'Norman Hunter you're a wanker, you're a wanker,' and how could anyone forget the moving and sympathetic, 'there's a hole in your heart dear Asa – dear Asa, there's a hole in your heart dear Asa, a hole.' These and other charming chants could be heard around the country every Saturday afternoon, oh and not forgetting the obligatory, 'the referee's a wanker.'

But I think all the afore-mentioned anthems and all the monkey chants pale into insignificance when compared to the cruel and abusive chant that Kevin Keegan had to endure that evening. Keegan's dad had died only a few days before the game and it was expected that Keegan would decide not to play. He surely must have regretted his decision to play against United because from the minute Keegan ran onto the Old Trafford pitch, the United supporters sang, 'Keegan, Keegan how's your Dad? Keegan how's your Dad?' and 'Keegan, Keegan how's your Dad? Keegan how's your Dad?' rang out round Old Trafford for most of the game.

And of course the Liverpool fans sang there Munich '58 song.

§

Ilkeston Fair, would be the last time I worked on the fair. I had been taken back into the fold by the Boss the previous autumn when I worked at the famous Nottingham Goose Fair. While working at the Goose Fair I stayed with my auntie Gladys and got the bus to and from Nottingham each day, which made it a twelve-hour day for me. For some reason the Boss didn't set up the kids' ride that I usually looked after, so I found myself making and serving toffee apples and candyfloss, which for a seasoned fairground worker like me was a bit of a comedown and it meant less opportunity to nick a quid or two. The only high point of my time at the Goose Fair was that I happened to 'get in shot' when local ATV news cameras were filming and a few of my mates back in Aldridge later told me 'they had seen me on the telly.'

When The Boss phoned and asked if I could help out at the Ilkeston Fair, he also informed me that I could share a caravan with a 'few of his boys'. Sharing with the 'Fairground Boys', this was a jump up into the big league and I readily agreed.

When I arrived at Ilkeston and I was shown my accommodation, my heart sank a little. I was expecting to stay in a large luxurious forty-foot trailer similar to what the Boss had. No such luck. I was told to throw my bag into a small tatty and smelly four-berth caravan, which was even smaller then the caravan that my parents owned. There was one double bed and a make-up bunk bed. My spirits lifted when I we was told ' I was going to be working on the children's ride. Next to my ride was a Dartboard Stall, which was looked after by the guy called Bugsy whose caravan I would be staying in. The Boss introduced me to Bugsy and I got on with him from the start; he was warm and funny and also looked like a right hardcase. Bugsy arms were covered with home-made tattoos and he had Bugs Bunny's face tattooed on each hand and it looked like a five year old had applied them.

On the other side of my ride was a large catering van owned by the Boss's sister and to my utter delight they sold my favourite food of the day, Wesley's Hamburgers. God knows what ingredients the Wesley Hamburger had in them but they came packed in a long round tin and the burgers were covered in a layer of yellow fat and were put into boiling water to cook. With all todays legislation stating what can and can't go into food, I doubt that Wesley's Hamburgers would be allowed on the supermarket shelves. But I didn't give a second thought to what went in to the burgers, I just thought they were fantastic and, like me, all of my mates thought it was the food of gods. The small Greasy Spoon next to the old Walsall bus station, produced the best ever Wesley's Hamburgers, so good in fact, that on more than one occasion, I spent my bus fare on a second burger and had to walk back to Aldridge. It was music to my ears when The Boss said 'if you're hungry just pop over next door and she'll sort you out.' Bostin–burgers morning noon and night!

After my ride had closed down for the night, Bugsy took me for pint and before I had even took a sip of my beer he said, 'never let your gaffer catch you stealing from him, if he catches you, you'll be out and he'll chop you're fuckin' fingers off.' 'I wont let him catch me,' I thought to myself. 'If you are going to steal, steal off the punters...' Bugsy continued and proceeded to showed me a few tricks of the trade. First he produced a ring that had a 50p piece attached to it. The ring was worn so the 50p coin was on the inside of the hand. The con worked like so - while wearing the 50p ring, a punter would be given their change. A few loose coins would be added to the palm of the hand, you would then hold out your hand, so the punter could see the money and pointing with one of your fingers, count out the change. They would see the 50p along with the other coins and think they were being given the correct change. Then the fairground worker would slap the coins into the punters hand and walk off. Because they had just seen the correct change, nine times out of ten the punter would put the change straight into their pocket, not realizing they had been swindled out of 50p – the cost of two or three pints, back then.

If a punter was stupid enough to hand over a £5.00 note, they would be stung even more. Only three £1.00 notes would be given, back, instead of four. The first two notes on show, would be legit, the third note would be one note folded in two. While still holding the £1.00 notes the fairground worker would count out 'four notes' then add the coins to the notes and as with the 50p con – slap the money into the punters hand and walk away. Faced with the fearsome looking, tattooed fairground boys, if any of the punters did notice the cons, they would rarely push their complaint.

While Bugsy was educating me, a young man called Boxer came and joined us. He was a younger version of 'Quint' (aka Robert Shaw) the shark hunter from the film *Jaws* and, as his name suggested, he was a fighting man. Bugsy later told me that a few weeks before, Boxer had got into an argument with some local lads and it turned into a fight. When two police officers came to break up the mêlée, Boxer battered the two coppers and left them unconscious on the floor along with two of his original assailants.

Boxer told Bugsy that 'when he'd finished work, he was going to charm a girl so could he bring her back to his caravan?' (Charm being fairground slang for 'fuck'.) Bugsy said 'no problem,' and boxer headed back to his waltzer ride. After a few pints Bugsy told me he was going to work on the big rides for a couple of hours and I should go back to the caravan. When I suggested that I'd accompany him he laughed and said, 'don't think that would be a good idea. If the boys see a new face, they usually give 'em a welcomin.' Not fully understanding what a 'welcomin' meant, I asked Bugsy to explain and he duly obliged. Basically a 'welcomin' is a crude initiation ceremony – the newcomer is debagged and a tube of tooth paste is spread all over his meat and two veg, which apparently is extremely painful, then a mixture of grease and engine oil is spread all over the victims arse. Finally the trousers are pulled back up and the newcomer is tied up with rope, more grease would be applied making it difficult to remove the trousers and allowing the gooey mess to sink into the skin. Straight out of the Eton handbook for boys.

When I got back to the caravan, Boxer's young lady was already waiting for him so I invited her in. It wasn't long before she started to tell me her horrifying life story. Having been in and out of care homes all her life, she was now living rough. She had regularly been sexually abused by those charged to take care of her and even though she was only just sixteen, she had already had two abortions, the most recent being only a few weeks ago.

Genuinely feeling sorry for her, but with ulterior motives I gave her £3.00 that I had nicked earlier from my ride. In my immature, selfish and calculated way of thinking, I mistakenly thought that if she had been through all those terrible things, 'if I'm nice to her, I'm sure she'll at least give me a wank.' She seemed very grateful for the cash, but indicated no amorous signs. I dropped a few subtle hints regarding my sexual needs, but she didn't seemed interested so I climbed into the top bunk, disappointed, frustrated and gagging for a wank.

Just as I was falling off to sleep Bugsy and Boxer came crashing into the caravan. Bugsy dived straight onto his double bed and Boxer got down to business with the girl, who was lying on the bunk below me. As Boxer pulled off the girls knickers he shouted out in utter surprise, 'what the fuck as happened to ya bush?' This produced howls of laughter from Bugsy and, laughing himself, Boxer said, 'come and have a look Bugsy.' Bugsy didn't need asking twice, he jumped out of bed and flicked on the light. Boxer moved aside so Bugsy could get a good look and carry out his best gynaecologist impression, which included a cheeky little internal examination, which seemed to amuse both Boxer and the girl.

Bugsy blurted out between his fits of laughter, 'she's got a bald fanny - I wouldn't shag that,' and Boxer added, 'I know, I may as well shag her arse.' While Boxer and Bugsy were still laughing about the girls lack of pubic hairs, she quietly told them that she had been shaved because she had recently had an abortion. This cut no ice with the fairground boys and they carried on laughing and taking the piss out of her shaven fanny.

Once the laughter had died down, Boxer announced, 'I'm going to charm her anyway, so switch off the light Bugsy.' I then had to endure fifteen-twenty minutes of the caravan rocking backwards and forwards, accompanied by puffing, panting and groaning. Boxer seemed very indifferent to the whole thing, even shouting out to Bugsy at one stage, 'I've got my finger up her arse,' to which a sleepy Bugsy mumbled, 'you dirty bastard.'

As I lay above the two 'star struck lovers', listening to Boxer treat the girl like a piece of meat, I grew resentful towards the girl. My child-like ego had been bruised; I couldn't understand why the girl had given herself to a coarse brute like Boxer and turned down my sensitive advances - and I'd given her three quid! When I woke up next morning I noticed the girls jeans on the caravan floor and poking out of her back pocket was the money I gave her. Still feeling hurt and sorry for myself, I took the dastardly decision to take the cash back. Checking that everyone else was still asleep, I quickly removed the £3.00 from the girl's pocket and quietly got back into my bunk.

Taking the £3.00 back would soon come back and bite me on the bum. Luckily for me the girl left the caravan without noticing the £3.00 was missing from her pocket. But when she did eventually discover the money had gone, she headed straight back to the fairground, where she found Boxer and his mates setting up the waltzers. Through tears of anger, the girl openly accused Boxer of stealing her money and called him all the low-life names under the sun. Understandably Boxer was none too pleased with her accusations and said he didn't believe that she ever had £3.00, to which the girl replied, 'yes I did, Steve gave it to me!'

The girl realised that she was not going to get any joy out of Boxer and left the fairground and Boxer came in search of me. He came bouncing towards me and, almost sticking his face in mine, snapped, 'did you give that slag £3.00?' When I replied, yes, Boxer shook his head and said, 'what the fuck for?, I explained that she had told me she was homeless and was completely broke. 'And what the fuck has that got to do with you? You don't even know her,' Boxer said through gritted teeth. 'I felt sorry for her' I nervously replied. Boxer called me a fuck-faced wanker about a dozen times, a chicken dick and zooie (someone that shags dogs and sheep) and told me to keep out of his way. Bugsy had been watching our little tête-à-tête and, after Boxer had stormed off, Bugsy said to me, 'he must like you, normally he would have just knocked you out, then asked questions when you came round.'

Over the next two days I was sure to follow Boxer's instructions and kept well out of his way. On the last day of the fair the Boss gave me an hour dinner break so I went to the pub for a couple of lager and limes with a local girl who had been hanging around my ride for the best part of the morning. While I was sipping on my drink, the girl from the caravan walked into the pub with a couple of her mates. I immediately felt extremely guilty about my previous behaviour and thought I must make it up to her. When the appropriate moment presented itself, I approached the girl and discreetly gave her a couple of quid and made her promise, she wouldn't tell anyone that I had given here any more money. She promised the money would be our secret and then gave me a long, hard smacker on the lips.

After I had helped the Boss close my ride up, I wandered over to the catering van and enquired if they needed any assistance. Sis was glad of my offer and after giving me my instructions she handed me two Wesley's Hamburgers, which I quickly scoffed. As I was fetching and carrying for Sis, she continued to offer me Hamburgers, saying 'they will only go to waste, if you don't eat them.' In just over an hour I devoured five Wesley's Hamburgers; there was no room left for a toffee apple.

§

May 1st, FA Cup Final day, and Ade and me were at Wembley to witness Manchester United appear in an FA Cup Final for the first time since 1963. The Cup Final was my 26th game of the season and, taking into account I had a round trip of over 160 miles for home games, for a fifteen-year-old school boy, I thought that was pretty good going. I certainly didn't know of anyone else in my school that travelled to see their team like Ade and me had.

Ade and me were over the moon when the FA Cup Final tickets landed on our doormats. We really didn't think that we would get them, as we were unsuccessful in obtaining tickets for United's semi-final clash at Hillsborough against Derby County. Ade and me still went up to Hillsborough on the Brummie Red coach, in the vain hope of picking up a ticket outside the ground. Sadly no tickets were available, so along with another few thousand United supporters, we spent the afternoon outside the ground.

While the game was taking place inside the stadium, many of the United fans that were locked out were looting local shops and having running battles with the Yorkshire coppers. I saw an old man walk past a group of United fans trying to break the window of a showroom. Disgusted by the behaviour, the old man lifted his walking stick and hit a United fan clean across his back. As the United fans turned round to confront their attacker, the old man said, 'you bastards wouldn't be behaving like this if you'd have been on the Somme,' to which United fan replied, 'forget the Somme you daft old sod, I've been to Millwall and Newcastle twice!' Clearly not impressed the old man carried on his merry way, whacking random United fans as he went.

I had seriously considered taking a walking stick to the game, not to use as a weapon but for its intended purpose. I had only recently got my leg out of plaster and I was still a little unsteady on my feet. A big ugly lump, three years my senior, (you know who you are Ray Francis) had clattered into me while playing football and his heavy challenge had resulted in torn ligaments in my ankle. Fearing the lads would take the piss out of me I had decided to leave my walking stick at home and the only support I had for my damaged ankle was my eleven hole Dockas. The day before the final I spent most of the day writing slogans on a butcher's coat that I had recently acquired. Most of the slogans sang the praise of United's hooligan army, but then it was a bit of culture, Ade drew a wonderful United crest on the back of the white coat.

ITV traditionally ran a programme the night before the Cup Final entitled 'Who Will Win The Cup?' Most United fans were super confident that United would be the ones. Our opponents, Southampton, were a mere mid-table second-division team; United on the other hand had finished third in Division One. Ade and me had no doubt it would be a walkover. But the football pundits on 'Who Will Win The Cup?' didn't think the final would be so clear-cut and they were split fifty-fifty to who they thought would lift the Cup. As soon as the programme finished, a panic stricken Ade phoned me, 'Grange, we could lose you know – we could actually lose' After listening to the pundits myself, I also had a few doubts but told Ade I thought it would be impossible for United to lose to Southampton. I think I convinced Ade and myself everything would be ok on the big day and bursting with excitement and anticipation I went off to bed.

The best laid plans of mice and men! Some how, United lost. Personally I put it down to Alex Stepney diving like a falling tree while trying in vain to stop Stokes 83-minute winning goal. Southampton lifted the cup and shook my world to its foundations, I was totally numb and for an hour or two, I lost my faith.

On the Monday morning after the Final, Ade and me decided we would go into school with our heads held high. I wore my denim jackets which was covered in sew-on Man United badges and had a scarf hanging off my belt and Ade wore several scarves, one of them wrapped round his head. As we walked down the main corridor it was like the parting of the Red Sea and you could hear a pin drop. The scene was just like two infamous gun-slingers walking into a town. As Ade and me sat in silence at the back of the classroom, trying to look mean, moody and magnificent our form teacher said to the rest of our rowdy classmates 'if you don't quiet down immediately, I'll set Grainger and Chambers onto you; I'm sure they're itching to take their frustrations out on someone.' Silence instantly fell over the classroom!

Even though my exams were getting extremely close, I was still avoiding most of my science classes, but I decided to go to a certain biology class after learning that we would be dissecting frogs and newts in the lesson. I didn't really enjoy or gain any knowledge by seeing the reptiles being cut open but I did come out of the class with something: one of the cut-throat razors that were used to dissect the frogs. Amazing the teacher didn't count the amounts of cut-throats that had been handed back in. I simply walked out of the classroom with a cut-throat razor in my pocket.

I had no intention of using the cut-throat razor for foul games; it was just bravado and wanting to show off in front of my mates. After playing around with the cut-throat on the way home from school, I took it home and hid it in my bedroom, forgetting about it for a few weeks. One boring Sunday afternoon a few mates had joined me in my bedroom to listen to a bit of music and I got the cut-throat razor out, just to liven things up a little. We all took turns playing the tough guy with the razor. Then a knock on the door made me put the cut-throat in my pocket.

Another couple of mates were at the door and they asked if I was going down the Croft to play football. I was up for that and we went to the centre of Aldridge for a kickabout. I was almost at the Croft, when I realized I still had the cut-throat razor in my pocket. I was too far from home to take it back and, for a few seconds, I thought of hiding the razor somewhere, but then I said to myself, 'oh bollocks to it – I'll be ok,' and carried on to the Croft.

After playing football, with the cut-throat razor in my pocket (which could have been nasty), my mates and me went and sat down with a few girls who had been watching us play for a while. On the ground near to where we were sitting there was a long branch that someone had broken off a nearby tree (like I told the officer - it wasn't me). Acting 'the big I am' in front of the girls, I dragged the branch over to where we were sitting, then got out my cut-throat razor and started to turn the branch into a spear. As I was whittling away, a dog walker approached us and I noticed him looking at the damaged tree, then he saw me carving up the branch. As he passed me the dog walker gave me a look of disgust and me, being full of bravado, responded by giving him the fingers.

I can only assume that the dog walker went straight home and called the police, because five minutes after he walked past me, a panda car turned up. And would you 'Adam and Eve it' one of the officers was none other than - Ken the Copper. As obnoxious as usual, Ken the Copper came swaggering over and said, 'which one of you mindless morons, broke the branch off that tree?' We all denied any knowledge of the damage but Ken's eagle-eyed mate noticed the wood shavings and the sharpened point on the end of the branch. 'Who's got the knife?' the officer asked.

Thinking it wasn't a major crime to try and make a spear from a branch I found on the ground and of course, being a cocky little bleeder, I owned up. I was told to stand up and Ken the Copper started to search me. I had put the cut-throat razor in my pocket as soon as I had seen the police car turn up, so it didn't take long for the razor to be discovered. 'What the fuck is this?' Ken snapped as he took the cut-throat razor from my pockets. 'It's a knife' I replied. 'It's not a fucking knife; it's a cutthroat razor!' Ken's mate added. Then I said something very stupid and really pissed off the two coppers: 'if you knew it was a cutthroat razor, why did you ask me what it was?'

My mates and the girls all laughed out loud, but Ken the Copper wasn't amused. He grabbed me by my collar and said, through gritted teeth, 'a mate of mine was cut to pieces by one of these last week.'

Showing no sympathy, I shrugged my shoulders and said, 'so? That's got nothing to do with me.' The two coppers stared at me for a few seconds then Ken said, 'I should charge you for carrying an offensive weapon'. As soon as my reply left my lips, I knew I had said the wrong thing. 'Do what you want; you always do anyway.'

I was immediately frog-marched over to the panda car and thrown in the back. After I was questioned (unaccompanied) and charged with carrying an offensive weapon and criminal damage (to the tree), the desk sergeant asked me for my parents' telephone number so that could come and collect me. I replied that my parents were out for the day and wouldn't be back until later, without checking whether I was telling the truth or not. The sergeants then asked for the telephone number of any relative that could come and collect me, so I gave them a telephone number of my Uncle Bill.

When Uncle Bill was shown into the room where I was waiting, he looked at the younger copper who had been sitting in the room with me and said to him, 'bleedin' hell son, they say you're getting old when the coppers look young – you don't look old enough to have left school!' The young copper went red in the face with embarrassment and probably anger, and I couldn't help having a little chuckle. Good old Uncle Bill.

Because of my previous appearance in juvenile court, a probation officer was sent round to my house. Understandably my parents were furious about this. It was bad enough to have a probation officer visit our house, but when the officer turned out to be a patronising, arrogant twat, it just added insult to injury. My Dad was particularly upset with all the personal questions; yet another reason for Dad to have nothing to do with me.

The week before my appearance in court I had another meeting with the probation officer and when I informed him that I still intended to plead not guilty regarding damaging the tree, he replied, 'don't be stupid. The magistrates won't believe you and you will get a bigger fine - just plead guilty to both offences and get it over and done with.'

I continued to argue my case, pointing out that there was obviously no witness to say that I had damaged the tree. The inefficient wanker wasn't interested and with a big exasperating sigh said 'just plead guilty!'

When I was in court and standing in front of the magistrates, I was asked if I was pleading guilty or not guilty to the charges. Burning up thinking about the injustice of me pleading guilty to something I hadn't done, I replied 'I've been told to plead guilty about damaging the tree, but I didn't do it - I'm only guilty of carrying an offensive weapon.' The magistrate gave me a long hard stare and said, 'So, are you pleading guilty or not guilty? If you didn't cause any damage, you should plead not guilty and the case will be adjourned.'

I had a police officer standing at the side of me and through gritted teeth he snarled, 'just plead guilty you little cunt.' Charming British justice in all it's glory. I was thinking about saying to the magistrate, 'after advice from my honourable council, I plead guilty to both charges,' but I thought better of it. Feeling I had no option, I pleaded guilty to both charges and received a £35 fine: £20.00 for carrying an offensive weapon and £15.00 for damaging the tree. Almost a week's wages for something I hadn't done! I wrote to the International Court of Justice in The Hague about the injustice of my case, but sadly I never got a reply. Dutch twats.

The day I took my last CSE exam at school was also the last time I had a fight with big brother. I was in the kitchen telling my Mom how badly I thought I'd done in my exam when my brother walked in. Hearing the conversation, he started calling me thick and after exchanging one or two insults, he started to push me. I pushed him back against the kitchen cupboards then he launched himself at me and we were at it, like cats and dogs. As me and Big Brother fell onto the kitchen floor in a loving embrace, I remember Mom screaming at us, then all of a sudden there was extra blows raining down on me. Mom had got hold of the broom and she was indiscriminately whacking both of us and calling us 'a pair of animals'. For once I was winning and on top of my brother, but thinking I was receiving most of the blows from our Mom I thought I needed to even the odds so I reached for a milk bottle that was sitting on the edge of the work surface. I had just managed to grab the bottle, when my brother punched me in the stomach, causing me to drop it. The milk bottle hit the floor and smashed on impact, sending glass and milk everywhere. Undeterred we carried on fighting and our Mom continued to hit us with the broom handle and scream at us. As we wrestled with each other, the broken glass cut us both and soon splatters of red ran through the pool of milk that covered the kitchen floor. What a bleedin' carry on - I wonder how many millions of hits that little scene would get on YouTube these days.

Knowing that my CSE exams had gone awfully, I thought I would be lucky if I got a pass in any subject. With this in the mind, Baz and me went off to the army recruitment office in Walsall and sat the army entrance exam. To my utter surprise I got over 90% in the exam and the recruitment sergeant suggested that I should return to the recruitment office with my parents as soon as possible and sign. 'Bleedin' hell, they must be a load of thick gits in the army if I got over 90%,' I thought to myself.

I was genuinely keen to sign up, but when I learnt that Baz had failed the exam, my enthusiasm wavered. I just didn't have the confidence to join up without one of my mates. A few years later one of my mates, Nick Giles, signed up, all on his lonesome and spent five years in the forces. Before joining the army Nick had worked in an engineering factories and he told me why he decided to enlist. 'I'm sick of all the rules and regulations at work.' Told you the Army was all full of Thicko's! I often wondered how life might have turned out, if I had taken the King's shilling and followed my uncles, granddad and great-granddad into the army.

When 'Results Day' final came round, I headed for the school with the rest of my mates. There were no sealed envelopes with your personal grades, everyone's exam result were pinned up on a makeshift notice board, which had been set up in the reception area so my failures were there for the entire world to see. When I arrived at school there were loads of kids crowded around the noticeboard, so I asked one of my classmates if he'd seen my results, his answer was predictable but still hurtful. 'Yes – you did crap,' he laughed.

Out of the seven exams I sat, I failed four and got three passes, two of the passes being the lowest grade possible to obtain in a CSE. So Cambridge was out of the question. But there was a bit of reassuring news when I went to the deputy heads office to collect my school-leaving certificates. Expecting the worst I opened the big A4 envelope and started to read the comments from various teachers. As I read I was pleasantly surprised; I thought I would have only received negative comments like, how disruptive I was and I was always skiving off and I was leaving school semi-illiterate, all of them true. But, instead, almost all the teachers had written positive things about me, especially my sport's teacher who stated 'how hard I worked in the sports lessons and I had represented the school for the last five years, playing for both the rugby and football teams and if I carried on with my football, I could possibly play at a good level. But the testimonial that really shocked me was from my long time adversary Mr. Winters (AKA Willy the Whip). He wrote, 'Steven is a born leader and when he matures and learns to use his natural abilities wisely, I'm sure he will do very well for himself.' 'Fucking Hell - I'M A BORN LEADER'. All the disappointments of my exam results immediately disappeared and all I could focus on was that Mr. Winters thought: 'I'M A BORN LEADER.

I felt ten feet tall and was quick to show my mates what Willy the Whip had written about me. They all seemed suitably impressed, which is more than I can say about my parents, who received the news that their second born was 'A Born Leader' with their usual indifference.

Even though I left school with extremely poor exam results, I still ended up with three job offers, two from small builders in Aldridge and one from a builder in Great Barr. And because the builder in Great Barr offered me the job first, I took that one. So at the tender age of fifteen-and-three-quarters, I officially started work for the princely sum of £16.00 per week. £5.00 went straight to my Mom for my board. Well she was doing my sarnies.

Monday to Friday I was up at 6:30 and out of the house by 7:00. Then I had a twenty-minute walk to get the 357 bus to Great Barr. I found the work all very straightforward and the men I worked with all seemed a good craic. The one I worked with most of the time was a Paddy from Dublin. For the first few weeks I couldn't understand a word he was saying.

My starting work coincided with the hottest summer temperature in the UK since records began. From early June to mid September most days were in the 80's and there were a few spells when it hit the mid 90's for seven or eight days on the trot and, for the most part, I was working outside with my shirt off and there wasn't a drop of sun cream to be seen anywhere.

The boss must have been pleased with me because, after only working for him for two months, when I hit sixteen he gave me a 25% pay raise - £20.00 a week. I was rolling in it. On the day of my 16th birthday we were working in Sutton opposite the White Lion Pub and at dinnertime the four men I was working with took me over to the pub and each brought me a pint of lager and lime. As it was my birthday, when we returned to work, my work colleagues let me sit in the shade of a large tree and sleep off the beer - it was like being on holiday.

While we are on the subject of the holidays, when my parents and sisters went away in August for their two-week annual holiday. Nick and me arranged a party or two (make that six or seven) at my house. For the previous three or four months Nick had been working at the Lazy Hill off-licence, which was at the top of my road. Every evening without fail, Nick would put a little something outside the back door of the shop and I would pick it up. A 'little something' could range from a few cans of beer, to bottle of vodka and this happened four times a week.

We stored our booze carefully in Nick's loft and most Friday nights when his parents were out, we would make a booze pyramid and as the weeks went by, the booze pyramid grew and grew in size. But we agreed that we wouldn't drink a drop and all the booze would-be used for a massive party fest when my family went away on holiday. To make ready for the party season, the night before my parents went on holiday, Nick, me and a couple of other lads smuggled the booze out of Nick's loft and into my garage. Up until then, only Nick and me had seen the size of our booze stack and our mates were amazed at just how much booze we had accumulated.

That first party was a great night. We had invited lots of girls from school and most of them turned up, meaning they outnumbered the boys by almost two to one. There were boys and girls in and out of all the bedrooms all night and I'm sure a good time was had by all. I suppose I really should have washed those bed sheets. The Sunday session was for the lads only and much to the annoyance of certain neighbours we had a great drunken and very rowdy game of football on the grass in front of my house. As it got dark we were threatened with the police at couple of times, but the coppers never turned up.

During the working week Nick and me only had a few beers each night, wanting to save our rations for the upcoming bank holiday weekend. On the Friday evening a few of the lads decided we would have a card night. We were having a great boozy time, except for continually disagreeing about the rules of poker and who had the winning hand.

After Drinking copious amounts of alcohol, hunger had set in and we were just deciding whether to go to the chippy before it closed when four or five cars pulled up opposite my house and about twenty blokes and a few girls started making their way to my front door.

The unwanted little mob mainly consisted of blokes three or four years older than me and a few girls who had been at the party the week before. Trying to impress the older guys, the girls had told them that my parents were away and I was having a party every night. The bastards fell on us like a swarm of locus, tramplining flowerbeds, pissing up the side of the porch and leaving bottles and cans all over the front lawn. I insisted there was no party but a couple of the gang that I knew by sight said 'they wanted to come in to check.' Pushing me aside, two of the gang entered my hallway, with this Ade dived off the stairs feet first and kicked one of the gang clean in the chest, sending him back into the porch. Me and a couple of my mates quickly pushed the second guy back into the porch and locked the front door. Luckily for me, Mr. Wood, who was one of my neighbours, was returning from the pub with a few of his drinking mates and they quickly came to my rescue. I think my mates and me would have been in big trouble if the cavalry hadn't arrived just in time.

As it was a bank holiday weekend, my mates and me agreed that on the Sunday we would stop up all night, drinking, playing cards and listening to our music. It was a long hard slog and most of us had forty winks during the early hours, The only one who actually went to bed was Kesh, who lived next door but one in the 'Grove' As the sun eventually appeared in the sky we all gave a big cheer and saluted the big yellow ball in the heavens. Then someone came up with a bright idea to celebrate stopping up all night by 'streakin'. Half a dozen of us stripped off in my back garden and ran naked around the grass island round at the Grove. We all jumped around like lunatics and made a right din. Nick overdid it a little bit and left a large pool of puke on the grass.

When we got back to my house, I was surprised to hear the phone ringing. When I answered it, Kesh's mom said in a very aggressive manner, ' tell Keith (Kesh) to come home now!' I told her that he was in bed, but she was having none of it and insisted that Keith went home that minute then slammed the phone down on me.

It took me ages to wake Kesh and when he finally came round, it was pretty apparent that he was still pissed. I must have told Kesh a dozen times that his mom had said that he 'must go home' before he finally got dressed and staggered the short distance. Even though Kesh had nothing to do with streaking around the grove, his mother greeted him at the front door with a smack around the head. When Kesh fell back from the force of his Mom's hand, his Mom noticed that he was drunk. She then called Kesh's dad down from his bed and he gave Kesh a good hiding. Sometimes it's just not your day.

The Cedar Tree pub, which was just a few minutes walk from my house, it became my local as soon as I started work, and on Friday evenings Nick and me would be propping up the bar by 7:00pm. We would regularly bump into a couple of older lads, Eddie and Peter, and they would become life-long friends and I would have a drink with them every Friday for over twenty years.

The Cedar Tree bar had it's fair share of characters. Mad Val, was a scrawny, badly dressed woman, who looked like a scary character from a Stephen King novel. Then there was Betty Wanklyn, she had a passing resemblance to Betty Davies's character from 'What Ever Happened to Baby Jane. Both of them were in and out of St Margaret's (nut hutch). Betty's on-off boyfriend, Herrman, could make a half-pint of bitter last all night. He was the only black man in Aldridge and he would often wear Betty's fluffy slippers, a tatty old dressing gown and white rimmed sunglasses. The 'Knife Grinder' was a strange, strange character. He would stand at the end of the bar all night talking to himself, drunk as a lord and then ride home on his three-wheeled bike, which incorporated his grinding stone.

The highlight of a Friday evening was when the cockle man made an appearance. Dressed in a white jacket and carrying a wicker basket full of seafood, he would pass through the bar selling his freshly thawed prawns, muscles and cockles. 'Alive, alive ohhh' they certainly were not. But once covered with vinegar, to our uneducated palate the freezing cold seafood was Cordon Bleu and the height of sophistication.

The Cedar Tree lounge was divided into two rooms, one full of bikers, the other full of boring middle-aged couples. Thinking back it was an odd place.

As I got to know Eddie and Peter better, after meeting in the Cedar Tree bar we would venture a little further and have a few pints in the oddly named Banks's pub, the 'Struggling Monkey', then onto the Elms and ending the night in the Whitehouse. We would usually do a little pub crawl on foot, but every now and then Eddie would drive us in his pride and joy and bird magnet - his Capri Ghia. The Whitehouse was quite a big pub and up until the mid 90's it attracted young people from all over Walsall. I loved it in there; it seemed half of my old school mates drank in there and I quickly made new acquaintances - and during the long hot summer of '76 'The Boys are Back in Town' seemed to be on the jukebox continually. Still to this day, I only have to hear the intro to Thin Lizzy's timeless classic and I am immediately transported back to those wonderful, carefree nights in the Whitehouse.

I had £15.00 a week to spend on what I liked. Beer was 22p a pint (in the Cedar Tree bar) I had no problem picking up a attractive girls, one of my mates had a Ford Capri Ghia, I could regularly afford to buy fashionable clothes, Elton John was at number one (along with Kiki Dee), I had just had my first proper tattoo - a lovely red rose, from the world-famous 'Tattoo Stan' - and the football season was just about to start. Life couldn't get any better.

United's first game of the '76-'77 season was Birmingham City; almost 59,000 packed Old Trafford to witness a 2–2 draw. The Birmingham comedian Jasper Carrot was in the crowd that day and he wrote a comical sketch about his experience. The one liner that sticks in my memory is, 'ay Carrot - they ay got no cowing Bovril.' Also in the crowd were two hundred Brummie Reds, The Birmingham branch had taken four coaches to the game and they had over five hundred members.

A few weeks later I went to see United at Derby and United fans invaded the pitch at the end of the game and ran the home supporters out of the ground. The next morning I was eating my breakfast when Kesh came round mine with the Sunday rag, The News of the World. 'Have you seen this yet,' Kesh asked as he passed me the newspaper. My eyes nearly popped out of my head - half the back page was taken up by a photo of the United mob on the pitch at Derby and who was in the centre of the picture? None other than little old me.

Until I went to Galatasaray in the mid 90's, the most frightening experience I had at a football match was at St. James's Park. I was with a mob of about two hundred United fans, who had a much-needed police escort from the nearby coach park. At one stage, police on horseback had to ride into a pub to hold the Geordies back and, as we queued to get into the Gallowgate End, the mad Geordies charged us every few minutes.

It threw it down before, during and after the match and rain wasn't the only thing falling down on us. Bottles bricks, batteries and coins were thrown at us and of course they were promptly thrown back over the dividing fence. The only people who seemed safe from the flying missiles were the half-a-dozen or so United fans who had scrambled up the floodlights. This is the last time I can remember football fans watching the game, while halfway up the stadiums floodlights.

When half-time arrived I went down to the back of the open terrace to see if I could find somewhere to shelter from the rain for a few minutes. I couldn't believe the sight that greeted me when I got to the bottom of the concrete steps - on the opposite side of the dividing fence was a large gang of young men and they were standing in silence, some of them gripping the fence, others lined up like a real-life terracotta army. All of them were staring menacingly at us.

The petrifying gang all had the same look: long straggly hair, kilts and shin-high hobnail boots. A few of them wore shirts, but even though it was pissing it down, most of them were bare chested. I looked at them in awe and fear for a few moments, then I got eye contact with one of them, I nearly crapped myself and immediately turned round and ran back up to the open terracing. I had nightmares for weeks after.

God knows how builder's merchants made any money in the '70s. It seemed every builder was robbing them blind, and the company I worked for was no exception. The company's main driver/chippy got an extra £25 - £30 added to his weekly salary because of all his thieving from the builder's yards. He was paid in cash at the end of each week for whatever he had stolen. I would often assist him loading the stolen items onto the company vehicles but the miserable bastard never shared any of his ill gotten gains with me.

The gaffa had asked the driver to get him a few wheelbarrows and half-a-dozen shovels. Unfortunately all the builder's merchants that we used had their tools and wheelbarrows locked in a separate storage unit, thus making it difficult to steal them. A few weeks had passed and still the driver had failed to nick any wheelbarrows so I took it upon myself to supply the gaffa with a wheelbarrow or two. There was a factory based near Redhouse that manufactured wheelbarrows and other tools, so one night under the cover of darkness Nick and me scrambled under the factory fence and had two wheelbarrows away. My house was well over a mile from the factory and we certainly got some strange looks from passing motorists as we pushed the wheelbarrows along the pavement. Not a sight you expect it to see at 10 o'clock at night.

The next evening the gaffa gave me a lift home and collected the wheelbarrows and I pocketed £6.00. The gaffa was pleased with the wheelbarrows and told me he could use as many as I could get and a few shovels were also required. This would take a little bit more planning. I really think Nick and me pushed our luck, openly pushing the wheelbarrows along the pavement. And if we were talking larger numbers, pushing them back to my house and hiding them in my Dad's garage wouldn't be an option.

The factory I was stealing the wheelbarrows from wasn't far from the abandoned Aldridge train station, so I decided to have a little reccie and went to explore the possibility of hiding the wheelbarrows and shovels in the old station once I had nicked them. I was disappointed to find that all doors and windows at the old station had been covered with plywood and it would have been difficult for me to gain entrance. Fortunately for me, there was another abandoned building near to the station – the Old Mortuary! I found an unsecured door at the back mortuary and, thinking there wouldn't be too many people wanting to visit the old mortuary, this would be an ideal place to hide the wheelbarrows until I could arrange transport to collect them.

A few nights later, I roped Nick into assisting me again and we removed eight wheelbarrows and as many shovels from the Redhouse factory. We perhaps could have taken more, but it had started to rain heavily and the little narrow pathway that we were using quickly became muddy and waterlogged and in our rush to get the wheelbarrows to our hiding place, both Nick and me slipped in the mud several times. By the time we had stashed wheelbarrow number eight, we were filthy and soaking wet.

The next evening I persuaded my Irish work colleague, Frank, to drive over from Great Barr and collect the wheelbarrows and shovels. Nick and me met Frank outside my house then we drove down into the village for the pickup. Frank insisted that he inspected the area before he commenced the pickup, so I pointed out that the only way a vehicle could reach the mortuary was by a single track lane that run alongside Harpers Bus Garage.

The short narrow lane that lead to the mortuary was in total darkness and for an age we sat in Frank's van, which was positioned about a hundred yards away from the entrance to the lane, and every few seconds Frank would shake his head and mutter in his strong Dublin accent, 'I don't like it Stiv – I just don't like it.' After finally convincing Frank it would only take a few minutes to load the wheelbarrows and promising him I'd get him a few porn mags, Frank revved his engine and shot down the narrow lane like a bat out of hell. Within a few seconds we were outside the mortuary, Frank followed Nick and me to the back of the building and we started to remove the wheelbarrows. As Frank entered the building, he said to me in a whisper 'what kind of building is this Stiv?' 'An old mortuary,' I replied. 'What the fekin' hell is a mortuary?' Frank asked. When I told him it was where dead bodies were kept before burial, he immediately dropped the wheelbarrow he had just grabbed and screamed out, 'I'm not staying in here' and ran out of the building empty handed.

Nick didn't have a clue why Frank had got so spooked and was totally baffled. Nick later told me he had only understood one word, that Frank spoke that night – 'Stiv' (Steve). I explained to Frank that the mortuary was no longer used but he flatly refused to go back into the building. Nick and me soon loaded up the van, then we jumped into the cab alongside Frank, who was still visibly shaken. After giving Nick a few quid and buying Frank his mags, I ended up with the equivalent of two weeks' wages in my pocket. The day after I gave Frank the porno mags, he asked me to order him a large jar of Rampant Rhino Horn aphrodisiac powder and a Peek-a-Boo bra. Kinky Bleeder.

1977

The work situation was still enjoyable and I really liked the varied work of a jobbing builder: one day concreting footings, the next day laying a few bricks, then up on the a roof, followed by a bit of plumbing or carpentry. Hard work, but it certainly wasn't boring. One of the easier tasks was taking loads of rubbish or soil to the tip in Streetly and once we had got past the Gatehouse I was usually allowed to drive the vehicle, which was often a three-ton tipper.

I had many 'driving lessons' on the tip and thought I was getting to be quite a good driver. Good enough in fact to take my Dad's small Moggy Minor van for a spin - what could possibly go wrong? Dad had gone out for the evening, so I asked Nick if he fancied coming for a spin in my old man's van. Nick knew that I hadn't had any proper driving lessons, but I reassured him that I had been driving lorries and vans at work for weeks and driving the Moggy Minor wouldn't be a problem.

I took the van keys from the kitchen and started up the van, which was sitting on the drive. Asking Nick to 'watch me', I gently started reversing off our long drive. Nick was anxiously looking on and instructing me, 'ok Grange, slowly – slowly, that's good…' I felt the back wheels bump down the kerb and onto the road and Nick shouted, ' you're doing great, just a little further,' then, 'ok. Stop!' On Nick's instruction I moved my foot off the accelerator but Nick continued to say, 'stop, stop' - although this time with a little of hint of panic in his voice. Then he screamed out, 'brake!' and dived to safety as the van hit the kerb on the opposite side of the road, mounted the footpath and crashed through our neighbour's garden wall.

At this point, I feel I should mention the fashionable shoes I was wearing that night. Colloquially they were known as Boat Shoes (nothing like what we call boat shoes today). They were curved at the front and unusually wide. Forget metal segs, you could have easily fitted a metal horseshoe to the sole of the shoe. It was those stupid bleedin' 'Rhythm and Blues' that were my downfall. For those of you who don't have a Morris Minor service manual readily to hand, let me describe in technical terms the distance between the accelerator pedal and the brake pedal: 'too fucking close', and this is not helped by the fact that the accelerator pedal is the fuckin' size of a very small postage stamp. So! as I put my foot on the brake pedal my super wide shoes still covered the accelerator pedal and thus I went hurtling backwards and crashed through the wall.

I must have hit the kerb at some speed as the van was catapulted backwards. It hit the stone wall about a foot off the ground and the van was precariously perched on the bottom few courses of the wall. I carefully got out of the see-sawing van and stood in the middle of the road with Nick, both of us staring at the damage I had caused and I was thinking, 'how the bleedin' hell am I going to get the van off the wall.' Then a voice from behind us said, 'what on earth is going on here?' Kesh's dad George had heard the loud bang as the van hit wall and he had come out to investigate. After George had made sure that Nick and me were both ok, with what seemed like super-human strength he managed to get the van off the wall and parked it back on our drive. Miraculously there wasn't a great deal of damage to the van.

Leaving all the damaged stonework in my neighbour's garden, Nick and me headed to the Cedar Tree bar. I was devastated and worried to death about my Dad's reaction and how much it would cost me to repair the wall. After copious amounts of Dutch courage, I finally went home to face the music.

Understandably Dad hit the roof and he got me out of bed early enough the next morning to tidy up our neighbour's garden and stone wall before I went off to work. It was dark and cold as I stacked the damage stone and tried to make the scene look a little bit more presentable. I had almost finished my task when Mr. Brown (the owner of the wall) suddenly appeared. Somehow Mr. Brown was not aware of the previous nights commotion and he had no knowledge of the damage to his side wall. He looked strangely perplexed as he stood in silence inspecting the gaping hole in his wall. 'That's strange. Everything was in order last night,' he muttered to himself. Then, quite bizarrely, he thanked me for tidying up the mess and offered me a lift to work! It was all too creepy and I declined his kind offer.

For the next three or four nights when I came home from work, which included a Friday evening, I had to dress (clean up) the damaged stone. Then over the weekend I had to assist my Dad to rebuild the wall, which meant missing the United game. Oh, and my Dad charged me for his time and the cost of the sand and cement for the compo.

A few weeks later Nick and me were involved in a more serious car accident. Nick's elder cousin, Martin, acquired a Reliant Robin (aka a 'Plastic Pig'). Martin was an experienced 'Biker' but hadn't passed his test in a car but because a Plastic Pig only had three wheels, you could drive one if you had a full motorcycle license, which Martin had.

Early one Saturday evening, Martin and his mate Steve turned up at the Cedar Tree bar and asked Nick and me to go into Birmingham with them. Always up for a little adventure Nick and me scrambled into the back of Martin's green Plastic Pig. It was a bloody horrible vehicle both inside and out but, as Martin pointed out after every criticism of the his new mode of transport, 'it's getting us from A to B, so shut the fuck up.'

We parked up in Birmingham and - after visiting usual haunts the Cabin, the Costermongers, the Pen & Wig, the Brown Derby and the O.C's and of course our driver had at least a pint in every pub, followed by a rum & pep - Martin dragged us to an Indian restaurant. I wasn't a fan of Indian food at the time so I ordered one of the two English items on the menu, omelette and chips, and it was bleeding awful. I left most of the meal and so did my fellow diners.

As was customary when visiting an Indian restaurant back then, at the end of the meal all four of us complained about our meals and refused to pay the bill. After insulting the poor Indian waiter for ten minutes, we left a few quid on the table and left the restaurant. The restaurant manager quickly followed us outside and repeatedly called us 'bloody white bastards!' 'That's a bit racist,' I thought. 'I'm glad I never left them a tip now.' A tip! - what a laugh, 'tip' to 99% of the teenagers in England meant where the dustbin wagons unloaded your weekly household waste and nothing more.

Martin was a big lad with a big appetite, so after leaving the Indian restaurant we jumped back in the Plastic Pig and headed for a fish-and-chip shop. The first chippy was near the Towers pub, but the chips were still in the fryer so it was back into the Pig and we headed for the chippy next to the Cat and Fiddle. Because it was so cramped in the back of the vehicle, we took it in turns to sit in the front passenger seat and it was my turn to sit up front.

Martin's mate Steve really didn't like it sitting in the back and offered to pay for my pie and chips if I let him sit in the front seat, for the short journey to the next chippy. I turned down Steve's offer and begrudgingly he got into the back seat and sat behind me. Martin had just turned onto the Queslett Road and we were tootling along quite nicely when a car full of young Asians overtook us. 'Cheeky Paki bastards!' Steve shouted in my ear. Then Steve turned to Martin and said, 'you're not going to let them cunts get away with that, are you?' 'I'm fuckin' not,' Martin snapped and 'put the metal to the floor'.

We all encouraged Martin to drive faster and we gave a collective cheer when the car full of Asians came in to view. Martin was like a jockey in the saddle, jumping up and down and encouraging his motorized steed to go a little faster. We got alongside the Asians just as the road dipped down towards the motorway bridge. Martin started to bang on his horn (Ooooh Matron) and we all gave them the 'V' sign and shouted abuse. The Asians looked bemused at our actions and I'm sure they were oblivious to the fact that we had been chasing them. All four of us in the Plastic Pig were going a little wild, then just before we went underneath the motorway bridge, Martin clipped the kerb and over we went.

As the car tumbled over, everything went into slow motion and there was a deathly quiet. The Plastic Pig overturned half a dozen times before coming to a stop at the bottom of a grass bank on the opposite side of the dual carriageway. Somehow we had managed to miss all the large concrete pillars that supported the motorway bridge. If we had struck one of those I'm sure we would all have been goners. I came round as a couple of ambulance men were putting me on to a stretcher and, from what I can remember, the grass bank was like this scene from a disaster movie: lots of people milling about, lots of flashing lights from ambulances, fire engines and police cars, and lots of debris.

I was taken off to hospital and after undergoing various examinations and x-rays, I was told I had only suffered a slight concussion, internal bruising and a few sprains, but they would keep me in a overnight just to keep an eye on me. The only damage to Nick and Martin was to their clothes. Sadly, Steve wasn't so fortunate. Steve broke his leg in several places, had three fractured ribs and his face looked like he'd done a few rounds with Joe Foreman. Steve spent almost three months in hospital with his leg in traction. If I had taken him up on his offer of 'free pie and chips' I would have most probably been the one stuck in a hospital bed for three months!

Nick and his dad collected me from hospital the next morning and on the way home Nick asked his dad to pass the crash site. We were all amazed at the state of Martin's Reliant Robin. On the grass bank was a pile of body panels, doors and seats and at the edge of the road sat what was left of the vehicle, which was basically the back wheels, the chassis and the engine block. 'Do you think it will be a write-off?' Nick jokingly said to his dad. Looking up at the near by motorway bridge and concrete columns, Nick's dad shook his head and said, 'I can't believe you all survived.'

The accident was reported in several local newspapers over the coming weeks and not one of the local rags got all our names correct. In quite a few reports I was named as Stewart Granger and Nick was named as Richard Burton. And in one newspaper, it was reported that a Richard Burton aged three died in the accident.

§

If I wasn't watching United on a Saturday afternoon, I would be on the top floor of the Walsall arcade, queuing up in Stan's tattoo parlour to get my old Indian ink jobs covered up. The little studio was always packed and a two-hour wait was not unusual. You could never describe Tattoo Stan as a great artist like some of the top tattooists of today, but he was Walsall's finest and he had been tattooing panthers, daggers, love hearts, swallows, ships, crucifixes and eagles on the good people of Walsall since the late 50's.

Stan was very much, a no nonsense sort of man and at times he could be a little scary. He was curt and cantankerous all the time and he would often question the design or the parts of the body that someone had chosen. Besides the dozens and dozens of tattoo designs on his studio wall, Tattoo Stan also had a large sign that read, 'no tattoos on hands, fingers, necks or face.' Blinkin' heck! If a sign like that was put up in a tattoo studio today, they would probably lose half their business.

Another thing that Stan was very reluctant to do was any type of football tattoo. Stan put a Red Devil on my arm but refused to put 'Man United', so Nick and me went to see Dodgy Vic in Wolverhampton. The entrance to Vic's tattoo studio (I use the word 'studio' very, very loosely.) was via a little alleyway and was no more than a tin shack/lean-to at the back of an old terraced house. The initial signs weren't good as we walked into Vic's little hovel. There was two Staffordshire bull terriers sitting on the floor, both of them had been shaved above the back legs and tattooed. Vic tattooed 'Man United' for me without question, but his work was so poor I got Stan to cover it up a few months later.

It took me well over a year to persuade Stan to do a United Crest for me but unfortunately it wasn't a great tattoo. The footballs depicted on the United Crest looked more like rugby balls and the whole tattoo was slightly skewwhiff.

On a couple of occasions when I was having my biggest Indian ink tattoos covered, I visited Stan during the week when he was a lot quieter and, if you were lucky, he would knock a quid or two off the price. The price of the tattoo was always shown next to the design, none of the nonsense you get today, paying the tattooist by the hour. My most memorable visit to Stan's was on such a week day. I'd taken the day off work and, feeling a little bored, I wandered into Stan's and, for once, it was completely empty. Without a word being exchanged between Stan and me I studied his wall-mounted designs. After about thirty minutes, Stan broke the silence. 'Have you come in here for a tattoo or not? he asked. When I replied 'I haven't got any money, I'm just looking' I was almost certain that Stan would give his usual reply to lads that were in the studio and not intending to get a tattoo, 'it's not an art gallery - fuck off!' But, to my astonishment, Stan said, 'roll your sleeves up and I'll do you a little tattoo.' I confirmed once again that I had no money and Stan snapped, 'just fuckin' sit down'.

I couldn't believe my luck - a freebie tattoo from grumpy old Stan! I'm sure there are not many people in this world who enjoyed that pleasure! Shortly after Stan had finished my tattoo, I was having a final little shuftie around his studio, when a timid and nervous-looking young man came through the door. The young man had only been in Stan's place for a few minutes when Stan growled at him 'are you having a fuckin' tattoo or just wasting my time?' The shy young man replied, 'it's my first tattoo, but I don't really know what to have.' Pointing at the various eagle designs, Stan said, 'what about, one of those?' After studying the designs for a minute or so, the young man said 'I like them, but I don't know which one to choose.' Stan replied, 'how much have you got to spend?' and his eyes lit up when the young man replied '£25.00'

A few weeks earlier I had only paid £8.00 for a massive tattoo that almost covered the inside of my arm and, previous to that, I had paid £5.00 for a large eagle on my upper arm. £25.00 was a small fortune for a tattoo. The young man looked visibly shocked as Stan said to him 'get your shirt off and I'll put a nice big eagle over your chest.' Patting the top of his arm, the tattoo virgin replied, 'I was thinking more of up here, on my arm.' 'Just get your shirt off,' Stan sternly replied. Almost in tears the young man removed his shirt and then, as instructed by Stan, sat in the old wooden chair that was just in front of the immoral and barbarous tattooist.

Stan's free-spending customer was now fully committed and trapped in the spider's web. Stan picked up a cheap old biro and started to roughly sketch out the overall outline of the massive eagle on the young man's chest. When Stan had finished his little masterpiece, he laughed and said in a very sadistic tone, 'hold tight to the seat of the chair and if you can feel anything under there - it's the fingertips of the last person that I tattooed on the chest!' Stan offered his tattoo gun up to chest of his customer/victim and in one foul swoop, he inflicted a line from the middle of the chest, right up to the shoulder blade. The colour immediately drained from the face of the hapless young man. It was brutal seeing the pain the young man was going through. But just as people stop and look at car crashes, I had a irresistible, morbid fascination with the look of agony on the young man's face and more than once I thought, 'thank fuck that's not me.' It puts me off having a chest job, for life.

§

At the end of the '76 –'77 season I'd been to forty-three United games which included trips to West Ham, Leeds, Man City, Newcastle, Sunderland and Arsenal, and all the FA Cup games, home and away. Loyal Supporter! United had an indifferent season and finished sixth in the league, but United finished the season on an high by beating Liverpool in the FA Cup Final, and by doing so stopped the Scousers from doing the double.

Sadly, a few days later Liverpool went on to lift the European Cup for the first time. Like most United supporters I was gutted, no longer could we sing 'Oh Man

United, the only English team to win the European cup.'
The final action of the season was the little matter of the
Home Internationals. England beat Northern Ireland away,
then lost to Wales at Wembley and in their final game, they
lost to Scotland at Wembley. It was bad enough losing to the
'sweaty socks' at home, but the fact that thousands of wild
jocks (including Rod Stewarts) invaded the Wembley pitch,
dug up the turf and smashed both sets of goalposts, just
added salt to the wounds. Where were Millwall, Tottenham,
Chelsea and West Ham while all this was going on?

With a few of my mates, I went into Birmingham to
watch the England – Scotland game. It was a few years off
from pubs showing football games. In any case the pubs
closed between 2:30 and 5:30. Any road up, my mates and
me joined scores of teenagers standing outside an electrical
shop that displayed TVs in the window. There was no sign
of trouble as we stood and watched the game, just a bit
of loud banter from the crowd, but the managers of the
electrical store got a little jittery and called the police to
move us on. Some of the coppers were very heavy handed,
pushing some of the 'telly watchers' to the floor and the
use of police dogs seemed totally unnecessary.

We tried to watch the game outside three or four
different electrical shops, but each time the police came
and moved us on. Being frustrated by being constantly
moved on by the police, me and a couple of my mates
went into the Grand Hotel on Colmore Row to see if they
were showing the game. There was nothing going on the
ground floor, so we decided to have a little mooch around
and after walking up and down a few corridors, I heard the
commentary of the football game coming from one of the

bedrooms. Being a cheeky sod, I knocked on the door and an anxious-looking man popped his head around the door.

'Can I help you?' the man said nervously. With three strange teenagers standing outside his hotel room, I suppose he had reason to be nervous. I politely told him that we were desperate to watch the England game but couldn't find anywhere to watch it and was there a possibility that we could watch the game in his room? The man turned away from us and spoke to someone in the room, then hesitantly he said, 'yes ok, but promise you will behave.' 'Scouts honour,' I said. The man moved aside and with a hand gesture invited us into his hotel room. As I entered the room I noticed there was another three men in there, one of them wearing a kilt! England were playing shockingly and the Scottish fan in the kilt wasn't slow to point out just how bad England were. I quickly noticed that one of our hosts was getting incensed with the jock, constantly taking the piss.

At the final whistle, the jock went mental diving all over his three English mates and none of them were very happy with this. But things got really heated as we all witnessed hordes of tartan-clad Scotland supporters running onto the hallowed turf. To the English supporters in the room this was a massive insult, but of course the kilt-wearing jock thought it was fantastic and he expressed how he wished he was on the Wembley pitch with his fellow countrymen. The jocks' wild celebrations were too much for one of his English mates and a right hander sent the jock flying across the room. The jock quickly got back onto his feet and launched himself at his attacker. Soon the pair of them were rolling round the bedroom floor and, after witnessing the little brawl, I can confirm that jocks don't wear anything under their kilts! The sight of the jock's Niagara's and hairy arse, was enough to put me off Haggis for life.

The two of them were having a right go at it, tables, chairs and lamps were all damaged in the mêlée. Their mates eventually separated the warring parties and set about tidying up the room. At bit ironic, my mates and me were told to behave ourselves and it was our hosts that ended up wrecking the room! A little shell-shocked we left the hotel and headed towards New Street and we soon realized that things had escalated from earlier in the afternoon. Police sirens seemed to be going off all over town. The teenage gangs that had been escorted away from the electrical shops, had returned once the police had left the scene and smashed windows and in a few cases stole TVs and other electrical items. It was going off everywhere - super exciting.

The police told many city-centre pubs not to open for the evening trade so Nick and me decided to walk down to Digbeth. As we walked through the Bullring market a lot of the stalls were packing up for the day and we noticed one stall was selling DIY goods, which included cans of spray paint. While the stallholder was packing away his other items, Nick and me grabbed a couple of spray cans each.

After a couple of pints, we spent the rest of the evening spraying United & Blues graffiti in various subways and de-facing walls in and around Digbeth. There must have been at least ten MUFC + GRANGE sprayed on walls in Brum. On a wall not far from the Blues ground, Nick sprayed 'Nick Burton – Aldridge – BCFC' I couldn't believe how naïve he was. 'Why don't you go the full hog and add your telephone number?' I said. I also pointed out that even Inspector Clouseau would be able to track down the perpetrator. But Nick, being full of beer and bravado brushed it off.

When our spray cans were empty we checked our finances and decided we could afford one more pint before getting the bus back to Aldridge. The first pub we came to was the Rainbow and for you history buffs out there, in the 1920's the Rainbow and the adjoining Adderley Street were home to the authentic Peaky Blinders. The top half of the entrance door to the Rainbow had an ornate, frosted glass panel that read, 'Pat Walsh's Irish Bar.'

'Let's go and have a pint with Pat Walsh,' I said to Nick. I had every intention of asking to see Pat Walsh, but when I noticed the size of the man-mountain barman, I changed my mind. I asked for two pints of lager and lime and the frightening looking barman glared at me for a moment and said in a soft, yet gruff Irish accent, 'they'll be no lager and lime in here!' 'Straight lager it is then,' I thought to myself. Without a response from Nick or me the barman went off to pull our two pints of lager.

While I was waiting for my drink I noticed the bloke standing next to me and he was like a caricature of an Irish labourer. He wore a donkey jacket that was at least two sizes too big for him and on his head he wore an oversized black beret with cut-outs to accommodate his massive ears. His muddy Wellies were turned over so the top half-exposed the inside of the boots and at the back of one of his boots was a large 'L' and on the back of the other boot there was a large 'R'. And when he spoke to the barman, it made my Dublin work colleague sound as if he was speaking the Queens English. I couldn't understand a word the old culchie was saying.

I discreetly pointed out the sartorial elegance of the Paddy standing next to me and when Nick took a sneaky peek at him, he burst out laughing. 'Have you seen his wellies?' Nick said to me. 'Yes, he's got 'L' & 'R' written on the back of them,' I replied. Nick looked at me and shook his head and said, 'but have you noticed the daft sod has got his wellies on the wrong feet?' Laugh! I nearly asked the barman for a shot of lime! When the barman put our drinks in front of us, we both took a gulp and immediately looked at each other in amazement. The lager tasted fantastic. We were enjoying the lager that much, when we were halfway down our drinks, we got our money out and checked to see if we could afford another pint. But sadly, after putting our bus fare to one side we only had 10p or 15p left.

We were cursing our luck that we didn't have enough money to buy another couple of pints, when an idea popped into my head. 'If we paid children's fares on the bus, we could afford a pint between us.' Nick agreed and we put our coppers on the bar. When the barman came over to us I ordered two halves of lager. The barman looked quizzically at us and said, 'what's the craic, can't you boys drink?' I explained that we thought the lager was fantastic, but we'd ran out of money. The barman took our little pile of money off the bar and went off to pour our drinks. When he returned with our drinks, he was holding pint not half glasses. As the barman put the two pints in front of us, I was just about to say 'we had only ordered halves' but the barman gave us a simple nod of the head, then walked away to his other customers.

What a result! After a bit of argy-bargy with the bus driver, he allowed us to pay child's fare. The bus driver had commented that 'he could smell alcohol on our breath' to which I replied 'we were underage drinkers' - which was true!

We had an unusually quiet journey back home to Aldridge as Nick seemed to be deep in thought. I didn't really think much of it and left Nick to his pondering. As usual, round about twelve-ish the next morning, I called round to Nick's house before going up to the Cedar Tree. I was a bit surprised when his mom told me, 'Nick went out on his own, about an hour ago.' This was very unusual behaviour. Like the 'lads Friday-night out' was now set in stone, so was our Sunday routine: a Wank, a fry up, read the back of the Sunday papers, meet the lads for a few pints up the Tree, watch Star Soccer and count how many times we could hear 'you're goin' get your fuckin' head kicked in', Sunday Dinner, a kick about down in the woods, Sunday tea, put out on my best Falmer baggy jeans with obligatory half-inch turn-ups, splash on some Brut - and head for The Elms disco.

I didn't see Nick until he sheepishly walked into the Elms late on the Sunday evening. Nick was embarrassed to admit that he had gone back to Birmingham to spray over his name that he had left on the wall near St. Andrews. When I asked him why had it and taken him so long, he replied that he had walked around Bordesley Green and Small Heath for hours trying to find somewhere that sold spray cans. Then travelling back on the bus from Birmingham, an inspector got on and discovered he had only paid for a child's ticket. Because Nick didn't have any more money with him, the inspector made him get off the bus in Kingstanding and Nick had to walk the rest of the way back to Aldridge. I thought to myself, 'Nick - for an ex-grammar school kid, you do some bloody stupid things.'

Throughout the summer, the Sun newspaper was obsessed with two things. One of them was teddy boys and punks having running battles up and down the King's Road in Chelsea. Never in a month of Sundays could I understand that fabricated punk-rock look. Vivienne Westwood and Malcolm McLaren must have been laughing all the way to the bank. Talk about the king's new clothes. The Sun's other obsession was Man United and Chelsea hooligans. While United had been running riot at away games in Division One, Chelsea had been doing exactly the same thing in Division Two but when Chelsea were promoted the Sun made a big deal about the bitter rivalry between the two sets of supporters. It published photographs of so-called Chelsea and United hooligans with scarfs around their faces to hide their identity. The Sun sensationally wrote that both sets of fans were planning their battle strategies and stockpiling all manner of weapons including petrol bombs, ready for when the country's most feared hooligans came face to face at Old Trafford in September. The Sun stated that the public would witness the worst outbreak of violence ever seen at the football ground. Like punk rock it was a load of bollocks. Sure there would be trouble when the two teams met, but it wasn't going to turn into World War Three as predicted by the Sun.

§

Aldridge was hardly the Bronx, but it had it's fair share of violent individuals and a few fighting gangs. I was closely associated with a gang of West Brom fans. Nick and me would regularly drink with them whenever we were in the Whitehouse. They were all at least a year older than me and their ranks included Mad Mick, Big Todd Yates, Nash, Kenny Bishop, Sammy Bradford, The Johnson Brothers, Brookhouse and Pollard. Mad Mick needs no introduction; Todd was at the head of the gang that once visited The St. Francis Catholic School and Todd had a bloody and bruising battle with their head-boy and many years later the head-boy became my bank manager; Nash carved a letter 'N' into the front soles of his Docka's. so when he gave someone a good kicking, his victim would be covered in small 'N's;

Kenny always reminded me of Troy Tempest from the puppet show Stingray, but Kenny had thicker eyebrows! As well as being a 'game lad' Kenny was also one for the ladies. Whether walking down the street, in a shop, or on a bus, if a girl took his fancy he would immediately approach her and start giving her his patter, he had no inhibitions when it came to the girls. I was with Kenny one time and he spent about fifteen minutes at a supermarket checkout trying to persuade a girl to give him her telephone number. The poor girl was extremely embarrassed and her face was red as a beetroot. He never did get her telephone number. 'It's all a numbers game,' Kenny would say; his hit rate was one in twenty.

Aldridge and Streetly had a long standing rivalry and we heard via Nick's new girlfriend that there was going to be a house party in Streetly and Nick was the only one invited. Me and a dozen of the West Brom boys decided to go to Streetly and gate-crash the party. After having a few drinks at the Buccaneer pub, we all made our way over. When we arrived at the house we were told in no uncertain manner that Nick was the only one with an invite and the rest of us weren't welcome. Nick tried to persuade the girl who was hosting the party to let us in, but to no avail.

We all resigned ourselves to the fact that we would have to find our entertainment elsewhere. That was, all of us except Nick, who decided to stay with his girlfriend and attend the party. A lot of the boys, especially Mad Mick, were very upset about Nick deserting the gang and said that he would be in serious trouble next time they saw him. We wandered back round to the Buccaneer pub and we just about to go inside when two car loads of Streetly kids pulled up in the car park.

Straight away a few of the West Brom lads recognized the kids in the two cars and rushed towards them. When one of the Streetly kids opened the car door and attempted to get out, Kenny immediately kicked the door back onto the kids leg and, just for good measure, slammed the door another couple of times against the passengers leg. The Streetly kid was screaming like a pig and soon his leg was covered in blood. The first car was only a two-door and because of the leg injury sustained by the front-seat passenger and the fact the driver was battered the second he got out of the car, the four kids in the backseat couldn't get out of the car. Mick jumped onto the boot of the front car and did his best to kick in the back window. He was soon joined by a couple of his mates, who were trying to break the side windows and pull the kids off the backseat and out of the car.

Meanwhile the Streetly kids in the second car were getting 'tools' out of the boot. But when Big Todd and a few other boys charged straight into them, the Streetly kids dropped their tools and tried to get back inside their car. One Streetly kid was dragged from the back of the car as it attempted to reverse off the car park and he ended up with little 'N's all over his face. By the time a few of the locals came out from the pub to break things up, three or four of the Streetly kids lay beaten on the floor and the first car had two broken windows and too many dents to count. Oh, and a very badly soiled backseat, where four of the Streetly kids had crapped themselves.

Next morning I called round for Nick and sarcastically asked him 'if he'd enjoyed the party'. I told Nick that he was now very unpopular with Mick, Big Todd and the rest of their gang and I suggested that he kept his distance for a few weeks. Much to my surprise Nick said he wanted to get it over and done with and would go and face them all at the Elms disco that evening. I couldn't decide if I thought Nick was very brave or very stupid. As Nick and me approached the Elms car park there was already half a dozen of the West Brom boys standing outside the pub. I think I was more nervous than Nick. As soon as we were noticed, one of the gang walked over to us and grabbed Nick by the throat, he was soon joined by one of his mates, who punched Nick straight in the face. I was totally helpless; all I could do was to stand by and watch my best mate get knocked about a bit. I'm sure I would have made things worse if I had of got involved.

Luckily, within a few minutes it was all over. Nick was called a deserting wanker and a cunt and told he wasn't welcome in their company again and that seemed to be the end of it. But when Nick and me were queuing to get into the disco, Mick appeared on the scene. Mick marched over to Nick and pulled out a knife. 'I've got a little something for you.' Mick told a terrified Nick. I had no doubts that Mick would use a knife; only a few weeks earlier I was in the back of Mick's knackered old Scrott (scooter) and Mick spotted a couple of lads walking towards us. 'We're going to have these two,' Mick shouted to me and drove onto the footpath. Dumping his Scrott on the floor, he approached the startled lads and within a few seconds they were both on the deck. Still wearing his crash helmet Mick head-butted one of them then proceeded to lay into the other kid with his cosh. My only involvement was to drag Mick away.

If Mick was capable of doing that to total strangers, I could well imagine what he would do to people who had upset or crossed him. Watching Nick being roughed up was one thing, but there was no way I could stand by and let him be stabbed, even if Mick was doing the stabbing. I had a lot of history with Mick and as soon has he had produced his knife, I tried to reason with him and, gambling on our friendship, I told Mick, that I couldn't just stand on the side-lines and watch my best mate being stabbed. Mick gave me a long hard stare and then an agreeable sadistic little smile appeared on his face and Mick put the knife back in his pocket, and Nick and me both gave a large sigh of relief.

§

After being given all the crap jobs to do, I had fallen out with Frank, my Irish workmate. So I got myself a job as an apprentice bricklayer with another building company based in Great Barr. But in the three or four months that I worked for them, I didn't lay a single brick, instead I found myself working on the Mods (modernization/refurbing of council houses) in Lozells and Winson Green, the latter being almost a two-hour bus journey from Aldridge.

I worked with men from mixed backgrounds and I quickly discovered they had little or no experience in the building Industry. On my first day I struck up a friendship with a happy-go-lucky but totally useless South African called Steve. Steve lived in a shabby bed-sit on Nechells Park Road and he happily boasted that in his neighbourhood there was a pub on every corner - which was handy for Steve as he was a borderline alcoholic.

Even in the 70's Nechells was very ethnic, and the smell of Asian cooking hit you as soon as you got off the Number 8 bus. In every sense, Nechells was a world away from Aldridge and a bloody long bus ride! So to save on bus-fare and travel time, I started to stay at Steve's little place a couple of nights a week.

There was two major drawbacks with this – one, I had to 'top and tail' and share Steve's grotty bed, and, two, Steve had a habit of pissing the bed and, depending on which way he was lying, I could receive an unwanted golden shower. The last time I stayed at Steve's place, I thought I would sleep on the settee to avoid the possibility of him pissing over me in the night. But a very drunk Steve got out of his bed in the 'wee small hours' and did his weeing on his settee with me on it! 'Would you Adam and Eve it?'

Another Nice but Dim (when it came to building work) fellow was called Dave Wakeling. He soon left the building game behind him and became the lead singer of the Birmingham Ska band, The Beat. I nearly fell off my chair the first time I saw my old mate Dave on Top of the Pops.

After a week or two working on the Mods, I found myself acting as a ganger (a head labourer) supervising all the other labourers. I was quite happy with this role and very 'hands on' until I realized that labourers got 30p per hour more than an apprentice. With overtime, the labourers were taking home £15.00 a week more than me and I was supervising them. Talk about taking the piss. I spoke to the works manager about the situation, stating 'I wanted to work with other bricklayers and be on the trowel or be paid the same as the labourers.' The works manager said he would work something out, but weeks went by and I was still on an apprentice's pay rate.

Being an enterprising and resourceful young man, I soon found ways, to top up my pay packet. I was digging up the slabs in one of the back gardens, when I came across some lead pipe. I immediately abandoned the task of lifting slabs and followed the route of the lead pipe. The pipe lead almost to the top of the long garden, where it formed a 'T' junction. I dug up the pipe to both the far left and right of the garden and, with a hammer and chisel, separated it. When water spurted out, I simply tapped the end of the pipe together with my hammer and thought no more of it. I rolled up all the lead pipe and hid it in one of the old outside toilets.

Some hours later a representative of the Water Board turned up and asked if we had running water on the property, because at least half the street had lost their water supply. Silly old me! I'd only gone and chopped through and nicked the main water pipe for the whole of Carpenters Road.

In between Afrikaans lessons, Steve and me would remove plaster decorations and ornate fireplaces and sell them to a tatter, who would call in and see us a couple of times a week, but the most lucrative find was a stash of pre-war one-pound notes. We were asked to remove a few rotten floorboards from an upstairs bedroom; in doing so we located a pile of cash. Originally there must have been hundreds of notes but sadly the mice had got to them before us. It was like confetti between the floor joists. Still there was about fifty or sixty notes in pretty good nick and we sold them to a collectors shop in the middle of Brum. Little did I know, that if I had taken the confetti money to a bank, it could have been weighed and we could have received even more cash.

After finding our cash bonanza, Steve and me spent the next week or so, ripping up floor boards in all the houses we were working in. We found one or two little goodies but no more cash, but instead of nailing the floorboards back down, we sold the 'aged floorboards' to the tatter man. All this was going on under the nose of that incompetent and or uncaring works manager.

One Thursday afternoon (pay day) he turned up late on-site and asked Steve and me if we would work over and move two tons of ready-mix concrete. I initially agreed, but when I open my pay packet, I was still only being paid apprentice rates. The works manager had been promising me for weeks to sort out my money and now I'd just about had enough. I told him where he could stick his job and his two-ton of ready-mix, which had just been delivered. On hearing this Steve said 'if he's not staying over, neither am I.'

The works manager was completely fucked. There was two ton of wet concrete at the side of the road and no one to shift it. Almost in tears he pleaded with us to assist, but we flatly refused. He had no choice but to do the job himself.

I took great delight in seeing him take off his jacket, roll up his sleeves and start filling a wheelbarrow with concrete. Just to add salt to his wounds, I lent against a lamppost for twenty minutes and applauded him, as he shovelled concrete. For some reason, the miserable bastard never sent me the 'glowing reference' he promised me.

Maybe it was my austere childhood, or that I was an instinctive hoarder, or I had a few mental health issues, or probably all three of them, but I would get emotionally attached to inanimate items such as my favourite toys. In later years it would be United memorabilia, clothes, records, paintings and porn mags. Losing any of the afore-mentioned items would feel like losing joyful memories or even a friend. The scientific explanation is that the brain forms an image of the body's homeostatic sensations in the 'primary interoceptive cortex'. This area is located in the insula, which is linked to emotion (the body's homeostasis), as well as empathy. This theory is supported by MRI imaging, which shows activity in the insular cortex when one is asked to feel one's own heartbeat or empathize with the pain or emotional state of others. There's another school of thought – that thinks 'FUCKIN NUTTER'.

I kept most of my 'precious things' in a large airing cupboard that was situated in my bedroom. My most valued positions included my Quick Draw integral gun holster with Colt 45 peacemakers, which I received on of my 10th birthday, and Little Joe and his black-and-white pinto horse along with the rest of my bonanza memorabilia. These I'd accumulated over several Christmas's. There was also a two-foot long Jaguar Sports car and just like 'Stinky Pete' it had never been out it's box.

One evening after returning home from work, I went to get some clothes out of the airing cupboard and I immediately noticed that all my Bonanza toys were missing along with my gun belt and my large racing car. I went straight downstairs and questioned Mom about the missing items. She casually informed me 'I didn't need them any more, so she'd given them away.' When I asked her who she had given the toys to, she replied, 'I don't know - it was a friend of Brenda's.' Some of my most cherished possessions and she didn't know who she'd given them to!

As the conversation continued Mom told me, that Brenda, her friend who lived in Pelsall, had called in a few days earlier with another woman and a young boy who she had not met before. To stop the young boy from getting bored (more like - stop him from interrupting their mindless gossiping) my Mom went in search of toys to keep him occupied. When my Mom gave the boy my toys to play with, the boy's mother commented 'he's got nothing like this at home' and without a second thought, Mom said, 'Steven is too old to play with them now, you can take them home with you if you like.' So as Brenda and her friend left to get the bus, my Mom slung the jewels of my childhood into a few old carrier bags and handed them over to someone she had never met before. I would have been a bit upset if I knew someone had even played with my prized possessions; but for my Mom to simply give them away, was unthinkable.

But the unthinkable had now happened. Initially I was boiling mad and demanded that my Mom contact Brenda and tell her to return the toys immediately. Whether true or not, Mom said she couldn't find Brenda's phone number. When I said she should drive round to Brenda's house she refused, stating 'it would be embarrassing.' My anger turned to melancholy shock. I was dismayed, despondent, disillusioned, heartbroken and then angry again. It seemed my Mom knew or cared little about me. How could she not know, how upset I would be if I lost cherished items that I'd kept safe for six or seven years? I couldn't have been more upset, if she had burned my United scarfs.

§

The only pub in the Walsall area where I had trouble getting in was the infamous Dilke. The sign on the door stated 'OVER 21'S ONLY' and I would say the average age of most of the clientele was early twenties. The Dilke was the only local pub, that put on live bands and also had a disco every night and on Thursdays, Fridays and Saturdays. The bar was open until 1:00 am. There was also a very under-used restaurant (small eating area)

With its heady cocktail of live music, scampi in baskets and a late bar, the Dilke attracted many young women. One young lady that caught my eye was named Anita. Soon there was a three-year, on-off love triangle involving Tina, Anita and me. Some fifteen years down the line, I ended up marrying Anita. What a rollercoaster ride that turned out to be.

Nick and me had only been to the Dilke a few times when we got caught up in a very nasty gang fight. We were just leaving the pub when we saw two cars parked near the pub doors and the occupants jumped out the cars and attacked two other lads. The other two lads were getting a real beating. Wearing our sheriff's badges and white

Stetsons, Nick and me, went to the aid of the outnumbered lads. Thinking back, getting involved with a gang fight in a dark car park was a very stupid thing to do; we didn't even know who was who, or what was going on. Nick and me could have easily ended up getting battered ourselves. Fortunately, when we pointed out to the gang that the other two lads had already had a good kicking, they pretty quickly got their boots off the heads of their prostrate adversary's.

One of the gang was quick to tell me that the two lads on the floor were part of a gang that, a few days earlier, had badly beaten one of their friends and who was now in hospital. On top of that, the two lads on the floor had just beaten up another one of their mates in the Dilke toilets.

While this conversation was taking place, one of the lads on the floor got up and started to run to safety. Unfortunately for him, one of the bouncers quickly rugby-tackled him to the ground and proceeded to bounce his head off the tarmac. The bouncer in question was the well known Rocky; he had a reputation for taking no nonsense and he scared the life out of me and my mates. The fired-up Rocky then dragged his prey towards the pub entrance and when the lad tried to struggle free, Rocky set about him again, this time using his fists and boots. Once again Nick and me intervened and, as politely as possible, informed Rocky that if he continued he would probably kill his victim. The lad pleaded for mercy and begged Nick and me to help him. This lad looked like he'd been in a car crash, he was so badly beaten he could barely stand.

Swapping our metaphorical Stetsons for St John's ambulance hats, Nick and me helped the lad to a seat inside the pub and the lights inside the pub emphasised his injuries even more. Nick and me were so shocked and incensed at the state of him that we agreed we would wait for the police and give a statement, telling how Rocky gave him an unnecessary beating. While we were sitting with the bruised and bloody lad, another one of the Dilke's infamous doormen, Abbey Heath, approached us. (And here's another one for you Peaky Blinder fans – there was an 'Abbey Heath' from the Black Country in Series 3.) Abbey Heath asked why we were sitting with this lad and I replied 'we were going to give a statement to the police when they turned up.'

'Have you seen what this cunt and his mates has gone to the kid in the toilets?' Abbey Heath growled through gritted teeth, then added, 'come and have a look at this!' He then led Nick and me into the toilets where we saw an unconscious man on the floor and he was almost as badly beaten as Rocky's punch-bag. 'That cunt sitting out there, deserved every thing he got,' Abbey Heath snapped at us. This put a completely different perspective on things – 'he who lives by the sword' and all that stuff. Nick and me went and sat at the bar and had a little rethink. Did we really want to get on the wrong side of people like Rocky and Abbey Heath? and if we did give a statement, we wouldn't get back into the Dilke again. Maybe the lad we helped back into the pub, did deserve everything he got. But it was Nick who swayed things. He pointed out we were only seventeen, thus underage drinkers. If we gave a statement, our true age would no doubt be revealed and we could end up in court ourselves.

Just as we were about to leave, the police appeared in the entrance of the pub and started talking to the bouncers. All the customers had now left the Dilke and, thinking we would look conspicuous walking past the police and the bouncers, I decided to look for an alternative exit. The nearest door I could see was behind the bar and it lead directly into the kitchen area. Leading Nick by the arm, we went behind the bar and through the door into the kitchen.

As soon as we walked into the kitchen I noticed several boxes of crisps stacked on top of each other. We all get the munchies after a few pints and I couldn't resist grabbing a few bags. Nick went straight past the crisps and opened the door of a large stainless steel fridge and stored inside it was the biggest piece of cheese I had ever seen. The giant lump of cheese must have been 2' long by a foot wide and six inches high. Without hesitation we pulled it out of the fridge and made our way out of the kitchen. Checking the coast was clear, we exited the back of the pub and started the hour-long walk home.

We soon wondered if we had done the right thing. The giant lump of cheese must have weighed almost a hundredweight and even taking it in turns to carry it, knackered us. So halfway home, we used the edge of a brick wall to crudely cut the cheese in a half (some thing you'll never see a TV chef do – bunch of poofs), and like a pair of giant mice we nibbled on our cheese until we arrived home. I must have eaten at least a pound of cheese and dreamt about giants mousetraps all night. The down side of bringing such a massive piece of cheese home was bleedin' cheese sandwiches for work for the next month.

After all the bollocks of Christmas Day dinner, Nick drove us off to Martin's new home, a pub just on the edge of Tipton. Nick's Uncle Gerry had previously run the Hobmoor, a very rough pub in Yardley, Birmingham. Gerry had being robbed several times while at the Hobmoor and in one of the robberies he got beaten up pretty bad and spent a few days in hospital. Moving to Tipton was like jumping out of the frying pan into the fire!

Fortunately, on my first visit only a few select customers were invited to the pub, and the bar had a nice party atmosphere. I thought I came from a dysfunctional family, but we had nothing on Martin and his siblings. The eldest of Martin's two brothers spent most of his time in a tent pitched In the back yard and more often than not he would have the family dog for company, which was a massive Pyrenean mountain dog. Martin's youngest brother spent most of his time hidden behind the sofa; at mealtimes his mom would have try and coax him out. 'Come on darling it's time to have something to eat,' his mom would calmly say. 'Fuck off - I'm not hungry,' was often the young cherub's reply. I never heard Martin's sister speak; she always had a vacant look her on her face and she just sat and stared at the telly, morning, noon and night, whether the TV was on or not, all in all a very weird chick. Martin's mom was a warm, fun-loving woman and a proper Mrs. Robinson. She had her tongue down my throat a couple of times that night and if it wasn't for my old lollipop lady from Kingstanding (aka Nick and Martin's Nan) it might well have gone further.

The pub had just taken delivery of one of those new-fangled pool tables. (Pool tables were going into many bars at the time.) To avoid paying 15p per game, Martin had furnished himself with a key to the paying device and with all the free practice, he'd become quite an accomplished player. When Martin was playing, and usually winning, against customers, the customers had to pay up and put

15p in the slot. One particular Irish gentlemen had waited his turn to play Martin at pool, but seemed to be having problems putting his 5p and 10p in the slot. 'It just wont go in,' the Paddy kept saying. When Martin went to his assistance, he noticed that somehow the Paddy had managed to squeeze his 10p in the 5p section and the 5p sat in 10p section and Martin pointed out that he'd got the coins the wrong way round. As Martin returned to the other side of the pool table, the Paddy fiddled about with the coins for a few more minutes, then exasperated shouted out, 'I turned the coins the other way round, but it still isn't feking working!' Frustrated, Martin marched back round the table to see what was going on and immediately noticed that the 10p was still sitting in the 5p section, 'You still haven't changed the coins around,' Martin snapped. 'Yes I have' replied the Paddy then added, 'last time the Heads were facing down and you told me they were the wrong way round – now the Heads are facing up and you're still telling me there the wrong way round.' At that Martin lost his patience. 'You bleedin' thick Mick – it doesn't matter if Heads or Tails are face up or down, but it does matter if you put the 10p in the 5p section and the 5p in the 10p section!' The whole bar burst into laughter, the only one who didn't see the funny side of it was the red faced Paddy.

We had a great night and I loved the fact that we could go behind the bar and pull our own pints. Nick, Martin and me could hardly stand by the time Martin's mom had thrown out the last of the customers but Martin wasn't done yet. There was an ITV program at that time called NAME THAT TUNE. For those of you that don't remember the show: the host read a clue to a song and the contestants alternated, bidding as to how few notes they needed to identify the song. Each contestant stated their bid to their opponent in the infamous format 'I can name that tune in?..' seven being the highest number of notes, one being least.

Martin picked up a half-pint glass and stopping at every optic on the back shelf, almost filled the glass to the rim. He then slammed the glass on the bar and said, 'I'll drink that drink in seven.' To which I replied, 'I'll drink that drink in six' and Nick slurred 'I'll drink that drink in five,' and on we went until Martin finally said, 'I'll drink that drink in one' - to which Nick and me both shouted out, 'Drink that Drink!' Being the piss head he was, Martin immediately picked up the glass of spirits and slowly started to 'Drink That Drink in One'! When he'd finished the drink, he slammed the empty glass back on the bar and gave us a triumphant smile, then much to mine and Nick's amusement, he promptly passed out on the floor.

We couldn't wake Martin and we certainly couldn't move the big lump, so Nick and me spent the night on the bench seats in the bar. When I eventually woke up next morning, I had the hangover from hell and I was on my second cup of strong tea when I noticed the time and realised I've missed the coach up to Everton. I was really disappointed that I was going to miss the game, It would have been my first trip to Scouse land. To add salt to my wounds, United had their biggest away win in years and beat Everton 6 – 2. I bet half the Everton team must have been playing 'drink that drink' the night before.

§

Some things in the building game were great, but working outside in the winter was horrible, months of freezing cold, wet and muddy conditions. Travelling home on the bus was always awkward and uncomfortable if my clothes were dirty and wet, as they were most nights. I was treated like a leper as I walked down the bus looking for a seat. I can remember people looking at me and I just knew what they were thinking, 'for fucks sake, don't sit next to me.' When I picked a seat, the person next to me would get as close to the window as possible to avoid contact with my grubby apparel.

When I arrived home there was a nightly ritual of work clothes over the radiators and muddy boots in front of the fire and, as there were three of us that worked in the building trade, our living room and hallway often looked like Mr. Wu's Chinese laundry. In an attempt to avoid working outside during the winter, I went for an interview in an engineering factory. The factory was nice and warm, but it was also very noisy, very smelly and was dimly lit and had no natural light. As the works manager was showing me around the shop floor and explaining the repetitive duties I would have to undertake, I felt a big black cloud engulf me and I literarily felt scared and panic stricken, as if I was alone in a spooky haunted house at midnight. I cut the works manager short: 'sorry to interrupt, but there's no way I could work in a place like this!' That said, I walked off the factory floor and into a long corridor that lead to the street.

As I walked down the warm and clean corridor, I noticed a young kid sitting in one of the offices. He looked a little younger than me and was smartly dressed in a suit and tie. The lucky sod was flirting with an attractive young secretary who had just handed him a cup of tea. I was green with envy and immediately thought of all the time I wasted at school. 'What I wouldn't give for a office job like that,' I thought to myself. Reality instantly kicked in and a voiced laughed inside my head and shouted out, 'you've got more chance of being signed by United, than you getting a desk job!'

I went straight to the job centre then looked in the job section of the Evening Mail and Express and Star, but no there was nothing doing. In desperation, that evening I called up Uncle Gra (aka Graham Walker), a family friend and a one-time working partner of Mickey Gibbs. Uncle Gra was a bricklayer, of sorts, and worked in a '4 and 2 gang' (four bricklayers and two hod carriers) on site throughout Birmingham and the surrounding areas. I asked Uncle Gra if he had any work going. Uncle Gra enquired 'what are you like on the hod (basically using a V-shaped open trough on a pole, to carrying bricks and compo on my shoulder). I'd occasionally done an hour or two here and there but never full time, but I told him a few white lies and he told me I could start the next day.

Uncle Gra and his long suffering wife, had been friends of my family for some years, so for the craic, I called Graham 'Uncle Gra', plus his wife, with her high-pitched cockney accent, always referred to him as 'Graaah'. Uncle Gra was no oil painting. At work he was disagreeable and curt, but he was good company in the pub and was every inch a rough-and-ready man's man.

There's probably hundreds of stories that I could tell about Uncle Gra, but the one I think that sums him up the best is this. After drinking very heavily at a New Year's Eve party at my parents house, Uncle Gra and his wife fell into their battered old Volvo and, in the early hours of New Year's Day, started to snake their way back home to Great Barr. They weren't far from home when Uncle Gra went straight over the traffic island that sat just outside the Tree's pub on the Queslett Road. The impact of the tyres bouncing over the perimeter kerb caused the front passenger door to fly open and Mrs. Walker was flung out of the car. In his Drunken stupor, Uncle Gra didn't notice his wife was no longer in the car and carried on driving towards home with the open passenger door bouncing off stationery cars. Uncle Gra parked his car outside his house, as only a drunk driver would, and made his way inside. As soon as he got inside his house, he started to shout for his wife, 'Moira, Moira – Moira where the fuck are you?' He was just about to take himself to bed when there was a loud knock on his front door. Uncle Gra staggered towards the door and flung it open, standing in front of him was a stranger - and Moira, who was covered from head to toe in mud. The good-hearted stranger had witnessed Uncle Gra's erratic driving and Moira being catapulted out of the speeding car and had gone to her rescue and even though she was filthy dirty and soaking wet from the sodden grass he had offered her a lift home. Uncle Gra made no comment about the state of his wife or who the stranger was, he just grabbed Moira by the arm and pulled her into the house and said 'I need my shoes taking off' then, without a thank you, a Happy New Year or a kiss my arse, he slammed the door in the face of the good Samaritan.

Thankfully I started my hod-carrying job on a Thursday and I got the weekend to recover. I thought I was fairly fit, but two days of running up a ladder with half a hundredweight of bricks on my shoulder absolutely knackered me. I'd almost worn my fingertips away from handling the coarse bricks and every muscle in my body ached. It wasn't just running up and down a ladder that took its toll. To avoid the long pole of the hod knocking over piles of brick on the narrow scaffolding the gang had reduced the size of the stale, so the hod only stood just over three-foot high; this meant I had to physically lift the hod from waist height up onto my shoulder. Because two of the brickies threw down bricks like machines, I had no chance of a breather. On the hod = 'hardest game in the world'.

One advantage of working with a bricklaying gang, if it rained or got too cold we took shelter in the site shanty (aka shed). If the brickies were fortunate enough to be on daywork, they would rub ice on the thermometer that sat next to the shanty door. If the temperature dropped below freezing we couldn't lay bricks because the frost would crack the mortar. It was fine skiving off in the shanty as long as the Irish ground workers weren't sharing air space. When the Jacks and the Culchies started to get a little excited and were having the craic with each other, us English boys couldn't understand a bleedin' word they were saying. They sounded like feral cats having a shag.

When we were working in Hockley and Handsworth, the site agent was always asking the Job Centre to send him labourers. Usually young Afro-Caribbean lads would turn up on site. They all seemed to have massive chips on their shoulders and 100% they didn't want to be on a building site. Some of them lasted the day but never returned, a few wandered off at dinnertime never to return and one or two of them left at breakfast (10:00) never to return.

One of lads from the job centre that did stay, was lad about my age and he was put in charge of the plants and the stores. When I asked him his name he told me everyone called him 'Molly'. I didn't ask why and he didn't tell me. Besides keeping the site tidy and making tea for the site agent, Molly was responsible for ensuring all dumper trucks were locked away in the compound each evening and checking in deliveries from the builder's merchants such as windows, doors and frames, lead, copper pipe and electrical items.

When the weather got a little better and the nights got a little lighter, I would stay behind after the brickies had left, then me and Molly would race the large dumper trucks around the site. It was great fun until Molly crashed his dumper truck into the site manager's portacabin. The corner of the portacabin was damaged and the side window had almost fallen out. Molly was almost in tears and pleaded with me not to tell anyone what he'd done. I reassured him that I wouldn't say anything then we did our best to patch up the damage. We pushed the window frame back into position and to hide the damage we lent a few bits and pieces against the damaged corner. Our efforts were all in vain, because when the site manager went into his portacabin the following morning and slammed the door shut, the window frame fell out and this caused the items we'd used to cover the damaged corner to fall over and expose the battered exterior.

Every day after work, I had to go into the centre of Brum to get the Harpers bus back to Aldridge. One evening I was walking along and counting the pennies in the palm of my hand to make sure I didn't have to try and pay child's fare on the bus. I'd just established I'd got enough money and I was just about to put the loose change back into my pocket when I walked past an old wrinkly newspaper seller sitting in his little wooden hut.

'Late - Eddyy – Shaanne,' he bellowed out just as I was passing him. I was in a little world of my own after counting my money and the ear-piercing sound of the newspaper vendor made me jump and caused my money to leap out of my hand and roll down the sloping pavement that lead to the dimly lit subway. I chased down the subway, desperately keeping and eye on my rolling bus fare.

Fortunately I manage to pick up my final coin from the floor, but as I looked up I saw the suit of my dreams in the window of Nelson House. It was a powder-blue three-piece with 16" flared trousers, a skin-tight waistcoat and lapels big enough to land a small plane on. The cost of the suit was well over a week's wages for me, but every day I would stop outside Nelson House and admire the 'whistle and flute' and in a Waynesque manner thought, 'it will be mine - oh yes - it will be mine.'

Somehow I needed more money, but where would I get it from? Now I didn't exactly blackmail Molly, but I did point out that I had kept quiet regarding the damage to the portacabin before I asked him to assist me removing some goodies, like lead and copper pipe from the stores. Molly was a willing accomplice and once I'd sorted my mate Kirby to lay on some transport, we removed all the lead and copper from the stores then smashed the door and padlock to fake a break in. I'd already got a builder lined up to take swag and when we dropped it off I got pocket full of cash and an order for ten internal doors. Molly was once again willing to assist but, to my amazement, he wouldn't accept any payment. Strange kid.

During working hours Molly put the doors in one of the garages on site and told me he wouldn't be around to help load the doors, that was solely down me. As he refused to take a 'back hander' I thought that was fair enough. Once again I roped in Kirby to supply the transport and another pair of hands for loading the doors into Kirby's van. All had gone to plan, Kirby was loading the last door into his van when I noticed a brand new sheet of inch ply that the doors that had been stacked on.

Thinking I could get an extra few quid for the sheet of plywood, I started to lift it up. For those of you who are not familiar with handling one-inch-thick sheets of plywood: as you lift, your hands follow your feet, so as you walk forward, lifting the sheet of ply in the process, your hands move up the sheet of ply and you usually look upwards. I followed this well-practiced manoeuvre but what I didn't know was that the sheet of plywood was put on the garage floor to cover an open manhole. While lifting the plywood I took a few steps forward, then CRASH – BANG – WALLOP I plunged down into a two-foot deep manhole and the heavy sheet of ply came clattering down on top of me. The plywood hit me square on the forehead and gave me the worst headache I had ever had. I also bashed and blooded both shins as I fell.

Kirby came to my rescue and, cursing the sheet of plywood, I left it on the garage floor. As Kirby was coming off the site, he decided to miss out the main entrance and take 'a safer shortcut' across a field. This meant driving through a small gap between the tree and a tall finger post.

As we approached the gap, I thought 'this is going to be tight, I hope he's going to slow down. It was and he didn't and both wing mirrors were knocked off his van. We had only gone a few miles, when we were pulled over by the coppers for having no wing mirrors. Kirby gave them some cock-and-bull story about his van being vandalized while he was working on the site and the two coppers seem to accept it and after a little look around the van, they sent us on our way. Why they didn't look inside the van, I'll never know.

That evening I had arranged to drive over and see a new girlfriend of mine, a very attractive girl from Erdington. Nick was also coming along as he was trying to get off with her friend. But with a large red mark across my forehead, battered shins and a headache from hell, I really didn't fancy it. But when Clev bought round his car for me to borrow for the evening, I thought, 'oh sod it, I might end up getting a hand job.'

Clev was Ade's brother-in-law and he'd been to a few United games with me and Ade, so I got to know him fairly well. Clev was the only person I knew who had tattoos on his hands and just like The Wanderer 'he tore open his shirt and he'd got "Rosie" tattooed on his chest'. He was quite a lad in his day and was still a scary character.

Even though I hadn't passed my test, amazingly Clev had still agreed to let me have his souped-up Hillman Imp to go over to Erdington. 'Give her one for me,' Clev said as he handed me his car keys, then added, 'don't get smashing up my car.' I confidently replied, 'I'll look after it for you.' Nick had passed his driving test and I don't think he was impressed with my driving, because several times he

251

suggested maybe he should drive, which would have been the sensible thing to do, but me being brash, full of bravado and foolish, I insisted on driving. I'd promised Clev I'd put some petrol in his car but being inexperienced at the petrol pumps, I almost put diesel in his petrol tank. Luckily for me, Nick spotted my mistake and put me right and told me we wouldn't have got very far if I had put in diesel - that's what a grammar school education does for you.

We were about half-an-hour late meeting the girls and they were not impressed with our tardiness and I wasn't impressed when my new girlfriend asked for a brandy and Babycham – it cost over a quid! The night didn't go well, I didn't even get a snog let alone a hand job, and I'm sure I didn't see the girl again. Not at a quid a drink, I didn't.

I was driving back home and struggling to find my gears, instead of slowing down or asking Nick to drive, I looked down at the gear stick for a few seconds, trying to work out what I was doing it wrong. Suddenly Nick screamed out, 'Grange!!! – Brake!!!!' I looked up and to my horror there was a car just a few feet in front of me, waiting to turn right. I smashed right into the back of him.

I sat there for a few seconds in total shock and then Nick said we should get out and check the damage. I had run into the back of an Austin Maxi, which was built like a small tank and there was hardly any damage to it, sadly the fragile Hillman Imp came off a lot worse; both wings and headlights were smashed and the bonnet was hanging on by a thread. I exchanged names and addresses with the other driver; I gave false details and then asked Nick to drive the rest of the way home. We limped home at about 10 mph and when we got to Clev's house, we sat outside for a good twenty minutes, while I plucked up the courage to knock on Clev's door and tell him what I'd done.

Feeling physically sick, I eventually knocked on the closed door and waited to face the music. 'You must have had a good night if you're this late,' Clev said jovially, when he opened the door. His mood soon changed when I told him what had happened. Clev pushed me aside and marched over to his car to inspect the damage. Shaking like leaf, I told Clev I'd pay for the damage. 'Fucking right you will,' Clev snapped. As Clev continued to inspect the damage then said, 'I think you'd better fuck off, before I lose my temper!'

I took the short walk round to my house and went straight to bed. I was absolutely shattered but worried about how I would pay the repair bill for Clev's car and whether Clev would give me a good hiding. It took me an eternity to get off to sleep.

When I woke the next morning, I was still in shock, sick, despondent and totally dejected. I had never felt so low in my life before. I lay in bed for ages, ignoring my Mom's calls to get up and go to work. Grasping at straws I lay there thinking, 'could that have happened last night? Surely it must have been a dream?' Then I started to think of all the things that had happened the day before: what if that sheet of plywood had knocked me out? what if the copper had discovered the stolen doors in Kirby's van? what if I had put diesel in Clev's motor? Was my guardian angel trying to stop me from getting behind the wheel of Clev's car? Surely one or all of them, must have been some kind a celestial warning. If they were, I quite obviously didn't take any bleedin' notice.

Even as I was walking round to Clev's house, I was still hoping and praying it was all a bad dream. The bad dream was soon to turn into a living nightmare. Clev's bashed up car was sitting outside his house and as I approached, the sight of the damaged car turned my stomach. Clev saw me coming towards his house and met me in the street with the estimate to repair his car in his hand. He passed me the estimate and I was shocked by the amount of items that were mentioned: bumper, radiator grill, radiator, new wings, new bonnet, lights, spray job, the list went on and on. Then I saw the dreaded total amount at the bottom of the page - £326.00, I nearly fainted - £326.00! That was the equivalents of ten weeks' wages for me. I could kiss my powder blue suit goodbye. £326.00! Surely it would be cheaper to buy a new bloody car. Totally and utterly shell-shocked, I told Clev to get the car repaired.

I could sort out the £26.00 ok, but I would need a loan to cover the £300.00. I spent the rest of the day visiting loan companies in Birmingham and Walsall. The story was always the same in all of the many offices I visited - a young smiling sales assistant would ask me a few financial questions, tick, or more like cross, a few boxes, wander off for thirty seconds to consult with their supervisor, then return and say 'you're fuckin' jokin' mate.' To be fair I was very naive and very desperate, thinking I could get a loan. I was only seventeen years old, I had no bank account, no real savings and once I started working with Uncle Gra, I was self-employed.

I returned home that evening mentally and physically drained, the one and only option left open to me was too tell my parents what had happened and ask them to lend me £300.00. Dad sat stony faced as I told him and Mom that I had crashed my friend's car and that I had spent all day in Birmingham and Walsall trying to arrange a loan, but with no success. After I told them I needed £300.00 there was silence, an uneasy silence, for a minute or two, then reluctantly my Mom said, 'we'll lend it you, out of our savings account, but you will have to pay it back.' My Dad immediately added, 'and you'll pay back the interest that we lose.' I instantly agreed and it felt like a ton weight had been lifted off my shoulders.

I had been steadily working off my debt at a fiver a week, when I got a massive stroke of luck. Out of the blue, Gary, my gaffer when I first left school, called me and asked me if I'd be interested in a little foreigner – he'd promised a couple of OAPs who lived next door to each other in Great Barr to point their chimneys and ridge tiles. Gary told me he was too busy to do the job and he'd let the OAPs down on a couple of occasions after promising to do the work. He also added 'I'm sure you could name your own price.' With that in mind and also thinking what Mickey Gibbs would have charged them, I went and paid the OAPs a visit. After viewing the properties from all different angles and a lot of 'oohs' and 'aahs' while discussing the work with the two sets of OAPs, I made my move and said '£200.00 cash'. Without hesitation the wrinklies all nodded their heads in agreement.

The following weekend I borrowed some ladders from Gary and roped in Nick to drive and assist me on the roof. I told Nick I'd give him £15.00 for the weekend's work, which he was more than happy with, but Nick's eyes almost popped out of his head when one of the OAPs handed me

£200.00 after we'd had finished on the Sunday afternoon. I was quick to tell Nick, that every penny would go towards paying off my £300.00 and pointed out, in real terms, he received £15.00 more than I did.

By the time I had finally paid back Mom and Dad, the 'casual era' had just started to kick in. Anita had brought me a pair of 'straight' wrangler jeans; Doc Martens were being replaced with 'Kickers'; and my desire for the powder-blue suit had dwindled. But the age of flared trousers and wide lapels wasn't dead in Aldridge. On the back of 'Saturday Night Fever' a drinking mate of mine from the Cedar Tree, Tommy O., bought himself a white suit. He also had the black shirt that was unbuttoned to navel, but instead of a medallion on his chest, he had the tattoo of a mermaid. The deluded Tommy thought he was God's gift to women; the rest of Aldridge thought that he looked a proper Herbert and he certainly made me think, I'd had a lucky escape with that powder-blue Suit.

§

I was travelling up to Old Trafford on the Brummie Red coach one Saturday morning, we were just approaching Stoke when it was announced on the radio that due to a frozen pitch, the United game had been cancelled. There was a collective groan from my fellow passengers and within a few minutes the coach had turned around and was heading back towards Birmingham. I was disappointed about missing a day up in Manchester and didn't fancy hanging around Birmingham, which most of the other boys were intending. The coach company we used was based in

Droitwich and that's where the coach was heading after the drop off in Birmingham. Thinking it would be a bit different and a good craic, Banka and me stayed on the coach and travelled down to Droitwich.

Banka (aka Michael Benson) and me were Kindred Spirits. He liked a drink, he had a great sense of adventure, he liked to have a good laugh, he had an eye for the ladies and, of course, he loved United. As I got to know Banka, I soon realized there was one or two differences between us: he was far more articulate than me and much better educated than I was. Banka/Bankclark got his nickname due to the fact that he had previously worked for the Williams & Glyn Bank as 'guess what?' Yes! a bank clerk, not very original I know. But if you met him, never in a million years would you guess his previous profession. Banka was sacked from the bank after going on the rampage with ten dodgy cheque books he'd acquired from the bank's printers.

Banka had been well aware that most of the branch's of Williams & Glyn Bank were in Manchester and the surrounding areas, and, just using public transport, he visited ten different branches and produced a different cheque-book at each of them. This was obviously all pre-computer days and all the bank clerks did back then was to stamp and date the receipt slip in your cheque book. Banka chose the day after his monthly salary was paid into his account, before he undertook his suicide cash-shopping trip and he pocketed almost £1,400.00, not far off a year's annual pay. As Banka had to sign every time he withdrew cash from the ten different branches, it was inevitable that he would get caught.

257

And he was. Banka was taken to court, but only received a small fine and wasn't forced to pay the stolen money back to the bank. Banker saw this as a result, even though his career in the banking profession was well and truly over.

Banka and me hit the pubs of Droitwich around noon and we were having a good time until the pubs closed up as usual at 2:30. We were wondering what to do with ourselves until the pubs opened again at 5:30, when Banka suddenly remembered that a mate of his worked in a clothes shop in Worcester which was only a few miles away from us. So off we went to Worcester. We met up with Banka's mate and luckily the closing of his shop coincided with the opening of the pubs. We were having a great craic and we had met a few girls who amazingly brought us drinks.

Come 7 o'clock Banka's mate said he was off home. Banka and me were enjoying the company of the girls and had no desire to leave. Unfortunately as the night rolled on and the drink hit us, Banka and me got louder and we had a little flirt with some other girls up the bar. When we eventually wandered back to chat with the girls we had met earlier, we discovered they had done one! After visiting a few more pubs we made our way back to Worcester station, hoping to catch the last train back to Birmingham. We had just missed the last train - we were only an hour-and-a-half late!

The thought of spending the night on a cold railway station didn't appeal, so we went in search of alternative accommodation. We tried a few B & B's but the avaricious bastards wanted us to pay in up front; we didn't have the price of the train fare, let alone the money to pay for B&B. After walking the streets for ages we decided we would have one last roll of the dice and walked into the reception of the biggest and, by the looks of it, the most expensive hotel in Worcester. Banka gave the young receptionist a bit of charm, then asked if they had a room for the night, without hesitation she replied 'yes of course' then produced two registration cards. As we were filling in the registration cards with false names and addresses the receptionist said, 'it's a twin room ok?' Banka and me both nodded and with that, she gave us a room key.

We kept a straight face long enough for the lift doors to close but as soon as the lift doors were shut, Banka and me jumped around the lift like a couple of lunatics and screamed with joy. Both of us were amazed how easy it was just to walk into a big posh hotel and blag a room. When I woke up the next morning and looked at my surroundings, I couldn't believe my eyes and I very quickly started to feel worried about our deception. Neither Banka nor me had ever stayed in such an elegant establishment and the excitement of being in a posh hotel room had now turned to anxiety and misgiving. We started to fill each other with doubt, as we were both fearful of a knock on the door or a member of the hotel staff questioning us as soon as we walked out of the lift doors.

From our hotel room we nervously planned our escape route from the hotel. After much deliberation we decided to leave the hotel five minutes apart and use different exits and if we were stopped by the hotel staff we would simply say we were going out to buy Sunday papers and we would return soon. Of course, our fears and woes were completely unfounded, there was no armed guards waiting for us as we got out of the lift and no checkpoint or barbed wire at the hotel exit; we simply wandered out of the hotel as if we were any other paying guests.

We hitch hiked back to Birmingham and I spent the afternoon propping up the bar and drinking free beer. Banka was the other side of the bar pulling pints. When Banka wasn't serving customers, we giggled like a pair of schoolgirls about the previous day's antics and we both agreed if it was that easy to get a room in a top hotel, we must do it again and soon.

Over the next few months we hitch hiked all over the Midlands, posing as sales reps for a shower company, and every night we stopped in a nice hotel. To look the part Banka and me dressed smartly sometimes even wearing suits. We did Peterborough, Cambridge, Gloucester, Cheltenham, Malvern, Ross-on-Wye and Bristol. The more hotels we did, the more confident we became and there was no more sneaking out of the hotel like in Worcester. We would have a full breakfast and put our evening meals and drinks on our bill, of course the bills were never paid. We were having the life of Reilly and all for free.

The only problem we ever had was in Gloucester. We had left our hotel in the morning and we were on the edge of town with our thumbs stuck out, trying to get a lift back to Birmingham, when the hotel manager from where we stayed the night before drove past and recognised us. I saw his brake lights come on and I thought, 'oh fuck – this means trouble,' but as he'd stopped on a dual carriageway, several drivers immediately beeped him and the hotel manager drove on, no doubt cursing Banka and me as he went. I was very worried that he would soon be making his way back to us, so I was mightily relieved when a kind-hearted driver stopped and picked us up.

The best trip by far was Malvern. We had checked into a hotel and because the pubs were closed we went for a little wander. While crossing an old railway bridge I noticed what looked like a disused station; the doors and all but one of the windows were boarded up. Having nothing else better to do, Banka and me decided to go and explore. We climbed over a small fence and scrambled down the embankment and made our way onto the platform of the deserted station. From the old signs dotted around, it seemed like the station belonged to an old school. Now this might seem like something out of Just William or Tom Brown's School Days, but it's true. We climbed through the window of the station and immediately saw a set of stairs. Even though the stairs were almost in darkness, we encouraged each other to go forward. Feeling our way with our hands we made it to the top of the stairs and found a large door. I pushed gently on the door handle and my surprise the door opened slightly.

I pushed the door open a little wider and was flabbergasted to see a huge and very grand room. It had a beautiful timber floor, tall ceilings and was highly decorated. It was the sort of room you would expect to see Mr Darcy and Eliza swirling around in. After taking in the grandeur of the stately room, we ventured a little further into the building. We entered a large kitchen via a short corridor, but unfortunately all the cupboards and fridges were padlocked. After coming across a few empty offices we found ourselves in the main reception area, but still, there was no one to be seen. Then we heard music coming from upstairs, so up we went. We timidly opened the first door we came to and observed half a dozen young girls playing various brass instruments. As we continued to explore upstairs, we discovered several more rooms, where young girls were practising playing various musical instruments, everything from pianos to flutes.

As Banka and me were mooching around the first floor corridors, we noticed that all the doors had keys in the locks, it was an opportunity not to be missed. Out of shear devilment, we locked all the doors we came across and took the keys. A childish prank I know, but we were giggling like a couple of five-year-olds as we made our way back down the stairs.

We were almost at the bottom of the stairs when three or four teenage girls appeared in the reception area. They all immediately screamed in unison and shouted out, 'Arrhh BOYS!' then rushed off out of sight. The screams prompted a few more girls into the reception area and their reaction was exactly the same - shrieking screams, followed by 'Arrhh BOYS!' and then they vanished.

Banka and me were standing bemused at the foot of the stairs when an elderly woman appeared. Looking every inch like a stuffy school mistress, she bellowed out in a very commanding voice 'who are you two? What are you doing here?' but before we had chance to reply, she snapped 'you're coming to see the head mistress. Follow me!' She then turned around and marched off down at one of the corridors, fully expecting us to follow her. Banka and me were so taken aback by the screaming girls and the autocratic school mistress, we did!

Still holding a handful of the keys each, we walked behind the stern woman for a short while, then Banka said 'what the hell are we doing?' On hearing us talking our escort shouted out 'silence!' That was it! Banka and me almost fell on the floor laughing and in our state of hysteria we dropped all the keys. In military-style fashion the school mistress suddenly stopped spun around and cried out 'what on earth do you think you're doing – stop it! Then she spun around again and did a sharp turn to her right and heading up a set of small stairs. This time we didn't follow her. We walked back towards the reception area, where a small group of teenage girls had congregated, once again, on seeing Banka and me they screamed their little heads off and ran for cover. Holding each other up and wiping away tears of laughter, Banka and me let ourselves out of the front door and wandered back into the real world.

After having a few drinks around Malvern in the evening, our funds were running low so we decided to head back to our hotel, to see if we could get a little credit from the bar. When we got back to our hotel, we found a wedding reception in full swing and one over-worked barmaid was serving at the main residents' bar and at the private bar serving the wedding guests. Getting impatient waiting to be served, Banka and me took it in turns going into the room where the wedding reception was being held and asking the barmaid to come and serve us, in the residents' bar. This of course interrupted the flow of drinks for the wedding guests. After we had visited the wedding bar half a dozen times, we were approached by the hotel manager. Expecting to be told to keep away from the wedding reception, Banka and me were pleasantly surprised when he said, 'as you're the only guests in the bar, would you like to join the wedding party?'

We didn't need asking twice and immediately joined the celebrations. The hotel manager was the uncle of the bride and along with introducing us to the happy couple, he also introduced Banka and me to the bridesmaids. We spent the rest of the evening, eating and drinking and generally having a great time mingling with the other guests and when the smoochy records came on at the end of the night, Banka took the one of the bridesmaids for a spin on the dance floor. The remaining bridesmaid then dragged me onto the dance floor.

Banka had hit the jackpot, while I was left with the booby prize. Banka's bridesmaid was a stunner. She was twenty years old, she had long blonde hair, big brown eyes and big round tits. My bridesmaid was thirty-one years old and looked liked 'Bobby Ball'. When the slow dances had finished and the bar had closed, the four of us took our drinks up to mine and Banka's shared room. Not surprisingly Banka was soon snogging the face off his gorgeous bridesmaid. I was fighting mine off, telling her, 'I was tired and I'd had too much to drink' but she took no notice and was all over me like a rash.

After a short time Banka's bridesmaid took him off to her room, leaving me with, a 'sex starved veteran man-eater' or in my case a 'teenage-eater'. After about half an hour my sex-mad momma had eventually worn me down. She had almost stripped of me naked, when the bedroom door flew open and in marched the beautiful bridesmaid wearing just her pants and Banka's unbuttoned shirt. 'What's wrong with me Steve?' she said as she casually removed the shirt. As I stared at her perfect form, she managed to do in seconds, what my old bag had failed to produce all night and I went as stiff as a board. 'I can't see anything wrong with you,' I said with my tongue hanging out. 'Michael won't make love to me,' she said while erotically running one of her finger round the top of her pants. I was just about to jump on her and rip her pants off when my old bag got up and quickly put Banka's shirt back over her near-naked friend, then gently pushed her friend out of our room. She suggested she return to her room and try to sort things out with Michael. Fuckin' Spoil Sport!

Very much with the beautiful young woman in mind, I lay back and let 'Bobby Ball' do what she had to do! When I woke up the next morning I was very relieved that I was on my own and I didn't have the misfortune of facing my old bag whilst sober. Still half asleep, I wondered into the bathroom and had a 'Jimmy Riddle' then I went to the basin to wash my face. As I threw the first few handfuls of cold water onto my face, I suddenly caught my reflection in the mirror, I couldn't believe my eyes. My tender sweet sex kitten had not only covered my neck in love bites, she had also covered most of my torso and upper arms in love bites. I looked like I'd got a bad case of German Measles. Well it gave Banka something to laugh about after his disastrous night of missed opportunities.

The last hotel we stayed at, with the intention of doing a midnight, or more like a 'midday flit', was Leicester. I had told Nick of mine and Banka's many adventures and Nick was keen to join us on one of our expeditions. Initially Banka wasn't too happy about Nick joining us. Three's a crowd and all that stuff. But when I told Banka that Nick had a car and we wouldn't have to worry about hitch-hiking, Banka soon changed his tune.

Nick drove the three of us to Leicester and we soon found an hotel in the middle of the town. Unfortunately when we went to book into the hotel, I really fucked things up. When the receptionist enquired who would have the twin room and who would have the single, I blurted out our real names, after already giving false names! The hotel manager had been within earshot of the whole conversation and on hearing three different names, he immediately intervened and said, 'we need payment up front.' We said this wouldn't be a problem and we would pay by cheque when we bought our luggage in from our car. Of course we didn't go back, neither did we try to check in to another hotel. We got a little paranoid thinking that the suspicious hotel manager might phone round and inform other hotels in the area that three fraudsters were on the prowl.

We had an uneventful time in Leicester. The highlight of the day was when I nicked a 'Shoplifters Will Be Prosecuted' sign. The nightlife was also disappointing and then we had to endure a very uncomfortable night cramped up in Nick's Mini.

I'm glad to say the weekend was saved by a very eventful trip back home to Aldridge. We were all awake soon after it got light and by 06:00ish we were driving out of Leicester. While messing around with the 'Shoplifters Will Be Prosecuted' sign we passed a shop sign that Banka took a shine to. Nick stopped the car, so Banka could get a better look. Thinking he could pull the sign off the wall, Banka got out of the car and started to pull and tug at the sign. Banka was Just about to give up when Nick shouted 'hold on a minute, I've got my tools in the back – I'll come and give you hand.' Nick soon produced a rake of spanners and screwdrivers and in no time we were on our way, with Banka sitting in the back seat holding the shop sign he so desired.

The shop sign was the first of many we collected that morning; we removed several more shop signs and a few house signs. Then as we drove into the countryside we started to dismantle and swap-round road signs. The *pièce de résistance* was when we swopped over the four-foot by three-foot Leicestershire and Warwickshire county signs. We could barely stand we were laughing so much as we unbolted the aluminium signs and carried them across the road and re- positioned them to their metal frames. We laughed all the way back to Birmingham as we discussed how much confusion it would cause having the county signs facing in the wrong direction.

By the time we got back to Birmingham, Nick's boot was full and most of his backseat was piled high with signs of all description and we'd also picked up a couple of traffic cones on our travels, which Banka used as a megaphone to frighten passing pedestrians.

It was only mid-morning when we arrived back in Brum and none of us had any thoughts about going home. Nick mentioned that he'd seen lots of signs in Sutton Park, so we headed down to have a gander. I can't remember why, but as soon as we entered Sutton Park Nick decided he wanted to show how robust his little Mini was and went off-roading. At some speed Nick was dodging in and out of the trees, flying up and down grassy banks. When we thought a small stream had blocked our path, Nick didn't just cross it, he drove down it.

We had driven a couple of hundred yards down the stream, when we came across a football match. I don't mean a few kids having a kick around; it was two full teams, in full kit, on a full pitch with goal nets and a ref. Nick guided his faithful little Mini out of the stream and straight onto the pitch. As we drove onto the pitch Banka used one of the traffic cones as a megaphone and started singing out of the car window, 'we're goin' on the pitch, we're goin' on the pitch,- and now you're goin' to believe us, we're goin' on the pitch!'

After the initial shock, most of the players seemed very amused to see a car riding round the pitch with Banka hanging out the car window and serenading the teams with his makeshift megaphone. The referee didn't seem to see the funny side of things and in a vain attempt to get us off the pitch he started chasing the car. On seeing this, Banka immediately started to sing, 'the referee's a wanker - the referee's a wanker.' This produced a loud cheer and applause from the footballers and, like the three of us in the car, the footballers were soon in fits of laughter.

1978

Towards the end of the 77–78 season the Brummie Reds organised a five-a-side competition for its members. The top team would represent the Birmingham Man United supporters club at the Cliff (then Man United's official training ground) where they would play against other United Supporters Clubs from all around the UK. Almost twenty teams competed for the honour of playing at the Cliff, but there could only be one champion.

Going by the name of 'Scoreboard Paddock' we took on all comers and with great saves from Maddog Bradbury, a sound defensive partnership of Mick Carol/Scrivener and a hat-full of goals from Speedy and yours truly, we conquered all before us. Scoreboard Paddock wore the United away-shirt, the top with its three vertical stripes, red pinstripe trim and the club crest. That top would become iconic and the first of the United football tops to be worn by fans as a fashion garment.

Every match we played we annoyed our opponents and all the other teams on the side-lines by imitating the United players pre-match greeting when we played at home. Single file we trotted into the centre of the pitch, then rotating 360° we waved to our adoring fans. This little ritual produced boos and hisses from the side-lines and the fingers from our opponents.

The night before the five-a-side competition at the Cliff, I could hardly sleep, I was so excited. Not only was I going to be playing at United's training ground, but we had been informed that several of the first-team players had promised to be in attendance. Besides the Scoreboard Paddock travelling up to Manchester, we took a coach-load of supporters - but I think the opportunity of visiting the Cliff and meeting some of the players might have had some influence on their decision to give up their Sunday.

When we arrived at the Cliff, there was so many coaches and United fans milling around, it looked like a match day at Old Trafford. Over forty supporters' clubs had sent teams to the Cliff, including a couple from Scandinavia. It was a great carnival atmosphere and, as promised, a few of the players turned up, as did Dave Sexton, the United Manager. Banka made a bee-line for Mr. Sexton as soon as he saw him. Banka wasn't going to pat the manager on the back or shake his hand or ask for an autograph, he wanted to give Sexton a bollocking for playing such shit-negative football! Banka marched over to the manager, but he had barely got two words out when a few of the committee members of the Brummie Reds, dragged him away.

It was definitely a different kettle of fish when the players turned up. Like the rest of us, Banka was a bit star struck when our Saturday heroes were around. Of the senior players, Pearson, Macari and Coppell made an appearance and several fringe players were also there, including Andy Richie, Ashley Grimes and the veteran Scottish defender, Alex Forsyth. All the players were happy to pose for photographs and give autographs but Forsyth was the only player who would have a kickabout with us. Sadly he refused to be our substitute.

Even though I say so myself Scoreboard Paddock played magnificently on the indoor pitches of the Cliff and we won all our games in the group stages. But due to an outrageous decision by a biased ref, the Telford branch narrowly beat us in our first knock-out game. Sick as a parrot, I did what all good footballers did in the 70's - and went off to the pub.

Just before my 18th birthday, I walked into the Cedar Tree bar. On seeing me, Flo, the old barmaid, immediately started pouring my drink which was light-and-bitter at the time, a bit of an old man's drink I will admit. But I had chosen this particular drink because I had clocked that when the doddering old customers ordered a combination of the draft beer and a bottle – such as L&B or Brown (Manns) - and mild, the barmaids would pour them almost a pint and only charge for a half. Look after the pennies and all that stuff. Any road up, back to Flo pouring my pint. It was a sign of recognition and pride on my part and I was truly a part of the Cedar Tree family. The fact that Flo knew my regular drink without me even asking made it feel like the Cedar Tree was truly my second home.

On the night of my 18th birthday I was celebrating in the Cedar Tree and, as was the tradition, I was buying friends and associates drinks. Joe the landlord was serving me and he asked me 'is it your birthday?' 'Yes – it's the big one!' I replied proudly. 'What - you've got the key to the door?' (meaning twenty-one) Joe said. 'No – eighteen' I answered a little surprised. 'Eighteen!' Joe shouted out. 'You cheeky sod, you've been coming in here for over two years, I've got a good mind to bar you!!' And I it wasn't really sure whether he was joking or serious. Then with his usual poker face, Joe said, 'you'd better buy me a bloody drink as well and some crisps, happy birthday!'

Just after my 18th birthday, I really upset my Dad by bringing a puppy home. It was an Alsatian-Labrador cross and I named him 'SUPER RED' – 'Red' for short. Fortunately my Mom and sisters immediately took to Red and they persuaded my Dad to let me keep him. I know there's an old saying that 'pets can look like their owners' that wasn't true in my case, however Red acted like his owner. He was extremely intelligent and was forever getting into scrapes. As soon as he was tall enough, he was using his teeth and paws to pull back the bolt and the latch on the back gate and off he'd go in search of his mates. After a while his little gang would come and call for him most mornings, a small pack of dogs would sit on the small green in front of our house and one of the dogs, usually a Jack Russell cross, would come to the porch door and start scratching on the glass until Red was let out.

Once Red was out with his gang, the dogs that would jump about and play on the green, for about ten minutes before going off on their travels. Red and his pack mates were the strangest bunch of dogs you could imagine; I'm sure the BBC could have made a cartoon programme based on their antics. There was a very elegant Afghan hound, there was Mad Butch a Staffs cross, a crazy Collie that tried to bite the tires of cars as they drove up and down the street, a mongrel of some description that would run round in circles trying to bite its own tail and the Jack Russell cross.

Red was a frequent visitor to the playground at Leighswood junior school. He would happily play with the school kids and was loved by both pupils and teachers. But one particular day Red overstepped the mark and followed the kids into morning assembly, he then proceeded to piss up the curtains. The next day we received a letter from the headmaster stating that everyone at the school was very fond of Red, but after his last escapade, we must keep Red under control and if Red was seen in the school playground again they would have no option but to call the police to remove him.

I had already fixed an extra bolt on the back gates, which was out of reach of Red, but Red didn't seem to have any problems scaling the back wall. So to stop Red from escaping from the back garden, I erected a two-foot-high timber fence, to sit on top of the five-foot-high brick wall. After I had finished my handiwork, I stood back and looked at what I thought would be an impregnable barrier to Red and I remember thinking, 'there's no way on earth he will get over that.'

I asked my Mom to lock the gate behind and I went and stood on the side garden, then once I knew the gate was securely bolted I shouted for Red. After a few unsuccessful attempts of trying to open the gate, Red took a run up and somehow scrambled over the seven-foot-high barrier. I just dropped to my knees in disbelief, if there had been a circus in town, I would have gone and sold Red to them.

Red certainly had an eye for the ladies, he would sit outside a house where a bitch was on heat for days, if he thought he would get his wicked way. One of the Poole girls, our neighbours from across the road, knocked on our front door and told me that Red had got into their back garden and done 'the business' with their prized racing whippet and she couldn't separate them. I followed her over the road and I wasn't expecting the sight that greeted me. In the excitement of carrying out the dirty deed, Red had ended up facing the opposite way to his love interest, with his little willy firmly stuck inside her. They looked like a oversized pair of book-ends.

As soon as Red spotted me, he dropped his head with embarrassment. Luckily after throwing a couple of buckets of cold water over them, we managed to separate the lustful couple. As they separated Red stared up at me for a moment and gave me a look, as if to say 'sorry' then off he bolted. I couldn't be too annoyed with Red; only the week before, I had to hide in Anita's wardrobe for a couple of hours when her parents came home unexpectedly.

It seemed a regular occurrence me hiding and sneaking about, while I was trying to have a bit of 'how's your father' with Anita. She had got a job as a receptionist at Baron's Court Hotel and whenever she was working on a late shift over the weekend, she would smuggle me into her hotel room. What a result. I could have a session with the lads on a Friday night or be out all day Saturday at the match, then I made my way to Anita's hotel at midnight. Even though Anita was the first girl I spent the whole night with, from memory we didn't have too many passionate nights as more often that not, I was too pissed to perform, especially after I had raided the mini-bar.

I had spent the evening at Anita's house in Shelfield and I told her that I wanted to watch a TV programme about Jackie Onassis. Anita said she didn't know who Jackie Onassis was' I told her she had previously been married to John Kennedy. Anita replied, 'I didn't know the Kennedy's had split up!' I laughed so much I missed the last bus home.

Another occasion when I also missed my last bus after visiting Anita, I was taking a midnight stroll back to Aldridge, when I was stopped and asked directions by a lorry driver. I knew exactly where he wanted to go and it wasn't very far from my house. So to save me a hour plus walking home, I offered to direct him to his destination. The driver was more than happy with my suggestion and I climbed up into his cab. He was only a few years older than me and we immediately struck up a rapport and by the time we'd got to the factory were he was picking up his next load, we were getting on like an house on fire. He told me that once he'd picked up the load in Aldridge he was off to Lisbon. Of course he had to explain to me where Lisbon was. I was still very much a thicko in most area's of education!

When he said Portugal, I was really impressed. I always wanted to go to Central America and see the lions, zebra's and penguins! I told him I hadn't done much travelling but would love to see more of the world. To my utter amazement he said, 'you can come to Lisbon with me if you want.' After establishing he wasn't joking and how long we would be away for - he said a week - I eagerly agreed.

The factory where the driver was picking up his new load, was on the Northgate which was only a short walk through the woods to my house, so while he was sorting out his load, I rushed home to get my passport. Being the middle of the week I had no money, so I had a look in Mom's purse and helped myself to the few notes in there. I left an IOU and stated, I will be back in a week. Then like a kid a Christmas, I ran back down to the factory on the Northgate.

After a short wait at the factory we hit the road and I could have burst I was so excited. The driver and me talked non-stop about 'cabbages and kings' and I was so jealous of all the places that he had visited. After driving for some time we came to a service station where the driver said 'this would be the last stop before we got onto the ferry and crossed the channel' and he advised me to go and get a drink while he was filling up with fuel and having a final check, over on his vehicle. 'You've got fifteen minutes, then next stop France,' he shouted out as I walked over to the service area.

As it was the early hours of the morning, the only place that was open was the canteen area which was situated on the overhead linking walkway between the north and south carriageways. The café was almost deserted and I sat dreaming of my adventures to come as I quickly downed my cuppa and made my way back to the lorry park. Much to my dismay I couldn't find the lorry, I walked, then ran, up and down the lines of trailers desperately trying to find my new mate. As I hurriedly moved through the rows of trucks, I keeping thinking to myself 'I was only gone ten minutes; the driver said fifteen minutes. I wasn't any longer than ten minutes.'

Where was he? Surely he wouldn't have gone without me – he wouldn't have done that! My heart was racing and my stomach was turning as I continued to search for the vehicle that was supposed to be taking me on the adventure of a lifetime. When the reality kicked in that the driver had left without me, I sat down on a bench and was totally shattered and the thoughts of the driver a abandoning me, made me feel sick. I know, I'd only known him for a few hours, but I really thought there was an immediate friendship between us. Feeling totally dejected and shell-shocked I decided to try and get myself home. I walked back over the linking walkway (to what I thought was the north carriageway) and went and stood at the end of the service stations with my thumb out. after a few minutes a small van pulled up and as I opened the passenger door the driver asked me 'where are you heading?' When I replied 'Walsall' the driver gave me an odd look and said 'Walsall? That's north, me and the road are heading south!' South! I was now on the south side of the service station? Then it hit me like a thunderbolt: when I came out of the overhead café, I must have turned left instead of right and I had been looking for the driver on the north side of the carriageway. What a thick twat!

I hitch-hiked back home and all the way I kept shaking my head and thinking, 'how could I be so stupid and fuck up such a great opportunity.' My Mom was still asleep as I walked through the front door, I put the money back in her purse, ripped up the IOU note and, feeling extremely disappointed with myself, I went off to bed to dream of what could have been

1979

I hadn't been back with Tina for long, but I was bursting with wanderlust and seeking adventure. So when I got a job travelling the length and breadth of the UK as an assistant steel erector, I couldn't believe my luck. Understandably Tina wasn't very happy, as she'd just given up the job she loved and moved back to Aldridge from London to be with me. My new job involved erecting metal water cooling tanks/ towers and ducting in various factories and warehouses.

On my first day in the job, I had my first trip north of the border and I spent the week working in a whiskey distillery in Glasgow. I was wide-eyed as we drove around the grubby city looking for the distillery and then, later, looking for digs. I was amazed to see the old Glaswegian tenements, I'd never seen anything like them. I was even more amazed when I discovered that people still lived in them. The tenements were black from years of smog and vehicle-pollution and every other window was boarded up. But there were still a few curtains hanging up in the windows and noisy and very scruffy kids playing in the streets and on the steps.

We eventually found a small B & B at the top end of Sauchiehall Street. Once we had settled into the B & B and paid for the rooms in advance, the two blokes I was working with, The Dangler & Knuckles (everyone had nicknames), took me for my first Indian meal. As we entered the Indian restaurant we were shown to a table, then an Indian waiter (about my age) approached us with some menus and said in a broad Glaswegian accent 'can I

get you boys any beers?' 'Well, I gew to Cannock!' I nearly
fell off my chair in disbelief. What a culture shock. I had
come across a few West Indians, but I could count on one
hand the amount of times I had come into contact with
Asians and the black face and the Glaswegian accent just
didn't fit; it was like peeling an orange and finding an apple
inside. That said, the young waiter seemed a decent sort
and recommended I try a lamb Rogan Josh, after I'd told
him I hadn't had a proper curry before. That was the start
of a life of spice.

I experienced another culture shock while in Glasgow.
I was reading the local evening paper and while flicking
through the job vacancies section, I noticed every other
job stated 'Catholics need not apply' Wow! It would have
been like reading 'Pakies or blacks need not apply' in the
Express & Star. The only 'Need Not Apply' advert I'd seen
before was a jovial one in the Birmingham Evening Mail,
it read - 'BRICKLAYERS WANTED – pipe smokers and
fisherman need not apply'.

Over the next few weeks I met the rest of the erecting
crew and got my nickname 'Pictures' because of the amount
of tattoos I had, and when my mate Nick came to work
with us for a couple of months he was first known as 'No
Eyes' because he could never find anything, then when
the Boson found out Nick's initials were NB his nickname
became 'Footnote' as in *Nota Bene*. A few other notable
nicknames were 'Scuttles/Batteries' (he was always asking
to stop the van, so he could buy batteries for his ghetto
blaster), 'Everest' (he was frightened of heights!), 'Robin
the Bastard/Damp-Down Pete' (he continually pissed the
bed) and the obnoxious 'TNUC' (his nickname was an

anagram!) the thick twat who was the only person who didn't realise, the significance of his nickname.

With this memorable band of misfits, I worked in some very unusual places: Bishops Abbey – then England's training ground, Ford Dagenham, various RAF camps up and down the east coast, a precious-metal factory in Surrey, an explosives factory, Leyland Trucks (bunch of lazy bastards), Cadbury's chocolate in Bristol, Coal mines in Lancashire and Yorkshire, British steel on the Isle of Sheppey, Sellafield (Sea Scale), Nuclear power plants (punk sheep), Euston Station and Tower, food-processing factories, the Giro Bank, and the NEC.

The precious-metal factory was located near Staines. It was a very non- descript building and it easily blended in with the other buildings on the small industrial estate. As you would expect, the security was extremely tight and we had to pass through a metal detector and X-ray machines when we entered and left the building. CCTV cameras were everywhere and we had an escort with us at all times; even if we wanted to go to the toilet, our escort would radio for another member of staff to accompany us to and from the bog. Large rolls of gold and silver thread were commonplace as were gold and silver rods and bronze and aluminum ingots.

After working there for three or four days we got quite friendly with a permanent escort and, on our last day, we persuaded him to show us the strong room where the gold bullion was stored. What a sight! There were three pallets standing about for four-foot high full of shiny gold; just one of those gold ingots would have set us up for life. The Dangler half-jokingly said to escort, 'why don't I drop a couple of those gold bars in a tin of our bitumen paint, your metal detectors wouldn't detect the gold through that thick bitumen.' The shocked look on our escort's face told us what he thought of the Dangler's suggestion and we were immediately hustled away from the strong room.

I had put on a stone in weight in the time we spent working at the Cadbury's factory in Bristol during the annual two-week 'shut-down'. Talk about kids in a sweet shop, and a giant sweet shop at that! Except for a couple of other maintenance teams the factory was deserted and throughout the day we helped ourselves to all types of chocolate bars. The security inside the building was non-existent, so every evening when we finished work we would throw dozens of boxes of chocolates into the back of our vans. My personal favourite at the time was the Curly Wurly (I also love the TV ad with Terry Scott, 'So does anyone want to buy a hat?') Usually covered with dustsheets or old blankets we would smuggle the stolen chocolate into our digs each night. By the end of the first week my wardrobe was full to bursting with boxes of Curly Wurlies A nosy cleaner in our B & B had a lucky escape when she opened my wardrobe door and was immediately buried under an avalanche of them. Fortunately she was also a fan of the chocolate bar and she ate her way to safety.

On our last morning at Cadbury's, a self important and overbearing security guard approached us. For a minute I thought we might be in a bit of trouble, but it wasn't to be. In a very patronizing and grandiose manner he said, 'I don't usually allow this – but as a special treat, you can go into the staff shop before you head off and buy chocolates at staff rates.' Buy from the staff shop! We probably had more chocolates in our two Transit vans then they had in their staff shop! The security guard seemed quite put out when we graciously declined his offer. He was even more put out, when Knuckles threw a large bar of chocolate at him as we drove through the exit gates.

All our family and personal details were passed to the Home Office for screening before we were allowed entry to the heavily guarded Seascale nuclear power station (later known as Sellafield). Now this will probably sound a bit strange, but as we approached the menacing looking Seascale nuclear power station for the first time, the thing that really struck me were the mad sheep. They didn't have nice rounded wooly coats like the sheep in the Midlands, instead they had a wild and unkempt look, they also had several different colours of dye splattered all over them and the large ID tag through their ears finished off the look. There was no doubt about it, they were - PUNK SHEEP! I told the Dangler to stop the van, so I could have the craic with the strange-looking creatures, but instead of running after the sheep and shouting 'Mint Sauce' like I usually would, I jumped into the field full of Punk Sheep and started pogoing and singing Sex Pistol songs and, to my great delight, the Punk Sheep started to join in, only with the pogoing of course. I hope you weren't thinking they were singing along as well, now that would a bit far fetched!

My pogoing with the Punk Sheep certainly put a smile on the lads' faces, but the jovial mood soon changed when we arrived at the main gate of Seascale and we were greeted by police carrying machine guns and sidearms. We were taken into the gatehouse and asked to produce our photo IDs that had been issued by the Home Office. While we were doing this, police dogs were sniffing inside and out of our vehicles. After a few minutes we were given the all clear and escorted to the medical block. The whole crew had to undergo a full medical, which included the doctor grabbing our bollocks and us bending over and touching our toes. I didn't like that!

After the medical we were issued with a Seascale uniform and it was stressed that this must be worn at all times when on-site and it even included boots, socks and pants. At the end of every shift we were instructed to put the uniforms into a large laundry basket, then the following day we collected a new uniform. The Seascale uniform was soon christened 'Nut-Plute Gear' As well as being given a new set of clothes each day, we were also given a futuristic-looking gas mask and a standard radiation detector and a strange plutonium safety detector. The first was like a two-inch-square, blue plastic badge and similar to what a nurse would wear in x-ray departments. The second was a four-inch long narrow tube that had a dial in the one end. Because of where we were working, we were informed both of these devices should be checked at least every thirty minutes. And all for £2.00 an hour and of course there was no mention of any extra safety money.

We had been working for a few days in one particular building which housed the entrance to a large tunnel - we speculated where the tunnel went to, but no one would venture into it - then one afternoon we heard a noise coming from it. As the noise grew louder, three men appeared in the entrance of it. They were all carrying automatic weapons and were wearing full protective clothing and face masks, behind them were two other men dressed the same but carrying a small metal box between them. It was like a scene from a science-fiction movie and it was very unnerving. I was always glad to get out of the nuclear station and get back to our B & B. It was probably the best B & B I had ever stayed in and for once I had the luxury of my own room. The guy who ran the B & B was a great bloke and very clued up. Because accommodation in and around Seascale was very limited, he knew he could charge a premium for the rooms, which he did. Luckily for us, he was a very generous soul and with the extra money he made from our boss, he gave the lads four pints of beer each night FOC and a free ten-minute phone call every other night.

But by far the most exciting attraction that our landlord would regularly lay on were blue movies. Porn on film was a real treat back in the 70's and for a teenager very difficult to get hold of. What an education it was watching those wonderful films and the icing on the cake was I had my own room, so I could have as many 'Tommy Tanks' as I liked. Nice One!

If Seascale was the best B & B, the worst one was in New Brighton. Only two of the six bedrooms had doors, the other four just had crudely hung curtains across the doorway. The chain-smoking scouse peasant that ran the B & B introduced himself as 'F-ing Franny' and added, 'they call me that, because I'm always fuckin' swearing.'

We were coming down the stairs of the B & B after dropping bags in our rooms and our charming host said, 'I've got fuck all in the kitchen, so if you bunch of tossers fucking horny f*cking about it want breakfast in the morning, one of you better run me down to the fuckin' shops.'

Surprisingly the breakfast was ok, but there was only one table and three side chairs in the so-called breakfast room. That meant two of us had to sit in the grubby armchairs and put the 'chipped' plates on our laps. Knuckles, who wore glasses like the bottom of milk bottles, was sitting in one of the armchairs and as F-ing Franny handed him his breakfast he said, 'listen you four eyed twat, don't you get spilling any fuckin' grub on my furniture, or I'll send you the fuckin' cleaning bill.' Then as F-ing Franny was leaving the room he said, 'if anyone finds a fuckin' mouse, I'll give 'em an extra fuckin' sausage.'

I'm glad to say the Dangler and me were called way to another job and I only had to spend one night in that shit hole. It was double good luck that the Dangler and me were called away, because the day after we left, the rest of the crew had a bit of misfortune. After overloading a scaffold inside the cooling tower they were erecting, six of the crew crashed fifteen feet onto the metal floor of the tower. Miraculously no one was badly injured and there wasn't even any broken bones, but there was plenty of cuts and bruises.

After the crew had released each other from the small mountain of metal panels, scaffold planks and poles, and checked they hadn't got any broken bones, the Boson, being a hard and unsympathetic taskmaster, insisted that they all carry on working; there was no way anyone was going to skive off and go to hospital, while they could still stand and hold a spanner. The incident was soon known as 'The New Brighton Plummet' and the Boson was known as a cunt by the rest of the crew.

While the rest of the crew were nursing their cuts and bruises up in New Brighton, the Dangler and me were working on a small job just south of Birmingham. This meant every morning we had to drive down the Stratford Road and every morning as we approached the Mermaid Pub, situated on the junction of Warwick Road, our transit van would be surrounded by Paddies looking for casual work. There must have been getting on for a hundred Irish labourers in the pub car park and every time they spotted a van they would run into the road and flag it down and shout 'give us the start! – give us the start!' The thing that bewildered me each morning was the number of Paddies wearing dirty old suits and carrying a pair of wellies. The poor sods probably only owned the clothes they stood up in.

At that time a lot the Paddies looking for casual work on a daily basis were living a hand-to-mouth existence and had no fixed abode. They worked for beer money and slept the night on a mate's floor or in a chair and some of the really hard drinkers spent the night in the drinking clubs around Sparkhill such as the Cascade and the Talk of The Town. When they were kicked out of the drinking clubs they would make their way to the Mermaid and try and get a few hours kip in the car park and pray they got 'the start'.

Sheerness on the Isle of Sheppey must have had some of the strangest people in Britain. I thought the boring, goggled-eyed Yorkshire twats took some beating. I was amazed to learn that virtually every pub in Yorkshire had a TV in the bar. I'd never seen a TV in a pub bar before I went to Yorkshire. In the land that time forgot, the landlord would usually play the TV at full volume, while the brain-dead, humdrum locals sat like statues gauping at Emmerdale or Coronation Street. On more than one occasion, an inbred Yorkshire landlord told us to stop talking while their favourite TV programme was on. Talk about killing the art of conversation!

Sheerness didn't have TVs in the bar but it had the most unfriendly and suspicious people. They dressed like they'd fallen into a jumble-sale box and they didn't know the war was over until the early 50s, at which time most of the inhabitants of Sheppey were living in Anderson shelters and there was rationing until the mid 60's.

Without fail, every time we walked into a pub the locals would turn and stare at us; they would stop talking for a few minutes then resume their conversations in a whisper. As if we were bleedin' interested in what the boring twats had to say! They obviously weren't used to seeing strangers and they may of thought we were escaped inmates from the Island's Category-A prison, or even we were long-lost relatives from the local loony bin.

It was the same in the shops and the canteen at the steel foundry, where we were working; nobody would give us the time of day. Even our landlady at our B & B hardly spoke to us, the ugly old cow. And she had webbed fingers and no doubt six toes on each foot and a cock.

The cooling tower I was working on at the steel foundry was the biggest tower I worked on and I was working at heights of forty foot without a harness or any safety net. I was expected to pull up large plastic coated RSJ's by hand while standing on a 8 x 6" beam. I must have been mad or too frightened to tell the Boson I wouldn't do it. The people who were definitely mad were the drivers of the massive open-backed trucks that carried the red-hot waste out of the foundry. The trucks drove about forty or fifty yards away from our tower, but we still had to turn our faces away from the heat, as they passed us. Fuck knows what type of protective clothing the truck drivers had to wear. Whatever they wore, I bet they glowed like the Ready Brek kid at the end of their shifts.

Just before I started steel erecting, I worked for a likeable but dodgy builder in Erdington and just before I left his employ I was pulled over by the police while driving one of the firm's vans; the tax disc was out of date so the police asked me to produce documents at the local police station. I soon discovered the van had no tax, insurance or MOT and I was sent a summons to appear in court. Unfortunately the court date coincided with me working away in Sheerness, so I had to get home under my own steam.

The cost of the train was ridiculous so I got out the trustee thumb once again. A lorry driver who was heading for Hertfordshire picked me up and he offered to drop me off at one of the services on the M1. This was long before the M25 came along and our route took us along Commercial Road, which is in the heart of the East End and, back then, was the centre of the rag trade in London. The Commercial Road was all hustle and bustle. It was a great experience to see dozens of young men running across the road and down the pavements wheeling rails full of fashion garments. Commercial Road was a real beehive of activity and no doubt full of great characters, but sadly the London rag trade and all its characters are lost forever.

The lorry driver dropped me off at the services on the M1 as promised and within a few minutes a car had pulled alongside me and a smartly dressed young man stopped and offered me a lift. I jumped into the passenger seat and off we went. After five or ten minutes I started to feel a little uneasy; when I tried to chat to the driver he replied with one word answers. From my experience of hitchhiking when somebody stopped to give you a lift, it was for the sake of company and usually the drivers never stopped talking, this guy just stared at the road.

Finally he spoke to me. 'I've done you a favour by picking you up, now will you do a favour for me?' the driver said to me. Thinking he was a sales rep and he was trying to sell me something, I replied, 'yes of course' and I was ready to give him a false name and address. But instead of giving me some sales patter he said in a soft voice, 'can I stroke your leg?' I was too shocked to speak for a minute or so and while I was still trying to work out what was happening, the driver said, 'it would really mean a lot to me, if I could just rub my hand up and down your leg.' Then I blurted out 'are you some kind of a puff? The driver then seemed a bit upset and said in a indignant manner, 'well, I wouldn't put it like that myself.' This was the first time I'd been approached by a 'Woolly Wuffta' and after several minutes of a stony silence, I innocently asked the driver, 'so why are you a puff then?' The driver replied quite sharply, 'I don't really like that word, I just am what I am and I like men.'

Even though we were speeding along the M1, I asked him to stop the car and let me out. But he refused stating he couldn't stop on the hard shoulder and he would drop me at the next service station. When we got to the services, I got out of his car arse first, I wasn't risking that homo pinching my bum as I got out. I had literally just dropped my bag on the floor when a massive Mercedes car pulled alongside me. The electric window on the passenger door opened and a middle-aged man lent forward and told me, 'he was heading for Birmingham and was that any good for me?' When I said yes, he told me to throw my bag in the boot.

As I threw my bag in the boot I saw a box of Champagne, a mink coat and a camelhair coat. 'Fuck me, this bloke must have some money' I thought to myself. When I got into the passenger seat, the first thing the man said to me was 'why did that man, just drop you off?' I was immediately struck with fear and for a few seconds thought the whole of the M1 must be full of puffs today and they're all searching for new meat. 'You don't know him, do you?' I nervously asked the new driver. 'No, I just thought it was strange that you was dropped off at the services,' the driver replied. I remained silence for a few minutes then said, 'that bloke in the other car was a puff and he asked me if he could feel my leg. A Little smile appeared on the drivers face and he enquired, 'and what did you say?' I snapped back, 'I told him to fuck off!' I wanted him to know straight away that there was no chance of him playing with my gearstick. Seeming a bit disappointed with my answer, the driver just said, 'Oh' Then for the next hour or so he proceeded to boast about how much money he had and about his holiday home in Jamaica and how generous he was with his friends - even new friends! Just before I got out of the flashy Merc in Birmingham, the dirty old sod handed me his business card and said to me I'm staying at the Grand Hotel for the next five nights, it would be lovely to see you again,' then added, 'help yourself to a bottle of bubbly out the boot.' I didn't answer him and I didn't take a bottle of bubbly, but I always wish I had done a runner with the expensive looking fur coat.

As I was travelled on the bus back into Birmingham the next morning for my court case, I was thinking of the injustice of me going to court and why should an employee be responsible for tax, insurance and MOT on a company vehicle. So when I got into Brum I went in search of a law book that might help me out. In WH Smiths I came across *The Policeman's Handbook on Law*. I quickly flicked through the 'car offence' section and there in black and white it stated, 'an employee cannot be held responsible if his employer does not tax, insure or MOT company vehicles.' Knowing that I wouldn't remember word for word, regulation D, sub section 1736H, paragraph 2 of the motor-vehicles offence, I slipped the policeman's law book under my jacket and made my way to the Victoria law courts at the back of Steel House Lane.

It was a funny old set-up in court; all the defendants who were going in front of the magistrates that morning had to sit together in a large Victorian court room which meant you got to hear all the other cases. The magistrates dealt with several cases before my name was called and I got to hear the ins and outs of a burglary, a couple of the shoplifters and an insurance fraud, but the best by far was a local prostitute was bought into the court room, flanked by a couple of coppers. The lady of the night had failed to attend court a few days earlier and she had been arrested that morning. When she was bought before the magistrates she said, 'I didn't attend court, when instructed because one of my customers had tied and gagged me and kept me prisoner for two days.' This statement bought a roar of laughter from the public gallery and the other defendants.

The magistrates made some sarcastic comments about the prostitute's lame excuse, then read out her charges: living off immoral earnings, possession of cannabis, shoplifting and resisting arrest. The prostitute's solicitor pleaded her case and then stated that she was trying to turn life around and she had now secured a full-time job. The solicitor then handed the magistrates a letter confirming details of the prostitute's new job. After the magistrate had read the letter, showing no emotion the magistrate said, 'working two hours a day as a Lollipop Lady can hardly be considered, a full time job.' Once again the court was in fits of laughter. With the court room still in uproar the lady of the night was taken into custody to await sentencing.

When it was my turn to stand in front of the magistrates, I nervously started to read from the *Policeman's Handbook*. I wasn't nervous because I was in front of the magistrate; I was nervous because I was such a crap reader. As soon as I had finished stating my innocence, the magistrates asked the Clerk of the Court to confirm if what I had said was correct. After The Clerk had consulted with the court solicitor and he confirmed to the magistrate, that in fact I had no case to answer. The magistrate gave the Clerk a real bollocking and told him he had wasted everyone's time and my case was thrown out.

Only a few weeks later I was up in court again. The very evening after my appearance in front of magistrates, I was having a drink with Nick and Ade and we got reminiscing about the old days, in particular the times we would break into our junior school and play football in the assembly room and take pot shots at the Stags Head that was mounted on the wall. As the night wore on, we were full with beer and full of bravado and as we left the Cedar Tree thought it would be great idea to go and have mooch around our old school.

We used the same route to get in to the school, that we had used six or seven years previously, a dodgy window in the assembly room. After ten minutes of poncing around in our old school, we decided we'd wandered down memory lane for long enough and we were making our exist via the dodgy window and onto to the flat roof of the school, when we heard a loud voice shout out, 'Get down from there, you bunch of bastards!' Then we saw loads of torch lights shining all over the playground and about half a dozen coppers running towards us. Nick, Ade and me jumped off the roof and made a run for it. I was running towards the perimeter fence, when I was stopped in my tracks, by a truncheon flying past the side of my head. A couple of coppers knocked me to the ground and handcuffed me. Nick and Ade were found by the coppers a short time later hiding in the woods.

After being photographed and fingerprinted, we all spent our first night in police custody. When Nick, Ade and me were charged the next morning with burglary, all three of us deeply regretted the previous night's shenanigans and the fact that we were going to have a conviction for burglary hung over us like a black cloud.

The day we appeared in court, I was thinking that, because of my two previous convictions and being put on probation, I might end up with a few weeks inside. Nick, Ade and me sat anxiously waiting to be called in front of the magistrate, but we seemed to be waiting outside the courtroom for ages and I was getting more stressed by the minute. So to help stop the nerves I started to mess around a little and did a few Bruce Lee impersonations. Ade and Nick joined in and soon there was a mock Kung Fu Battle in the corridors. Things got out of hand when I sent Nick flying into a man who was getting a plastic cup from the drink dispensing machine. The man's hot drink spilt all down his trousers and he was not amused. When the man complained, Ade told him to stop moaning and that the drink could easily be wiped off his trousers in the toilets. Not long after the incident with the spilt drink, we were called into court. Would you Adam & Eve it? the man we caused to spill his drink and who Ade had told to 'stop moaning' was none other than the prosecuting solicitor!

Not surprisingly, the solicitor laid it on thick to the magistrates and said 'we would probably have caused thousands of pounds of damage at the school if we hadn't been intercepted by the boys in blue.' Fortunately he didn't have any record of my previous convictions and you could see the disappointment in his face when he had to tell the magistrates, 'none of the three - have any prior convictions.' When all three of us expressed sincere regrets and remorse for our actions and stressed it was completely out of character, the magistrates believed us and we got away with a fine.

My third appearance in court in almost as many months came about after I had been barred from the Whitehouse. Forgetting all about the little altercation with the sour-faced barmaid from the week before, I walked into the Whitehouse and asked for a pint. 'You're barred,' the sour faced barmaid told me. 'What the bleedin' hell for? I enquired.

Then I remembered our tête-à-tête from previous week. She had called the landlady over to deal with an argumentative customer and while the landlady was remonstrating with the customer the young 'ugly' sour-faced barmaid stood watching on with her arms folded.

The pub was packed and it must have been four-deep at the bar and I had been waiting ages to be served. So when I saw the barmaid standing idle, I shouted over, 'instead of standing there with your arms folded, any chance of a bit of service? She heard me but 'cocked a deaf 'un'. As the pompous sour-faced cow stood statue-like behind the bar, I got more pissed off with her and called out, 'are you doin' any work tonight you lazy sod?' Once again she ignored me.

When the landlady had eventually finished arguing with the objectionable customer the sour face barmaid, only went and served him although he had caused her to stand idle for ten minutes. Then she came over to me and said, 'I'm not serving you,' and started serving the person next to me. 'Bollocks to the stupid cow,' I thought and went off into the bar to get served.

I was flabbergasted that the miserable sod wouldn't serve me. Thinking the landlord would be sympathetic to my plight, I told him, one of his barmaids had refused to serve me, but to my shock and disbelief he replied, 'well you had better leave the pub!' I tried explaining what had happened the previous week, but the landlord simply wasn't interested and told me he would call the police if I refused to leave. Not taking any notice of the landlord's threat, I asked one of my mates to buy the drinks.

I was on my second pint when four or five coppers came walking into the pub, Thinking nothing of it I carried on drinking and chatting to the lads. Then I spotted the landlord talking to the coppers and the landlord pointing at me. The coppers approached me and one of them said, 'the landlord said you're barred and you refused to leave the pub.' I replied 'it was a joke, but I'll just finish my drink, then I'll be off.' 'No!' said the copper firmly, 'you leave now,' then the copper went to take my drink from my hand. As he did so, Nick intervened and said, 'let him finish his drink.' Obviously the copper ignored Nick and made another grab for my drink. Nick then grabbed my glass and the copper and Nick wrestled with each other for control of my pint.

To my amazement Nick and the copper ended up on the pub floor and my pint was spilt all over the copper's uniform. The other coppers immediately dived on Nick and carried him kicking and screaming out of the pub and threw him in the back of their van. Now that was really out of character for Nick. Slightly shocked, me and my mates stood speechless for a minute, then a couple of the coppers returned, put my arms up my back and frog-marched me out of the pub. As soon as I was pushed into the police van and still had my arms behind my back, I said, 'this is a fuckin' joke, I haven't done anything.' Then a young copper smacked me in the mouth and said, 'stop swearing you drunken cunt.' I was furious and tried to break free from the coppers holding my arms. All the way to the cop shop, I told the young copper what I thought of him, but all it got me was a few more digs from the other coppers.

As soon as I got to the station, I told the sergeant that I'd been assaulted but the coppers in the van said I had been resisting arrest and they were restraining me and that was the end of the matter. After another night in the cells, I was charged with being drunk and disorderly (even though I'd only had a pint and a bit!) and refusing to leave licensed premises. Nick was also charged with being drunk and disorderly and with 'obstructing a police officer while in the line of duty.' The desk sergeant said to Nick, he was very lucky he wasn't charged with 'assaulting a police officer' which of course was a far more serious charge.

Nick and me couldn't argue about being charged with 'refusing to leave a licenced premises' or 'obstructing a police officer while in the line of duty' but we both objected to be charged with being 'drunk and disorderly' when we'd had little more than a pint each. So off we went to the local solicitors for some advice and after hearing our story the solicitor said, 'you haven't got a leg to stand on. Even if the police can't smell alcohol on your breath they can claim that you are drunk. And if you plead innocent, it will be the police's word against your and we all know who the judge will believe!' So much for Great British justice.

When Nick and myself appeared in court, reluctantly we pleaded guilty to all charges and to add insult to injury my least favourite policeman, Ken the Copper, was reading out the statements of the coppers who had arrested us. And the bastard really made a meal of it. He said I was swaying as the police entered the pub, my speech was badly slurred and I had a wild look in my eyes and Nick was made out to be the new Harry Roberts. All complete bollocks! In the grand scheme of things our court appearance was a nothing, but still the police were lying bastards. I got off lightly with a £25.00 fine, Nick on the other hand was fined a whopping £135.00

There were more visits to the police cells, but fortunately only for a couple of hours and I wasn't charged. Most Friday nights after the pubs closed me and the lads would end up at the Phoenix Chinese restaurant, which was right next door to Aldridge Police Station, this was very handy for the owners as every week, without fail, there was a fight and the occasional mass brawl. One brawl occurred after my mate Tony Martin had a chair smashed across his shoulders, just as he was tucking in to his beef chow mein. A couple of lads were thrown down the stairs and plates, glasses, chairs and tables were thrown across the restaurant. It was the nearest thing I've seen to a Wild West saloon brawl, the only things missing were John Wayne and Audie Murphy. The US cavalry in the shape of the Old Bill always came to the rescue of the poor restaurant owners.

The other regular occurrence was people doing a 'runna' (off on their toes without paying for the meal). One drunken Friday night, me and a few mates were just about to walk into the Phoenix when a mate of ours 'Dave' was walking out, or I should say staggering out. We all chatted for a few seconds then Dave said 'he still had a pint left on the table and he would come back inside and join us.' Dave had already eaten and paid for his meal! After we had eaten our food and downed a few beers, we decided we would do a runner. As soon as the waiters had left the restaurant and gone back into the kitchen we jumped up and ran out. By this time Dave was quite pissed and didn't really know what was happening, but out of a sheer knee-jerk reaction, Dave also ran out of the restaurant, closely followed by the Chinese waiters. Unfortunately Dave, the only one who had paid for his meals and drink, was the only one apprehended by the waiters. The waiters immediately dragged Dave to the police station and demanded he paid his friends' bill. Dave was wobbling all over the place and was soon thrown into the cells for the night.

The next morning the police gave Dave the option 'pay the bill in full, now! Or be charged with theft.' Dave agreed to pay the bill and the police drove him to his house to get the money. Dave handed over almost £20.00 to the police and that was the end of the matter. Whether the police passed on the money to the Chinese restaurants we will never know.

Me and the rest of the lads thanked Dave for paying the bill and told him we would pay him back, but I'm pretty certain none of us ever did. The following week Nick, Rigga and me were back in the Phoenix and nothing was said by the Chinese waiters about previous weeks 'Runna'. They simply didn't recognise us, I suppose all of us drunken, loutish whities looked the same to them! After we finished our meals, we checked our finances and discovered we didn't have enough to pay. We weren't in the mood for a runna so we came up with a cunning plan. Nick would just stroll out of the restaurant and when the bill came, we would deny knowing the third person (Nick) and say that 'he had casually joined us at our table.'

Of course, the waiters weren't having any of it and when we refused to pay the bill in full they called on their friends from next door. A copper soon arrived and after Rigga and me had told him our flimsy story, he asked what was the name of the mysterious diner who as disappeared into the night. Rigga and me both blurted out a name instantly, unfortunately I said 'Pete' and Rigga said 'Alan.' 'Pete Alan,' I said quickly. Or was it, 'Alan Peters?' Rigga added and grinned like a Cheshire Cat. Rigga and me might have been amused, but the copper certainly wasn't. He shook his head then marched us round to the police station. We were put into the cells and told we would stay there until we agreed to pay the bill in full.

Rigga and me thought it was a bit of a laugh for an hour or two, but as we got cold and tired, we caved in. In the early hours of the morning Rigga phone his dad from the police station and asked him 'to come and pay the rest of the bill'. Rigga's Dad eventually turned up at the police station and paid the outstanding amount on the bill and Rigga and me were released from the cells. Understandably Rigga's Dad was well miffed and much to my amusement, he refused to give his troublesome son a lift home.

I had taken the afternoon off work to visit the opticians for the first time. As I was a little early, I did a silly thing and went and had a couple of pints so by the time I got to sit in the opticians big chair in the darkened room I was a bit tipsy. The optician was young attractive lady and I soon started to flirt with her. But when she started rotating her head and rocking backwards and forwards while examining my eyes with her hand held ophthalmoscope, I got the giggles. She tried to examine my eyes a few times but halfway through the procedure I burst out laughing. At one stage she switched the lights back on and told me to take the examination seriously. So I put on a straight face and tried as hard as I could not to laugh, but each time she approached me and she started to rotate her ahead, I lost control. Then just when I thought I had my laughter under control, the optician got the giggles which set me off again. A few giggles from the optician, turned into hysterical laughter and she was almost on the floor and when she said 'stop it, I'm going to wee myself,' the tears were rolling down my face and I almost fell out of the chair. Still trying to hold back the laughter, she told me 'she had no choice, but to cancel the examination.' As she was booking me another appointment she made me promise, I wouldn't have a drink before the next eye test.

As I walking back home from the opticians, I passed my old junior school and my jovial mood soon changed to anger, as I spotted one of my old teachers in his classroom. I don't hold a grudge against many people, but Mr Low (aka Lowbags) is definitely one of them. He was a bully and he loved to humiliate children. Lowbags would make a child stand on their chair in the middle of the classroom then encouraged their classmates to laugh and shout at them. Often the humiliated child would end up in floods of tears. Lowbags, the bastard, used this type of psychological torture on me and my mates when I was in the junior school and here he was, ten years down the line, still doing exactly the same bleedin' thing. I snapped and started to shout all types of obscenities at the old bastard, which he did his best to ignore. But when I turned round and started to walk back towards the school gates, Lowbags quickly started to close the large open windows. Aiming all the expletives I could think of at the horrible bastard, I approached his classroom and started banging on the window. The kids in the classroom were loving the situation and I noticed a few of the boys literally jumping and screaming with joy and clapping their hands as Lowbags face turned white. It was a satisfying sight seeing the fear in Lowbags eyes but to this day, I still regret not going into the classroom and kicking the evil bastard in the bollocks.

Even though I was working away for most of the week, there was still a lot of friction at home, especially with my Dad, so I applied for a council flat. I told the council a little white lie, that my auntie had moved into our house and she had moved into my bedroom and I was sleeping on the settee. My aunty Peggy had moved in with us for a while, but she hadn't taken my bedroom and the council never bothered to check this out. So a few weeks after sending in my application form, the council offered me a three-bedroom flat in a tower block in Brownhills, 66 Bailey house.

I was getting very serious with Tina and I was sure she would be moving in with me. With this in mind, I thought I would have one last boys' holiday before I really started to settle down, and what a holiday. Along with four of my United mates from Manchester – Ged, Wilkie, Knockers and Clarkie - I planned to go swanning off around the Greek islands for five weeks. When I finally got round to telling Tina of my holiday plans, she was extremely upset and asked me several times if she could come with me, but I kept replying, 'it' s a lads Holiday!' It was the first time I'd flown and as I sat on the aeroplane I said to the air hostess, 'those people down there look like ants.' The airhostess smiled and said, 'they are ants sir, we haven't taken off yet!'

Oh we did have fun. We spent the first few nights in Athens and our resting place was the roof of youth hostel and we were charged the grand sum of 60p per night. After visiting every bar in Plaka, Athens old quarter, and getting thrown out of a lot of them, me and the Manchester boys headed down to the nearby port of Piraeus, where we jumped on a boat and started our island-hopping adventure. First port of call was Mykonos and we couldn't wait to get off the island. Every bar we went in was full of leather-clad German and Scandinavian men snogging each other.

We then went onto Paros, Hydra, Poros, Naxos, Milos, Kea, Andros, Siros, Zante and Spetses. The islands seemed very similar and we would usually only spend a couple of nights on each one. As the small boats approached an individual island, we could always see the black-clad old women waiting to offer us accommodation. Back in 1970s, hardly any of the small islands had any hotels let alone airports. Fishing and farming was the main occupations and everything was ridiculously cheap.

We were spending less than £10.00 a day on accommodation, food and drink and we were pissed morning, noon and night for the first couple of weeks. Very few of the old Greek women spoke English, they just held a small card that read, 'Room – Zimmer – Chambre.' The second we got off a boat, a little old lady would usually latch onto me. Then, after examining my tattoos and shaking their heads in disbelief, they would lead me through the narrow winding backstreets to their home. The same procedure obviously happened to the Manchester lads as well.

Sometimes, there was a family in the small house and sometimes just the old dear and a husband. Always the accommodation was extremely basic, but what could you expect for less than a quid a night? We never spent any time in our accommodation, we would drop off our packs and immediately head back to the harbour to meet up with the other lads, and then we would be off in search of the local bars and taverns.

When I say we never used accommodation sometimes this was literally the fact. It was a regular occurrence that on our first night on an island, we would find it extremely difficult to find our little houses. After ten hours of drinking, all those narrow little streets looked the same, especially at four in the morning. So we would often end up sleeping on the beach or around the habour, but without fail the mothering instinct would always kick in and the next morning our individual little old ladies would come and find us and lead us back to their little homes.

And on every island we visited, I would queue up for at least an hour at a time to use an international telephone to call Tina, who I was missing like mad. Queuing for the phone was a real pain, the locals made up a majority of the people using the public phone and they would often, push in, be very loud and very animated, bloody foreigners. The only island we visited where all five of us stayed in the same accommodation was Spetse and we stayed there for over a week. The old couple that took us in, treated us like their own. The only time they got angry with us was when they caught us using tap water to wash our clothes. Spetse didn't have any fresh water; a boat would deliver drinking water to the island on a daily basis. Water to shower and wash clothes came from rainwater. So during the summer, there was a lot of smelly people in the town.

Spetse town was a bit bigger than most of the harbour towns we visited and it had an open air cinema on the edge of town. Positioned where it was, the cinema had little or no light pollution, but I didn't spend much time watching the grainy film with English subtitles, instead I was totally captivated by the Greek night sky. Even to this day, I have never seen a night sky to beat the one over Spetse, the stars were absolutely stunning.

When it was time to say goodbye to our wonderful hosts, they both started to cry. I had never seen adults cry like that before and I was totally embarrassed by the outpourings of emotions from the old couple. I wanted the earth to swallow me up after the old man gave me a big hug, then kissed me on both cheeks.

Our last day in Greece was spent in Athens, where we stayed in a very down-and-out youth hostel. The only beds the hostel had available were two bunk beds in a room, more like a glorified shoebox, for six people. It was a tatty little hole. The manager told us that two young, oriental men were using the third bunk bed, but if acceptable to us, they would put a spare mattress onto the floor. We said this was fine and we were charged the princely sum of 25p each.

When we arrived back at the hostel in the early hours of the morning, worse for wear of course, the two oriental lads were sound asleep in their bunk. Knowing that one of us would have to sleep on the floor, as soon as we staggered into our small room, the five of us made a rush for our two bunks. After much pulling, pushing, kicking and swearing, Ged was left with the flimsy, thin mattress on the floor. And when I say mattress, it was just that, no sheets, no blanket, not even a pillow. Ged was not a happy bunny. 'There's no fuckin' way I'm sleepin' on that fuckin' thing, when them chinky cunts have got proper beds,' Ged proclaimed. Then Ged pulled the oriental chap out of the bottom bunk.

The little yellow fellow made a hell of a noise, all of it in foreign, and it seemed he was calling to his mate on the top bunk to come to his aid. There was a bit of 'wum ping tow' – 'taring pol tang wow li ime' - 'lim cum san sim' – 'jo la tin cho faa' between the two orientals. Which I think loosely translated meant, 'help me get this fat, hairy white devil out of my bed!' Bleary eyed, the man on the top bunk eventually jumped down and started to assist his friend in trying to drag Ged out of the bottom bunk. The two little Orientals were screaming like neutered cats as they pulled and tugged at Ged. The four of us in the two other bunks were in fits of laughter, but our mood, quickly changed when fists began to fly. Then it was our turn to go to our mate's assistance. After a brief struggle the two Orientals and their luggage were thrown out of the room. The little sods wouldn't give in though, they banged on the door and screamed at us in their own lingo, but they got the message when Wilkie opened the door and smashed one of them over the head with a metal water jug.

While I was in Greece, I'd left Tina and her dad decorating my/our new flat, cheeky sod I know. To my delight when I' returned Tina and her Dad had decorated the living room, kitchen and main bedroom. On the down side, Tina announced she wasn't going to be moving in with me. A few weeks later Tina told me that while I was with the boys in Greece, she had met someone else and he was only a bleedin' member of the Royal Marines acrobatic team and that was the end of Steve and Tina. Trust Tina to run off with 'the King of the Swingers' and after all those times I queued up at the telephone booths in Greece to call her. What a Tart!

Even though I was heart-broken over losing Tina, I made the most of having my own flat and I soon had plenty of girls in my life. Over one weekend I had a different girl in my bed on Friday, Saturday and Sunday. It was a nice hattrick to achieve, but I must admit the girl from Cannock that knocked on my door on the Sunday evening I didn't recognise. Apparently I had given her my address in a pub a few weeks previously and I'd told her to come and visit me. I must have had my 'Beer Goggles' on when I was chatting her up, because unlike the Friday and Saturday girls, the Sunday girl was no looker and the fact she had hairy nipples, was a really turnoff. Well two out of three isn't bad, I suppose.

Even though I was happy-ish with lots of casual girlfriends, there was one girl that I really took a shine to, but she really played hard to get. I would always see her when I went to the Dilke and because she always mentioned she was from 'West Brom' that became her nickname for my mates and me. West Brom lived in a tower block overlooking the M5 and she had a broad Black Country accent. The first time I spoke to her she said to me 'yow tork posh, were am ya from?'

One night West Brom's flatmate was in the Dilke with her, and the flatmate really fancied my mate Tony. After a lot of pestering from me and her flatmate, West Brom let us go back to her flat. The flatmate was immediately all over Tony and she kept saying 'give us a kiss ,gorgeous,' to which Tony replied each time, 'I told you, I don't want to kiss you, I just want to fuck you, now get your knickers off.' The flatmate giggled out of embarrassment at Tony' s crude and blunt approach and said, 'oh Tony, don't be like that; just give me a little kiss'

This little exchange was repeated throughout the night, as was Dean Friedman's hit record 'Lucky Stars'. West Brom was obsessed with the song and much to the annoyance and the frustration of Tony and me, she left the record on repeat play and it played continually for six hours. During those six hours, I used all my charm and powers of persuasion to get into West Brom's knickers, but after endured 'Lucky Stars' for six hours, all I got was a snog and a cuddle.

It took me another year before I finally got West Brom into bed. My mate Eddie and me met West Brom and her very attractive friend in the Dilke. After a great evening of dancing, drinking and quite deep conversation, West Brom agreed to come back to my flat in Aldridge. Eddie and West Brom's friend joined us; they had to – Eddie had the wheels! With dimly lit lights in my living room and Eddie's Marvin Gaye record playing in the background, the romantic scene, seemed to be set. West Brom and me were snogging on the settee and Eddie and West Brom's mate were getting to grips with each other on the armchair. But the ambience was well and truly shattered when West Brom's mate shouted out alarmingly, 'if you think you're sticking those fingers up me, you've got another thing coming!'

After sucking one of Eddies fingers, she had discovered that his fingertips were blackened and cracked, this was due to Eddie being a toolmaker. As Eddie went off to the kitchen to scrub his grimy hands with Ajax, West Brom whispered to me 'let's go to your bedroom.' An hour or so later, as we lay in bed, West Brom said, 'if I'd have know it was going to be this good, I would have let you have me ages ago!' Something had definitely clicked both physically and mentally that night and I really thought that this would be the start of something special between me and West Brom.

Unfortunately, because of work commitments, Eddie and me had to take the girls back home but on the journey, West Brom kept repeating how much she enjoyed the evening and she couldn't wait to see me again. It was just starting to get light when we dropped the girls off and both Eddie and me promised we would meet them at West Brom's flat that Saturday.

When Saturday came around fate dealt a cruel hand, Eddie's car had broken down so we couldn't get over to see West Brom and her friend. Neither me or West Brom had a phone and I wouldn't have known what buses to catch to get me over to the flats next to the M5 from Aldridge. Every time I went to the Dilke I expected to see her, but our paths never crossed again.

When I moved into my flat in Brownhills one thing that remained the same was 'Friday night was lads night'. After visiting our usual haunts and getting dropped back in Brownhills, I would visit the 'Old' Anchor Pub, which was almost opposite the tower block where I lived. The 'Anchor Inn' that I'm referring to was the original Anchor Inn, that was built in the early 1900s and was demolished in the mid 1980s to make way for the modern Anchor Inn.

The Anchor was a good old-fashioned Banks's pub and from the first time I went in the place, the old locals really made me feel welcome. The Banks's bitter they served in The Anchor was fantastic, but I started to wonder if the landlord was dropping something in my pints. Every Saturday morning after I'd been drinking in the Anchor, I would wake up to discover my clothes lying in a heap at the foot of my bed and they would be soaking wet. And if that wasn't weird enough, my bath would be full of water. The water would always finish level with the overflow. Getting up in the middle of the night and pissing on my clothes can, perhaps explain how they got wet. But, I would have had to piss like a horse to get my clothes as wet as they were. The bath full of water, I have no idea what went on there. Whenever I discovered the bath full of water, with out fail, the taps were always turned off. Therefore me, or someone or something else, must have patiently watched the bath fill up with water, then turned the taps off, as soon as the water reached the overflow. Spooky stuff. Funny thing was, as soon as I stopped going in the Anchor, there were no more piles of wet clothes and no more baths full of water.

At the Elms Sunday disco, Harry S. told everyone that he was going to throw a party the following Thursday while his parents were away. Thursday night was a strange night to throw a party, but Nick and me decided to go along anyway. Money was always tight on a Thursday so en route to Harry's house we called into an off-licence with the aim of picking up some cheap booze. As Nick and me walked into the off-licence, I noticed a large metal basket full of red wine, I also noticed the offy was packed and because of the amount of bodies in front of the counter, the man serving would find it difficult to see as far as the door.

I'd never drank wine before, but the opportunity to lift a few bottles of alcohol to take to a party was too good to miss. I grabbed a couple of bottles of wine and gestured to Nick to do the same. Within a matter of seconds, we had walked into the offy, helped ourselves to four bottles of wine and walked out again. Bearing on the side of caution and greed, Nick and me decided to secrete a couple of bottles of wine near to Harry's house.

When we arrived, Harry opened the front door while Nick and me were still walking up his drive. Looking worried and embarrassed Harry said in a hushed voice, 'sorry lads the parties off.' Then we heard a loud gruff voice from inside the house, 'if that's someone else looking for a party, tell them to fuck off.' Harry went as red as a beetroot and disappeared behind the closed door. Not having spent any

money on booze for the party, Nick and me had a couple
of quid between on us to get a few pints, so, still holding a
bottle of red wine each, we walked it down to the Dilke. We
smuggled a bottle of wine into the pub and hid the other in
the car park. After buying a couple of pints, I approached
at one of the barmaids I knew and told her I was off to a
party and just in case they didn't have a corkscrew, could
she open the bottle of wine for us' and she duly obliged.

I wasn't impressed with my first taste of red wine, but
by the time Nick and me had drunk almost of the bottle,
it started to taste a bit better. We weren't exactly discreet,
openly swigging the wine from the bottle in the middle of
the pub and it was luck more than good judgement that
we had virtually finished the bottle before we were spotted
by the bouncers and unceremoniously thrown out the pub.

We collected the bottle of wine that we had hidden in
the car park and walked back up to the Whitehouse. As far
as I knew, I was still barred from the place, so Nick went up
to the bar and got a couple of pints. Then he repeated what
I had said to the barmaid in The Dilke, but the bar staff in
the Whitehouse refused to open the bottle of wine for him.
A mixture of running out of money, being a bit pissed up and
getting a taste for the red wine, led us to desperate measures.
We broke the top off the wine by smashing it on the edge of
a low level stone inside the pub. That in itself was outrageous
behaviour, but then and very carefully, we started to drink out
of the jagged-edged bottle. We did eventually bring a little
decorum into the procedure, when we finished our beer, we
poured the rest of the wine into our empty glasses.

By the time we had finished the wine, Nick and me were
in a bit of a state and certainly weren't looking forward to

the hour-long walk home. So we were delighted when a couple of girls we knew said their dad had just come to pick them up and they would give us a lift home. Nick and me were obnoxious and loud as soon as we got into the car and we had barely driven off the car park when we passed the place where we had hidden the other two bottles of wine. Nick suddenly shouted out 'stop! stop! we've got to pick up our wine!' The girl's dad carried on driving for a few hundred yards, but when both Nick and me continued bawling 'stop! We've got to get our wine,' the car stopped and Nick and me jumped out and as we did so, I shouted to the girls dad, 'don't drive off, we'll be back in a minute.' But my request fell on deaf ears, the car door slammed shut and the car drove off into the night.

Nick and me walked back and retrieved the other two bottles of red wine, repeating the same method of opening the bottles as we had done in the Whitehouse. Then like a couple of hoboes we sat on a garden wall and drank from the broken bottles, spilling as much as we were drinking. When the wine bottles were empty, we threw them in a random front garden and started to stagger towards home.

It was late, Nick and me were pissed and it was freezing cold. By the time we'd got to the village, we were holding each other up and taking two steps forward and three steps back. As we reached the telephone boxes at the post office, Nick said he couldn't go on any further and he would call his dad to come and get us. So we bounced off each other and eventually got into the telephone box and Nick started to dial his home telephone number.

I slipped onto the floor in a heap and passed out. I don't know how long we spent in the telephone box, but when I woke up I was freezing cold and there was an inch of snow on the ground. Nick had fallen asleep, while still standing and still holding the telephone to his ear. I somehow managed to wake him up and told him we had to make it home or we would freeze to death. Clinging to each other for support and warmth, we ventured out into the snow.

I had never been so glad to see my bed and I'd never been so disheartened and full of dread at the sound of my alarm clock. I had the worst hangover I had ever experienced, but even though I was in a very, very delicate state, I dragged myself out of bed and went to work. I really wish I'd stayed in bed, as I was landed with one of the worst jobs you could think of when you've got an hangover: putting up plasterboard ceilings. Every time my hammer hit a nail, it would ring in my head and make my legs turn to jelly and the ever-present taste of red wine off my lips sent shockwaves through my entire body. The hangover had gone the next day, but the taste of red wine on my lips stayed with me for another two days. And it would be over twenty years before I sipped a claret again.

As soon as I had moved into my council flat in Brownhills, I applied for a relocation to Aldridge. After being in the flat for only a few months, the council offered me a two-bedroomed flat in a low-level building in Aldridge and it was just around the corner from the Struggling Monkey. It was like an early Christmas present and I certainly needed something to cheer me up. The day before I received the relocation offer from the council, I had been laid off from work and it was only two weeks till Christmas.

Another bit of good news was, Ged had invited Maddog and me up to Manchester for Christmas and when I heard that my mate Tony would be back for Christmas, Ged told me to bring him along as well. Tony had recently joined the merchant Navy and he arrived back in Aldridge with a hatful of stories and pockets full of cash. The fact that Tony was loaded was great news, because like Maddog, Tony was very generous and I was skint.

In the three or four months that Tony had been sailing the seven seas in the merchant Navy, he had visited most on the big ports in Europe and he had a brass in everyone. Tony had also been lucky to visit Singapore, Hong Kong and Manila, where some of the best tattooists in the world worked. But after a dinnertime session Tony decided to get his first bit of ink from Tattoo Stan. Being just a few days before Christmas, Stan's tattoo studio was deserted and the miserable git actually smiled at us when we walked into the studio. That was definitely a first.

After studying the tattooed designs on the wall for some time, Tony finally decided he would have a 'girly' unicorn's head tattooed on each shoulder. Stan traced out the design and started work on the first unicorn. Because Tony wanted the unicorns heads facing each other, Stan needed a mirror image of his first tracing. So while Stan was tattooing Tony's first unicorn, he asked me to trace up the other unicorn's head. I told Stan, I was crap at drawing and I was half pissed, so it wouldn't be a good idea. But after both Tony and Stan had encouraged me to do the tracing, I gave it my best shot.

I thought the tracing was terrible but Stan still used it, saying he only needed a rough outline. When Stan had finished his handiwork, he told Tony to have a look at his new tattoos the mirror. Tony ponced around looking at his shoulders in the mirror for about five minutes then said to

Stan 'I like them but there's one problem: one head's bigger than the other.' Stan's flippant response was, 'you can tell everybody, one's a male and one's a female!' That was Stan, forever the perfectionist.

Tony drove Maddog and me up to Manchester in his pride and joy, a 2.3L Viva Magnum Coupe. Tony always pushed his cars to the limit and we didn't do less than a ton all the time we were on the M6. At one stage he was driving so fast, the vehicles on the opposite carriageway looked like they were stationary.

When we arrived at Ged's place late on Christmas eve, the first thing Tony said was, 'fuck me, will my car be safe around here?' Ged and most of the Manchester lads I knew lived in old terraced houses in Gorton. I must admit, the first time I visited Gorton, I also thought it looked a bit rough and dodgy. But I had stayed at Ged's loads of time after United games and I had never had any problem. But that was probably because I was with Ged and the boys.

I assured Tony his pride and joy would be safe and we went to meet Ged in his local, the wonderful 'Hare & Hounds'. The pub was only a few minutes walk from Ged's place and was set in a row of terraced houses and it usually stopped open until the last person staggered out of the door or collapsed at the bar. There was always a great friendly atmosphere in the Hare & Hounds and the Boddingtons bitter was to die for, not like the chemical-based crap, we get today. Every other song on the pub jukebox, was a great sing-along record from the 50s and 60s like *Little old wine-drinking me* and *Memories are made of this* by Deano, and a load of Jim Reeves including my favourites *He'll have to go, King of the Road, From a Jack to a King* and *Build me up Buttercup* also *Sunny Afternoon* by the Kinks and loads more. What a great boozer. I can't remember what time we left the Hare and Hounds, but I bet Santa and his little helpers were in bed before us. When we all finally got up on Christmas morning, Tony said to Ged, 'I hope you've got the turkey all sorted for us.' Ged replied, 'no - I've a Capon instead.' 'What the fuck is a Capon?' I enquired. 'It's a fat cock,' Ged replied. 'And are we having steamed bollocks for pudding?' Maddog exclaimed.

After the confusion over the Capon had been sorted out (it's actually a fattened castrated cockerel) and Aunty Ged had prepared the veg, it was back off to the pub. The pubs in and around Aldridge were only open for a limited time on Christmas day, usually from 12:00 – 1:30, then everyone trudged back home for their Christmas dinner. It was 5:00 before we left the Hare & Hounds, by which time the Capon was like a giant shrivelled prune and when we all fell asleep after Ged had started to cook the vegetables, the scene was set for world's worst Christmas dinner.

The slop that Ged served up, would have put a workhouse meal to shame. We almost broke out teeth on the burnt Capon and the vegetables were so overcooked they were almost like a soup. It was time for another kip, then back up to the Hare and Hounds. Once again it was a great craic in there, but towards the end of proceedings, both myself and Tony had fallen off our stools a couple of times, because we were so drunk and tired. Ged said we were the last to leave but it was all a blur to me.

After a mammoth Boxing Day pub crawl down Ashton Old Road where there was literally a pub on each corner, Tony, Maddog and me headed back down the M6. Even though I had moved into my new flat in Aldridge, I still had one or two items I needed to pick up from the Brownhills flat. So after Tony had dropped Maddog off in Birmingham, we drove to Brownhills to get the last few bits and pieces.

When we had loaded my stuff into Tony's car I went back up to my flat for one last look around. After confirming I hadn't left anything behind, I looked out of the twelfth-storey window and as the winter sun sparkled off the supermarket trolleys which had been deposited in the Anglesey canal.

I thought to myself: 'I've lost my first love; I've got no job, no money and it seems no real prospects. WHAT ON EARTH IS TO BECOME OF ME?'

supermarket trolleys which had been deposited in the